E. Nadelman

W9-AZF-456

# GREAT IDEAS
## OF
# OPERATIONS
# RESEARCH

*by*
*JAGJIT SINGH*

*Revised and Enlarged Edition*

DOVER PUBLICATIONS, INC.
NEW YORK

Published in Canada by General Publishing Company,
Ltd., 30 Lesmill Road, Don Mills, Toronto, Ontario.


This Dover edition, first published in 1972, is a revised
and enlarged republication of the work originally published
by Dover Publications, Inc., in 1968. Chapters 2 and 3 of
the 1968 edition have been rewritten as Chapters 2-4; and a
new chapter (Chapter 5: Network Analysis) has been added.
The revised work was published in England by Penguin
Books, Ltd., in 1971 under the title *Operations Research*.


*International Standard Book Number: 0-486-21886-4*
*Library of Congress Catalog Card Number: 68-14995*

Manufactured in the United States of America
Dover Publications, Inc.
180 Varick Street
New York, N. Y. 10014

TO

*Indira Gandhi*

# Contents

## *Preface*

DESPITE the pretended aloofness of mathematicians from the workaday world of business and affairs implied in G. H. Hardy's celebrated toast, 'Here's to pure mathematics, may it never find an application', mathematics has been applied more than any other science in the development of modern technology. Some mathematicians have even gone a step further. They have recently shown that the increasingly complex technologies of today need nearly as much mathematics for their effective utilization as was required for their initial creation. A case in point is that of the product-mix problem. Given production facilities that can be used to produce a wide diversity of items, each having different costs, revenues, and market demands, a manager will naturally wish to allocate the available capacity to various products within the limits of market demands and production constraints in such a way as to maximize his profit or bring about, in the case of a welfare-oriented institution, some other utility or good. He cannot hope to do so in any actual case by mere guess-work or intuition. To discover the optimal allocation he will have to resort to a mathematical technique called linear programming. Or one might take another species of industrial problems compendiously called 'bottleneck' problems. These can be solved only by means of the mathematical theory of queues; and so on.

Such permeation of management, business, industry and administration by mathematics as the increasing use of these techniques indicates has come about in part because of the pressures of growing competition in both the domestic and export markets. But more importantly, it is a reflection of a new awareness on the part of managers that their job has become so complex that to be truly effective no man, however gifted, can rely solely on flair, intuition, and inspiration to see him through. One simply cannot afford to neglect the new mathematical tools now available for

7

correcting what may be called an amateur approach to management problems.

This book is an explication of a constellation of some mathematical techniques and their underlying ideas. The explication is intended for the new management *élite* now beginning to emerge, so that its members may know what is in the tool box and what broad purpose each tool can serve. The fact that all the diverse aids available are so useful does not mean that every manager has to be a mathematical expert. In fact, it is obvious that most should not even try. But each manager has to understand what scientific aid can be had in order to call for assistance in case of need. This is the only way he can detect and correct the source of dissonance in his managerial orchestration as well as protect himself against pretentious impositions of pseudo-experts.

The presentation of mathematical techniques made here is designed to give the non-mathematical manager an understanding of the main ideas underlying them rather than mere facility in mathematical manipulation. Consequently, in explaining these ideas I have assumed the reader to have no more than a rudimentary knowledge of algebra and geometry such as may be found in any high-school textbook on the subject. Although I have tried to show by concrete illustrations the relevance of these techniques to management, the exposition may nevertheless seem at times to suggest that the problems which mathematical techniques are designed to solve are artificial and have been constructed by mathematicians themselves for their own amusement. The idea at first encounter with these techniques is natural, because they are often presented in an abstract form in order to subsume the properties of a wide diversity of systems under one generic form. This is the method of abstraction, which is the very life breath of modern mathematics and the main source of its power. For by abstraction, that is, by cutting off contact with concrete reality or experience from which the theory may have actually sprung, we universalize our experience. We develop a body of knowledge which can be transferred from one field to another, as we have actually done in creating such peaks of abstraction as our present-day geometry and calculus by de-empiricizing our daily experience of space and time. But it has its pitfalls for the manager. For the drive towards abstraction is very often inspired by aesthetic motives, so that the mathematician is tempted to pay insufficient regard to the immediate needs of the manager. The manager, for his part, is naturally more interested in applications of mathematics here and now than in any fundamental mathematical creation for aesthetic delight. But if the manager will take the trouble to learn even the rudiments of the mathematician's language so that the two will be able to communicate, he will have little difficulty in orienting the work of the mathematician towards applicational goals. It is in directing and motivating the mathematical expert in his employ towards solving a manager's problems that his acquaintance with the broad ideas underlying these mathematical techniques, even if he comprehends them only partially, is likely to stand him in good stead. He can then ensure that the work his mathematical expert does will be commercially profitable to the concern rather than merely a source of joy to its creator. But he must also remember that the mathematician can often combine profit and delight even as the manager himself occasionally blends his business with pleasure. The mathematician combines them more easily. For practical work is usually inefficient without some theoretical knowledge that at the outset may seem academic; and theoretical work may remain purely ornamental without some seminal fertilization from practical experience. It is one of the tasks of the top managers of today to see that theory and practice, like delight and utility, are not too widely separated. If this book helps promote communication between the manager and the mathematician in his employ the result will be a better blend of the two and a richer reward for both.

*New Delhi*                                                    JAGJIT SINGH
*January 1967*

*Part I*

# INTRODUCTION

# CHAPTER 1

## *What is Operations Research?*

EVERY director, business executive, and works manager knows that the output of his factory or the efficiency of his office could be improved. The question is: How? Vague memories of various mystiques such as work study, management science, methods engineering, operations research, and O-and-M arise. This book aims to clarify the general attitudes and principles of only one of them – operations research – to enable the reader to employ such attitudes and principles in his daily work. But to start with, let us clear the air by answering the natural question of a beginner: what is operations research?

Operations research, or O R in its abbreviated form, is the name given to an omnibus, if sprawling, activity initially designed to apply science in the service of war in an entirely novel way. Application of science to invent new weapons of war is, of course, nothing new. It began with Archimedes or even earlier and has continued in increasing measure ever since. Operations research, however, is a different kind of scientific work in that it adapts the scientific method of exhaustive investigation and experimentation, not to inventing new armaments, but to improving the utilization of existing ones.

An early example of this deliberate turning to science to increase the effectiveness of existing weapons occurred during the Second World War and concerned how to set the time fuse of a bomb to be dropped from an aircraft on to a submarine. The Coastal Command of the Royal Air Force had decided that the fuse should be set to explode at a depth of 100 feet below the water surface, on the plausible expectation that the submarine would sight the approaching plane about two minutes before the instant of the attack and thus dive that far below the water surface by the time the encounter with the bomb could take place. But as the actual results of the offensive were disappointing, the problem was handed over to a team of scientists since nicknamed Blackett's Circus. After exhaustive field observations Blackett's team found that in actual combat the bomber had only a small chance of aiming the bomb right if the submarine dived as promptly as the theory underlying the existing practice assumed. It had a good chance of hitting the target only if the submarine remained close to the surface at the time of the encounter. It therefore followed that when the aim could be true, the bomb exploded too far below the surface to affect the submarine. On the other hand, when the aim was necessarily poor, it exploded at the right depth but at the wrong location (see Figure 1). It was a case of heads-I-lose, tails-you-win. It is obvious that in such a situation it would be better to set the fuse to detonate almost on impact instead of 100 feet below water,

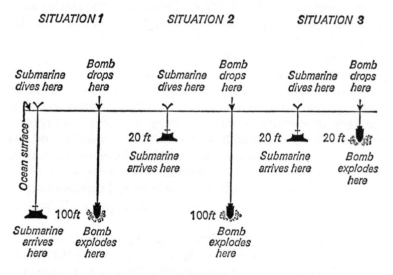

*Figure 1.* Conjugate incompatibility of depth and surface coordinates.

because it is precisely on such occasions, when the submarine has not yet dived fully, that there is any chance of seeing the submarine and aiming true. No wonder the result of the subsequent change doubled the number of submarine kills.

There are plenty of other examples of successful wartime use, in operations, of the concept of this scientific study of processes as they take place *not* in the laboratory but in the field or on the bench –

hence the name 'operations research'. Broadly speaking, their success was due to a neo-scientific attitude of mind towards the relation between men and the machines that they operate and the emergence of a body of methods for the solution of problems that arise in that relationship. It was but natural that after the war these methods that proved their efficacy in one sector should find wider application in others such as business, industry, management, and even civil administration. In all these new spheres of activity operations research has sought to optimize the over-all goal of the industrial system, factory, or plant by a controlled compromise between the diverse departmental objectives of its various offshoots, even as it earlier maximized the over-all effectiveness of a given weapon complex. We need hardly be surprised at the present proliferation of operations-research activity. For if the scientific outlook in fundamental research could transform Western civilization during the last fifty years more than in all the preceding millennia it is but natural that its infiltration in the day-to-day work of the field, factory, and office should have yielded reasonably rich pay-offs, albeit on a comparatively mundane plane.

Since operations research is by definition the *scientific* study of processes and methods of work in the field, office, or on the bench in order to increase efficiency, to the extent it does succeed in discovering ways of improvement it naturally implies a tacit if friendly criticism of the existing state of affairs. Consequently, an operations-research worker has to be extremely tactful and cautious in making such criticism when presenting his discovery. Not that we do not want our friends to tell us our faults so that we may reform ourselves. We only resent that particular stickler for accuracy who actually does so, as Henry James discovered long ago. This is why the first problem of a good operations-research worker is how to be that kind of stickler without provoking resentment. To do so one needs to combine, in a manner of speaking, the detachment of an ascetic with the commitment of a partisan. It is true that scientific neutrality and executive involvement do not go together easily. Nevertheless, it is important for an operations-research worker to blend the two. The reason is that while for discovering truth he needs to remain disengaged, for its implementation he has to have the fury of an engaged partisan. Clearly, a worker in this field, unlike the fundamental researcher, cannot wait for posterity to prove him right. He cannot, like Leonardo da Vinci, Galois, or Babbage, spell out his ideas, as it were, over the heads of his contemporaries, hoping that they will be hailed a century or two later. He is pragmatic and is interested in having his way and his ideas implemented here and now. If he does not, he labours in vain. If Blackett, for example, had not succeeded in persuading the Coastal Command to accept the recommended change in the setting of the time fuse no one would have known the value of his undoubtedly great discovery. Nor could posterity have evaluated it later as with the concepts Babbage and Leonardo presented ahead of their time. Operations research that is not acted upon at once is like an unborn idea that is never missed. An operations-research worker cannot therefore shirk the responsibility for getting his conclusions studied, respected, understood, and fully considered by his colleagues, superiors, and even his own subordinates with whose collaboration alone he can secure their acceptance. In subtle ways he must spare no effort in influencing and persuading the policy-makers without treading on their toes. Some zealous scientists may regard this as unethical and would advocate calling a spade a spade. But in the practical business of daily life no good ever comes of being tactless and needlessly making one's superiors lose face. This is why the art of communicating operations-research results to policy-makers is an imaginative and artistic exercise requiring all the gifts of successful persuaders. However, before an operations-research expert has anything to communicate, he has first to discover it.

How does one make an operations-research discovery worth communicating? Does it need the abracadabra of higher mathematics? The answer is, curiously enough, both yes and no. The truth is that current work in this field, like the tusks of an elephant, is of two kinds: one kind for grinding and the other for display. The latter kind of work, which appears in the published literature, has an impressive façade. There is a great display of technical virtuosity to delight the mathematician. But the practical value of such work in industrial and field practice in many cases is marginal. The former kind, the grinding sort that is rarely if ever published, is much more rewarding in practice. The reason – apart from the need to keep trade secrets – is that profitable, practical operations-research work is often arrived at by so simple, even crude, an analysis that very often its author himself would hesitate to write a paper about it for publication in a learned journal. And if he did it might well be rejected for its simplicity and lack of mathematical sophistication! I will illustrate this paradox with two examples of operations-research work of my own. One of these concerned the problem of increasing the humping or switching capacity of the Moghalsarai marshalling yard in India, the other that of falling speeds of freight trains on Indian railways. In the former case, as will be shown more clearly in Chapter 8, the service time of the yard, that is, the interval between consecutive switchings of two trains, which naturally determined the switching capacity of the yard, was reduced by ten minutes by providing an additional switch engine in the yard. By doing so the need to reverse the same switch engine on to the next train on the receiving line in the yard (a process that took ten minutes) was obviated.* While the financial gains of this research ran into millions of dollars in preventing detentions of freight trains that were queueing up daily at several stations in the neighbourhood, I could never persuade myself to write for publication in a learned journal a paper on the subject. On the other hand, I did write one on the speeds of freight trains, as the theme was mathematically somewhat sophisticated even though the pragmatic value of the research was practically nil. It merely proved that the speed deterioration noticed was spurious and did not indicate any real drop in standards of operational efficiency. But for improving it there was not a clue. Nevertheless, the paper was considered of sufficient merit to require reissue in a monthly international railway bulletin and translation into French.

The reason is that while learned periodicals and journals value mathematical refinement and academicism for their own sake, industrial enterprises look for only commercial gains. It is as inappropriate to carry the academic approach of a pure mathematician in operations research as it is to adopt the workshop ideology in doing pure mathematics. Such inversion of aims will result in as ludicrous work as that of an operations researcher who

*See page 153.

visited a symphony concert at the Royal Festival Hall in London and is said to have reported as follows:

For considerable periods the four oboe players had nothing to do. The number should be reduced and the work spread evenly over the whole of the concert, thus eliminating peaks of activity. ... Much effort was absorbed in the playing of demi-semi quavers; this seems to be an unnecessary refinement. It is recommended that all notes should be rounded to the nearest semi-quaver ...

Much of the operations-research work published in the periodical literature nowadays seems to the pragmatic industrialist like the above report only viewed from the other side of the hill. It is therefore important to realize that the quality of an operations-research project is judged not by the power of mathematics it employs but by the financial dividends including fringe benefits its adoption yields. As a great industrial captain who is also a great mathematician once told me, there is no doubt that any competent mathematician, if left alone in any large organization, will find something worth *his* while to do. The more important job, however, is to motivate him into doing what is worth his employer's while. If he is properly motivated he will find that he does not have to put a mathematical mountain in labour to secure several operations-research nuggets; quite the contrary. Nearly all the classical O R work done during the Second World War that has given operations research its present prestige was the application of mere common sense to war time problems, often without recourse to recondite mathematics. You may readily verify it by a glance at the pamphlet by Mehta, Thiagarajan, and Jaiswal, 'A Collection of Some Operational Research Problems from World War II'.*

However, constituted as we are, common sense while necessary is not sufficient for serious operations-research work. We also need to muster courage to act in a common-sense way. For even though our initial planning and procedures may be common-sensical and correct, they do not remain so for all time. Our industrial, administrative, and business world is not a complex of ready-made practices and procedures that last forever. It is a world in constant

* My own recent pamphlet entitled 'Operations Research on the South Eastern Railway' is a fresh demonstration of the power of this approach.

flux and of revolutionary leaps, crying aloud for decisions that will permit adaptation to changed situations. Yet we often do not make the decisions because we dare not face the confusion and trouble of change. Hence the first axiom in this field: that operations research is common-sense management pursued with *un*common courage.

Now if operations research is merely common sense pursued with uncommon courage, many of you who now hear of operations research for the first time may say, and in most cases with reason, that it is the sort of thing you have been doing all your life. Like Monsieur Jourdain you have been speaking prose without knowing it. Nevertheless, when one hears for the first time that there is something called prose, one also learns that there are associated with it such ancillary disciplines as grammar, syntax, phonetics, and orthography, the cultivation of which vastly improves its practice. Likewise, when one hears of operations research one also learns of its associated disciplines.

In the chapters that follow we shall be concerned with some of the better-known operations-research disciplines and techniques that have been developed during the past decade or two. We shall begin with the discipline of numeracy, the art of deciphering the meaning of strings of numbers, exactly as the complementary art of literacy is that of understanding what collections of words mean. Indeed, it is an art whose practice is in some ways even more essential than that of language, because if words are wise men's tokens for traffic in ideas, numbers are their real estate. But this need impose no great hardship. For luckily the art of numeracy, like that of language, may be practised at many levels. Just as there are grades of literacy, ranging from people just about able to sign their cheques to people worthy of the Nobel Prize for literature, so also there are people barely numerate enough to check their shopping bills at one extreme and contributors to the journals of the Royal Statistical Society at the other. Between these two terminals of numeracy there is many a habitable half-way house where one may lodge oneself comfortably according to one's taste or requirement. But at whatever point of the numerate continuum one decides to rest oneself, one ought to know enough of the basic principles of numeracy – its syntax and grammar – to make sense of any given large array of numbers. We shall describe in the next three chapters the principles that will enable a manager to read the regularities that often lurk in numerical counts of reasonably large aggregates and detect even frauds that would otherwise remain unnoticed.* This will be followed by an account of network analysis, linear programming, theory of games and rational decisions, queueing theory, Monte Carlo simulation, and finally some examples of applications of operations research to specific problems. While the techniques of numeracy, network analysis, linear programming, logic of decisions, and the like, have been widely adopted to solve management problems, operations research is no mere creation of an armoury of prefabricated tools and techniques that one seeks to apply willy-nilly to the problems that one faces. It is, on the other hand, a free creation of the executive mind in the field of industry, production, management, and administration by a wise exercise of judgement, common sense, and knowledge of the specific field to which it is applied. I am aware that some will consider this view rather unhelpful. It will be objected that if operations research is simply applied common sense and does not prescribe any routine procedures and methods capable of yielding the solutions we desire, we remain very much where we were. Cultivation of the ancillary disciplines of numeracy, logic of rational decisions, and so on, might amplify our inborn gift of common sense. But it can be no substitute for specific procedures, techniques, and methods that can tell us what to do in any given situation. This is a demand that is legitimate and is by no means peculiar to operations research. It is made in all fields of scientific endeavour although it is nowhere met in full, even in fields where routines, methods, and procedures have been most developed. The truth is that in geometry, where the innovation of Cartesian coordinates and the calculus carried the methods, procedures, and techniques as far as they could go, the role of geometric intuition or Euclidean common sense on which it was exclusively based before Descartes is all but undiminished. This is not to say that methods and procedures have no value; they do. But only when the problem in hand matches the method in our repertoire. In operations research, in particular, the danger of applying unwarily the wrong procedure or method is great because it is quite likely that the assumptions

*For an example see page 33.

underlying the methods do not hold in the case of the problem under study. The only safeguard against such misapplication is a general understanding of the ideas underlying operations-research methods. The object of this book is to unravel their mystique. But to begin with I should like to amend my earlier definition of operations research as a *management* activity pursued in two complementary ways – one half by the free and bold exercise of common sense untrammelled by any routine, and the other half by the application of a repertoire of well-established pre-created methods and techniques to be described later. I am willing, in deference to certain quarters, to let the latter half become the better half, provided the common-sense half continues to rule. If we practise operations research on these lines it can provide a great service to all fields of planning, technology, and development, particularly in the underdeveloped countries of Asia, Africa, and Latin America. Here the field of opportunity is still as simple, virgin, and lavish as that which the operations-research pioneers of the Second World War found when they were first drafted to war work.

# CHAPTER 2

# The Art of Numeracy:
## Statistical Summarization

THE art of numeracy has a discipline of its own no less rigorous than that of the parallel art of literacy. For deciphering the meaning of a string of numbers, usually called statistics, is in many ways similar to understanding the semantic content of a collection of words. And yet the laws of numeracy – its syntax and grammar – have been slow acoming. Despite the existence of some numerical facts like crude censuses of Vedic vintage no real progress in formulating them was made till about 300 years ago, when two independent lines of advance began to emerge. While John Graunt and Halley laid, on the one hand, the foundations of the empirical method of uncovering regularities that often lurk in numerical counts of large populations, Fermat and Pascal, on the other, devised a new probability calculus designed to compute the likely outcome of games of chance. The art of numeracy is a product of the fusion of these two trends – the empirical English method with Continental theory. The former has led to what is nowadays known as the problem of statistical summarization, including its offshoot, statistical specification, and the latter to that of statistical inference. Solution of both is the heart of numeracy.

Consider first the problem of statistical summarization, that is, the problem of deriving facts from figures. The problem arises because if we have an array of figures about any phenomenon we must first find a way of compressing the mass of figures presented us to a reasonable size in order to read their message, if any. Suppose, for instance, we are given the monthly earnings of 1,000,000 people in a town. Such a chaotic plethora of numbers in the raw can convey nothing meaningful to any human mind. In order not to miss the wood for the trees it is necessary to replace this unorganized string of numbers in the raw by a few selected figures – preferably by a single figure. How shall we proceed so as to discover a single figure that could in some way be taken as a representative of the entire array? There are several ways of doing this. First, there is the well-known method of replacing the entire array by its average or *arithmetic* mean. To calculate it we add *all* the figures in the array and divide it by the number of figures so added, as every schoolboy knows.

However, the (arithmetic) average or mean is only one among the several possible ways of replacing a vast array of figures by a single representative figure. Although it is most frequently used it is by no means the most representative. In some cases it is even palpably misleading to use the arithmetic average as a representative of the entire set. For instance, suppose the speed of a car going up on a hilly section was 20 miles per hour and coming down the same distance 30 miles per hour. What is the average speed on the round trip? If we say it is 25 we shall fall in error as may be seen by a little calculation. Suppose the section was 60 miles long. Going up our car therefore took 3 hours and coming down 2 hours – in all 5 hours over a distance of 120 miles. The average speed on the round trip was therefore 120/5 = 24 miles per hour and not 25 as we erroneously calculated by taking the simple average of the two average speeds. In such cases it is necessary to juggle with the figures a bit before striking the average. We first convert the original figures, viz. 20 and 30, into their reciprocals, that is, into 1/20, 1/30. We then calculate the average of these reciprocals and invert the average so derived. We thus obtain 24 which, as we saw, is the true average over-all speed on the round trip. The average obtained in this way is known as the harmonic mean. It can be shown that the harmonic mean of any set of figures is always less than the straightforward arithmetic average of the same set. As a result we are apt to be erroneously satisfied with our results if we take the ordinary arithmetic average in cases where we should, in fact, take the harmonic mean. This is not merely a theoretical point. There are actual managerial situations where such erroneous substitution of arithmetic for the harmonic average does occur. The Indian Railways, for example, compile average speeds of their freight trains run on various sections during each ten-day period in order to keep a watch on the mobility of the sections. Average speed of freight trains is quite a useful index of its mobility. But the way the index is actually compiled is erroneous. For the average speed of all the through trains run on any day is first calculated. Then the average of these ten daily averages is taken as the average over-all speed for the ten-day period as a whole instead of the harmonic average of the ten daily averages. For the sake of definiteness, let us assume that the average speed on a section was 12 miles on the first day and 15 miles on the second day. What is the average speed on the 2 days in question? The usual practice is to take the arithmetic mean of 12 and 15, viz. 13·5, and adopt it as the average speed during the 2-day period. But this is incorrect. For suppose the section is 125 miles long. The average time taken per train on the first day is 125/12 hours and on the second day 125/15. Now the average time taken by the trains run on

2 days is $\frac{1}{2}\left(\dfrac{125}{12}+\dfrac{125}{15}\right)$. The average speed is therefore:

$$\frac{125}{\dfrac{125}{2}\left(\dfrac{1}{12}+\dfrac{1}{15}\right)} \;=\; \frac{1}{\frac{1}{2}\left(\dfrac{1}{12}+\dfrac{1}{15}\right)} \;=\; 13\cdot3.^{*}$$

In this case the difference between the true (harmonic) average and the arithmetic average is rather small, being only 0·2 m.p.h. But in a 10-day period it may be appreciable. A case in point is the following performance during a 10-day period: 16 m.p.h. on 4 days, 15 m.p.h. on 3 days, 12 m.p.h. on 2 days and 10 m.p.h. on 1 day. The arithmetic average is 14·3 m.p.h. but the actual, that is, harmonic average during the 10-day period is 13·7 m.p.h., which is appreciably lower.

Some people imagine that the error is due to taking the average of averages, which in their opinion is one of the seven deadly sins which a statistician must never commit. This is only partly correct. There are numerous cases where it is perfectly legitimate to take the average of averages. Suppose, for instance, you had the average monthly earnings of a departmental store during each of the four quarters of a year. The monthly average of the earnings during the year is simply the arithmetic average of the four monthly averages during the four quarters. But in cases where an average is obtained by dividing one fundamental statistic by another, e.g. average cost

---

* Throughout this book decimal points are raised in the British fashion; multiplication is indicated by the (×) sign rather than the centered dot (·).

of running a departmental store per employee, it is *not* permissible to average the averages. In such cases the averages have to be 'weighted' in order to get the correct average of the averages. Suppose, for instance, we are given the average cost per employee of running 5 departmental stores in a chain. What is the average cost per employee of the chain as a whole? Let the 5 average costs be $c_1, c_2, c_3, c_4, c_5$ rupees per employee. The arithmetic average of the 5 averages is

$$\frac{c_1 + c_2 + c_3 + c_4 + c_5}{5}.$$

But it is not necessarily the correct average unless all the departmental stores had the *same* number of employees. As in fact the numbers of employees working in the different stores are different, the average of averages is not the correct over-all average cost per employee for the chain as a whole. Let the number of employees working in the 5 stores be $n_1, n_2, n_3, n_4, n_5$.

The total cost of each of the 5 stores would be

$$n_1 c_1, \; n_2 c_2, \; n_3 c_3, \; n_4 c_4, \; n_5 c_5.$$

The total number of employees is

$$n_1 + n_2 + n_3 + n_4 + n_5.$$

Hence the average over-all cost per employee for the 5 stores in the chain as a whole is

$$\frac{n_1 c_1 + n_2 c_2 + n_3 c_3 + n_4 c_4 + n_5 c_5}{n_1 + n_2 + n_3 + n_4 + n_5}.$$

Here we have multiplied (or 'weighted') each of the 5 averages, viz. $c_1, c_2, c_3, c_4, c_5$ to be averaged by its corresponding 'weight' viz. $n_1, n_2, n_3, n_4, n_5$ and divided the total of the products by the sum of the 'weights'. This is known as the 'weighted' average of the 5 average costs per employee.

'Weighting' thus is a device to check against the excessive egalitarian tendency of the arithmetic average. The plain truth is that the arithmetic average is rather too much of a leveller. Like the communist, it treats every item to be averaged as on a par with every other. But in a world bristling with inequalities even a communist is obliged to concede that a Stalin is more 'equal' (to use an expression of George Orwell) than a Molotov. So if we have to redress the balance between the counterparts of 'Stalins' and 'Molotovs' in a set of items to be averaged, we must assign bigger 'weights' to the big items and smaller weights to the little items before averaging the lot. What 'weights' are to be given to the various items is a question which can be decided only by a consideration of all the factors involved in any given concrete situation.

In the foregoing we have given some instances of cases where it is erroneous to replace the given set of figures by its arithmetic average. In general, we should always beware of averaging figures that are not homogeneous or widely disparate. For instance, there is no point in averaging the incomes of two persons as poles apart as the Nizam of Hyderabad and a rural slum dweller. When a set of figures is obviously heterogeneous it is better not to replace it by the arithmetic average of the set. The reason is that the average in such cases is not, generally speaking, a real representative of the central tendency of the set and is apt to be over-influenced by a few isolated figures. Suppose, for instance, we had two groups of people. Suppose further that in one of these 99 per cent of the people earned 160 rupees a month and 1 per cent 6,000 rupees a month, while in the second 50 per cent earned 180 rupees per month and the other 50 per cent 220 rupees per month. We can only say that the people in the first group earned more than those in the second if the earnings were divided evenly, but that is a big 'if'. Although the average earnings in the former case are higher being 218 rupees against 200 rupees of the latter, on the whole the people in the former group earn *less* than in the latter. If you pick a person at random from each group it is 99-to-1 that the person from the second group earned more.

How can we choose a representative figure so as to get over fallacies of this kind? In such cases we replace our array of figures by another kind of average which is not influenced by extreme items of the set. One such average is known as the *median*. It is the earning of the middle item, if we arrange all earners in order of their earnings. Thus consider a group of 101 persons with their monthly earnings as given in Table 1: (see opposite).

If we arranged these 101 persons in ascending order of their earnings the earning of the middle, that is the 51st person in this

*Table 1*

| Number of persons | Monthly earnings in rupees |
|:---:|:---:|
| 25 | 140 |
| 15 | 150 |
| 12 | 240 |
| 18 | 360 |
| 20 | 400 |
| 11 | 470 |

ordering, is known as the *median*. It is easy to see that the 51st person would be one of the 12 who earn 240 rupees a month each. The median value is therefore 240 rupees. In the same way we observe that in the case of the 2 groups cited above the median value for the first group is 160 rupees and that for the second 180 rupees. If we compare the median earnings of the 2 groups instead of their arithmetic averages we shall avoid the fallacy pointed out earlier.

Another way of replacing our array of monthly earnings re-referred to above is to replace it by the so-called *mode*. By mode is meant that value of the earning which pertains to the largest number of persons in the group. In the example of 101 persons whose earnings have been shown in Table 1 it is the group of 25 persons who earn 140 rupees per month each. This is, therefore, the fashionable or modal value, *mode* in French meaning 'fashion'. The mode, that is, the value of monthly earnings common to the largest numbers of persons, is thus 140 rupees. From the way in which the median and the mode are obtained it is clear that they are not influenced by the extreme elements of the array. They are, therefore, in some cases better representatives of the entire array of figures than the more usual arithmetic mean.

From the foregoing account it might appear that the arithmetic average is a highly over-rated entity in statistics and that other kinds of averages such as the harmonic mean, the median and the mode have been unduly neglected. Nevertheless, it is true that even a statistician almost exclusively operates with the arithmetic average. In the standard textbooks on the subject one finds an account of other kinds of averages such as the harmonic mean, the median and mode, etc., and the circumstances under which they may be put to use. But after the first chapter they somehow seem to forget the existence of these more sophisticated types of averages and fall back upon the good old arithmetic average or mean. The reason is that arithmetic average alone is suited to computational work. You cannot get far in statistics without using the arithmetic average. But to mitigate its over-egalitarian predilection statisticians have had to resort to other artifices. For no matter by what type of average, whether median, mean, mode or whatever we choose to represent any array of figures, it can only give a somewhat oversimplified picture of the facts they embody. If we want a deeper grasp of these facts we have to relax the restriction we imposed at the outset, namely, to make do with a single number. Suppose then we were permitted to summarize our array of figures by means of two or more numbers instead of only one. How shall we proceed? In the first place, we may take the average (the arithmetic, harmonic, median, or mode) as one of the two or three numbers permitted us in preparing our summary. How shall we select the others? That depends on whether we want to have only one or two additional figures. If we want our summary to consist of two additional figures, we can select the maximum and minimum value from our array of figures in addition to the average. Thus suppose we are given the following daily wages in rupees of 10 persons:

$$2, 3, 4, 6, 5, 3, 4, 4, 5, 4.$$

We may replace the entire array by a summarized picture:

| | |
|---|---|
| average daily wage | 4 rupees |
| maximum daily wage | 6 rupees |
| minimum daily wage | 2 rupees. |

But if we want to limit our summary to only 2 numbers we can take the difference between the maximum and minimum, viz. $6-2 = 4$, as a measure of the *range* within which the daily wages vary. Thus we can say the average daily wage of 10 persons in the group is 4 rupees with a range of variation of 4 rupees. For technical reasons that will be clearer in the sequel statisticians have not taken kindly to the idea of using range, that is the difference between the maximum and minimum, as a measure of the variance or 'spread' of a given array of figures. They prefer to use another measure, called the standard deviation, for this purpose. The idea of standard deviation may most simply be explained as follows.

Taking the figures of the array of the daily wages of 10 persons given above as an illustration we may say that the average of our figures is 4 rupees. If we take the deviation or difference of the individual figures from our average we have another set of figures equal in number to our original set. These 10 deviations are obtained by subtracting the average 4 from each item in succession. They are reproduced below:

$$(2-4), (3-4), (4-4), (6-4), (5-4),$$
or,      $-2$    $-1$    $0$    $+2$    $+1$

$$(3-4), (4-4), (4-4), (5-4) \ (4-4).$$
or,      $-1$    $0$    $0$    $+1$    $0$

We could replace this new set, the set of deviations (or differences from the mean), by a single figure as a representative of the entire set. This latter figure could then be taken as a measure of the 'spread' of the original figures from their arithmetic mean. How shall we replace our set of deviations or differences from the average by means of a single figure? If we took the average of these differences (each difference with its appropriate sign), we should get 0 as the average of these differences, as a glance at the figures shows. In fact, this would be so not only in this particular case but in every case on account of the very nature of the arithmetic average. You can try this by taking any set of figures and striking their average. Now take the differences of these figures from the average. Some of these differences will be plus and others minus. If we sum up these differences having regard to their respective signs, the sum would be 0. It is therefore no use taking the average of these differences or deviations, as we shall always get one and the same result, namely, 0. To avoid this difficulty we could ignore the minus sign of the differences and strike their arithmetic average *as if* all the differences were positive. This would give us a measure of the variance or 'spread' of our original array of figures. For instance, the average value of the 10 deviations quoted above regardless of their signs would be $\frac{8}{10} = 0\cdot8$. The number $0\cdot8$ so derived may be taken as a representative of the set of individual deviations from the mean and therefore as a measure of the 'spread' of daily wages round the mean. It is known as the mean deviation.

However, tampering with the signs of deviations brings its own nemesis in the long run. It makes this measure of variance or 'spread' mathematically intractable. Statisticians therefore do not favour the idea. They prefer to solve the difficulty in another way. If some of the differences are positive and others negative, and if the sum of the positive differences always cancels out that of the negative differences, we could make them all positive by squaring the differences. You will recall that the product of 2 negative numbers is positive, so that the square of a negative difference like $(-2)^2$ is $+4$. We could now deal with the squares of differences which are all positive. We could sum up these squares. Dividing this by the number of differences added up we would get the average of these squared differences. But to undo the initial squaring of the deviations in order to make them all positive, we now take the *square root* of the average of the squared deviations. It is known as the *standard deviation* and gives a measure of the 'spread' of the given set of figures round the average. Using the 10 figures of daily wages of our illustration quoted above we have the following array of differences or deviations from the arithmetic average (4):

$$-2, \ -1, \ 0, \ +2, \ +1, \ -1, \ 0, \ 0, \ +1, \ 0.$$

We note that some of them are positive and others negative. We square these differences to make them all positive. The result is:

$$4, \ 1, \ 0, \ 4, \ 1, \ 1, \ 0, \ 0, \ 1, \ 0.$$

The sum of these 10 squares of differences is 12. The average is, of course, $\frac{12}{10} = 1\cdot2$. The square root of $1\cdot2$ is $1\cdot1$ which is thus the value of our standard deviation.

Now you have every right to demand as to why statisticians

prefer to use this roundabout method of calculating the standard deviation as a measure of the 'spread' of the given array of figures to the simple method of calculating the mean deviation. The reason is that the standard deviation enables us to state that about 50 per cent of the figures of our array would normally lie within the range $m - \frac{2}{3}s$ and $m + \frac{2}{3}s$, where $m$ is the mean or arithmetic average and $s$ the standard deviation of the array. Similarly about 95 per cent of the figures lie within the range $m - 2s$ and $m + 2s$ and 99 per cent within $m - 3s$ and $m + 3s$. This is a rough rule, of course, but it is one which is found to work well enough in practice in most cases. In the case of our set of 10 daily wages quoted above we found $m = 4$ and $s = 1 \cdot 1$, the range $m \pm \frac{2}{3}s$, i.e. $(3 \cdot 3, 4 \cdot 7)$ contains 4 items of the set. This works to 40 per cent in place of 50 per cent postulated by the rule. Likewise, the range $m \pm 2s$, viz. $(1 \cdot 8, 6 \cdot 2)$ contains $\frac{10}{10}$ items of the array, corresponding to a 100 per cent score instead of the 95 per cent postulated by the rule.

In fact, a knowledge of the arithmetic mean $m$ and standard deviation $s$ of any given array would enable us to state in most cases, at least approximately, the percentage of figures lying in any stated range such as $m \pm ks$. If we assign to $k$ different values like $k = \frac{2}{3}$, 1, 1·5, 2, etc., we get different ranges. Tables exist which enable us to state the percentage of figures of our array lying in the range $m \pm ks$ for various values of $k$. Armed with such tables we could summarize our array of figures by computing only two statistics, namely the arithmetic mean ($m$) and the standard deviation ($s$). This is why standard deviation is a much more sophisticated measure of the spread or scatter of the numbers in our array than the range. If the range is like a go–no–go gauge, standard deviation is like a graduated scale in the measurement of the scatter or spread of any given set of numbers. However summarization of an array of numbers by merely computing their mean and standard deviation has two drawbacks. First, the validity of the summary depends on the chance that the numbers in the array happen to conform to the pattern assumed in the computation of these tables, although such a chance is quite considerable, as we shall see later. Secondly, even if it is valid it is not sufficiently graphic to reveal the regularities, patterns, or 'laws' that often lie buried deep under a debris, if not a mountain, of numbers.

Consider, for example, the plight of the manager of a by-no-means-apocryphal cartridge factory, who could make neither head nor tail of the readings of hardness indices of cartridge cases logged by his inspectors in order to ensure that only those with index number 80 or above were accepted. He was naturally puzzled when he was presented with scores of such recordings like the set of 100 numbers shown below:

*Indices of hardness*

86, 83, 84, 77, 87, 82, 83, 81, 85, 84
80, 80, 82, 85, 80, 82, 80, 83, 84, 85
81, 82, 82. 83, 80, 84, 80, 81, 85. 81
86, 82, 81, 80, 83, 82, 79, 81, 81, 83
85, 84, 80, 78, 84, 80, 80, 77. 81, 83
81, 81, 85, 81, 82, 81, 81, 81, 84, 82
80, 79, 80, 80, 82, 88, 81, 80, 82, 85
84, 80, 82, 78, 80, 84, 81, 83, 83, 81
80, 81, 82, 83, 83, 82, 78. 83, 82, 81
81, 83, 84, 82, 83, 80, 79, 80, 80, 82

Nothing very revealing would emerge if he summarized the afore-mentioned array of 100 numbers by computing their mean and standard deviation although even this computation would be a lot easier if only he set them in tabular form showing the frequency with which each value of the hardness index occurred in the array. Such tabulation is easily done. We find that the numbers in the array vary within the range 77 to 88. We can therefore tabulate them in the form of a frequency distribution indicating on how many occasions each of the 12 measurements 77 to 88, both inclusive, occurred in the above logging. Thus we observe that 77 occurred twice, 78 and 79 each thrice, 80 and 81 each 20 times, and so on for other integers as shown in the table opposite of their frequency of occurrence.

Since the import of the data is more quickly grasped if the frequency distribution is presented in a graphical form, an entirely equivalent way of presenting Table 2 is to diagram it as in Figure 2 by recourse to the chart-room principle. The chart-room

*Table 2.* Frequency distribution of hardness indices.

| Hardness index | Number of times occurring or frequency |
|:---:|:---:|
| 77 | 2 |
| 78 | 3 |
| 79 | 3 |
| 80 | 20 |
| 81 | 20 |
| 82 | 17 |
| 83 | 14 |
| 84 | 10 |
| 85 | 7 |
| 86 | 2 |
| 87 | 1 |
| 88 | 1 |
| total | 100 |

principle, by the way, is the principle of graphs you learnt at school. If you have a series of associated number pairs like the numbers in Table 2, where the hardness index 77 is associated with the frequency number 2, and so on for the other 11 pairs of numbers, each pair may be represented by a point on a graph paper. We draw two perpendicular lines $OX$ and $OY$ on a graph paper. If we measure a length $OM = x$ along $OX$ to represent the first number of the pair, that is the hardness index, and another length $MP = y$ parallel to $OY$ to represent the second number of the pair, that is the frequency, we obtain a set of 12 points $P_1, P_2 \ldots P_{12}$ to represent the 12 pairs of numbers listed in Table 2. A glance at Figure 2 shows that there is an abrupt precipice at $P_4$ corresponding to 80 hardness, the critical level below which cartridges are rejected.

While the frequencies to the right of indices 80 and 81 taper off gradually, those to the left fall much too brusquely in comparison. There could not possibly be anything in the production process favouring numbers exceeding the critical level of 80 so much more pronouncedly than those below it. Such a discontinuity in the frequency distribution at the *critical acceptance* point could arise only because of deliberate deception. *Prima facie* the inspectors were marking cartridge cases which were in reality of hardness 77, 78, and 79 as 80, 81 or more. Further inquiry fully confirmed the surmise. The incident shows how even a visual examination of the distribution pattern of numbers of a large array may reveal at a glance some of the operating conditions that have produced them. In other words, the form of frequency distribution is often an index of the shape of things already happened. If, therefore, we

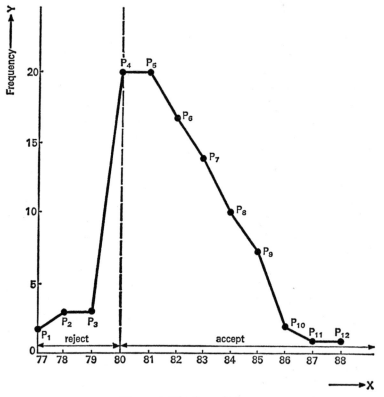

*Figure 2.* Hardness index.

can deduce a number of theoretical frequency distributions that are likely to arise from pre-assigned operating conditions, by comparing any observed distribution with its nearest relative among the theoretical ones we can obtain a fair idea of the prevailing state of affairs that have occasioned it. This is why the problem of statistical summarization in its broader sense boils down to identifying a given distribution with some one of a number of typical theoretical frequency distributions which serve as norms of comparison. Specification or derivation of such theoretical distributions is therefore but a prelude to the recovery of power through knowledge from the Niagara of numbers that would otherwise run inevitably to waste.

Among the theoretical frequencies available for comparison to ferret laws and regularities from numerical tables we may list the so-called 'normal' distribution of errors of observation, the exponential distribution for telephone calls arriving at random at an exchange, the Poisson distribution for the numbers of emitted particles from a radioactive substance, the binomial distribution for the number of defectives in batches of goods sampled for inspection, the negative binomial distribution for the number of accidents to munition workers, the geometric distribution for a batsman's score per innings, the Pareto distribution for the size of incomes, etc. Each of these distributions is the outcome of special conditions of the case. It therefore follows that if we can identify the actual frequency distribution with some one of these theoretical possibilities we can infer the conditions which have led to the distribution we have obtained, like the steeply discontinuous distribution of cartridge cases under conditions of fudging. Such statistical specifications are therefore now fundamental in the physical, biological, and social sciences; and even when they are apt to be incomplete and insufficient as in the case of fields like economics, sociology, administration, and management they are of great value for partial descriptions adequate for particular purposes such as detecting fraudulent inspections by officials inspecting production or other shortcomings in industrial practice. We shall therefore describe below some of the typical standard distributions with a brief indication of the circumstances of their origin.

Broadly speaking, frequency distributions are of two main types – either discrete or continuous – depending on the nature of the variate under measurement. If the measurements made are necessarily discrete such as those of births and deaths or even putatively so as was the case with the hardness index of our earlier illustration, which was restricted to only integral values like 77, 78, 79, etc., the resultant frequency distribution is said to be discrete. If, on the other hand, the variate being measured can assume any value in the real number continuum within the range of its variation, the frequency distribution obtained is continuous. In either case we normalize the frequency distribution to make it independent of the number of measurements taken and thus be rid of the arbitrariness of the choice made. We do so by expressing the frequencies in the form of ratios instead of absolute numbers. Thus instead of showing in Table 2 or Figure 2 the absolute frequency (20) of any measurement, say, 80, it is usual to show its *relative* frequency, that is, the ratio of the number of occasions (20) the index 80 was observed to the total number of observations (100). Thus instead of tabulating or diagramming the absolute frequency 20 against the measurement 80 we use its relative frequency, viz. the ratio $\frac{20}{100} = 0.2$. As a result the sum of all the relative frequencies equals 1 in every case no matter what number of measurements are made. Such normalization by recourse to relative frequencies in lieu of their absolute values naturally facilitates the comparison of actual distributions with theoretical ones because we do not have to depend on the arbitrary number of measurements we choose to make.

Only when the variate is continuous the normalization is secured by a slight variant of the procedure adopted in the discrete case. Instead of representing the relative frequency observed by the *length* of the ordinate line drawn against the corresponding integral value of the variate we represent it by the *area* of a rectangle. Consider, for example, the following 80 measurements of height which being a continuous variable is no longer restricted to take only discrete integral values:

*Measurements of heights in inches*

| | | | | | | | | | |
|---|---|---|---|---|---|---|---|---|---|
| 64·2 | 65·8 | 66·3 | 66·6 | 66·9 | 67·0 | 67·4 | 67·5 | 67·6 | 67·8 |
| 67·9 | 67·9 | 68·2 | 68·2 | 68·3 | 68·4 | 68·5 | 68·5 | 68·6 | 68·6 |
| 68·6 | 68·7 | 68·7 | 68·8 | 68·9 | 68·9 | 68·9 | 69·0 | 69·0 | 69·0 |
| 69·1 | 69·1 | 69·1 | 69·2 | 69·3 | 69·3 | 69·4 | 69·5 | 69·5 | 69·5 |
| 69·5 | 69·6 | 69·7 | 69·8 | 69·9 | 69·9 | 70·0 | 70·0 | 70·1 | 70·1 |
| 70·2 | 70·3 | 70·4 | 70·4 | 70·5 | 70·5 | 70·6 | 70·6 | 70·9 | 70·9 |
| 71·0 | 71·0 | 71·1 | 71·2 | 71·4 | 71·4 | 71·4 | 71·6 | 71·7 | 71·8 |
| 72·0 | 72·1 | 72·2 | 72·4 | 72·5 | 72·8 | 73·0 | 73·4 | 74·2 | 74·9 |

To make sense of the array of numbers given above we observe that all measurements lie within the range 64·2 to 74·9. We could therefore divide the entire interval of its variation into 12 equal sub-intervals:

63·5 to 64·5, 64·5 to 65·5, 65·5 to 66·5, 66·5 to 67·5
..., 73·5 to 74·5, 74·5 to 75·5

and count the frequency of occurrence of values in each sub-interval. If we do so we will find that the height data could be tabulated as shown below:

*Table 3*

| (i) Height in inches | (ii) Frequency (Number of occasions occurring) | (iii) Frequency ratio = $\dfrac{\text{column (ii)}}{80}$ |
|:---:|:---:|:---:|
| 63·5–64·5 | 1 | 0·01 |
| 64·5–65·5 | 0 | 0·00 |
| 65·5–66·5 | 2 | 0·03 |
| 66·5–67·5 | 5 | 0·06 |
| 67·5–68·5 | 10 | 0·12 |
| 68·5–69·5 | 23 | 0·29 |
| 69·5–70·5 | 15 | 0·19 |
| 70·5–71·5 | 11 | 0·14 |
| 71·5–72·5 | 8 | 0·10 |
| 72·5–73·5 | 3 | 0·04 |
| 73·5–74·5 | 1 | 0·01 |
| 74·5–75·5 | 1 | 0·01 |
| total | 80 | 1·00 |

In graphing the contents of Table 3 all we need do is to erect rectangles on the sub-intervals in such a way that the area of each rectangle represents the frequency ratio of the corresponding sub-interval as shown in Figure 3. The figure obtained is called a histogram and presents the height pattern in a graphic form, which is far more readily intelligible than the original hodge-podge of numbers from which it has been derived. If we had a much larger array of measurements, say, 10,000 or more, we could have split the range of variation of the variate into a still smaller size of, say, a $\frac{1}{2}$ inch or $\frac{1}{4}$ inch width. The narrower the width of the sub-interval adopted

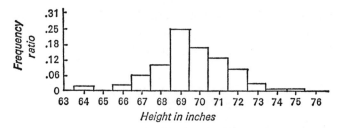

*Figure 3.* Frequency histogram.

and therefore the larger their number, the closer will each rectangle erected thereon correspond to the ordinate line. In the limiting case when the number of sub-intervals is very large, or, to use the mathematician's lingo, 'infinitely' large, the width of the rectangles of the histogram shrinks indefinitely so that the conglomeration of infinitely narrow adjacent rectangles becomes a smooth curve. Such a curve is known as a frequency curve. Figure 4 shows the

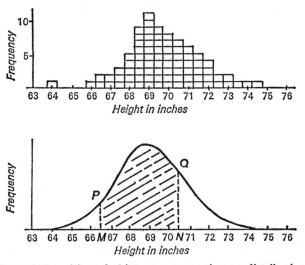

*Figure 4.* Transition of a histogram to continuous distribution.

progress of a histogram towards a smooth frequency curve. The merit of the latter is that it readily gives the proportion (or frequency ratio) of items lying within any stated range. Suppose we wanted the frequency ratio of persons with heights lying within the range 66·4 to 70·6. All we have to do is to draw 2 ordinate lines from the point $M$, where $OM$ represents 66·4 and from point $N$ where $ON$ represents 70·6. The area enclosed by the frequency curve between these 2 ordinates $MP$, $NQ$, and $OX$ is the required frequency ratio. Hence if we could draw the frequency curve of heights it would give us all we wanted to know about them.

At this stage it might be objected that the frequency-curve method of summarizing our data is in the end self-defeating. For it requires a very large number of figures. We have to have a frequency ratio in each of the numerous sub-intervals into which we split the entire range of the variable before the curve can be drawn. The summary therefore has to employ a larger array of figures than even the original. If the object was economy of figures it has been completely defeated and to call the frequency curve (or the table of figures on which it is based) a summary of the original array is a misnomer.

There is force in this objection but fortunately there are two ways of specifying a curve. One is to have a table giving the pairs of associated numbers, or coordinates of a large number of points lying on it. We plot the points on a graph paper and join them by a freehand curve. The other is to give the equation of the curve. That is, we specify a mathematical formula whereby we can calculate the ordinate ($y$) of any point on the curve provided its abscissa ($x$) is given. For example, this formula may be:

$$y = 2x+3,$$

or,

$$y = 4x^2+5,$$

or any of the numerous more recondite expressions invented by mathematicians. Now it may happen that after we have drawn our frequency curve by making use of the given table of figures in the manner indicated above and noted its approximate shape, we may be able to state its equation in a mathematical form. We may, for instance, be able to say that the frequency curve of heights shown in Figure 4 is of the form

$$y = \frac{1}{\sqrt{2\pi}(1·86)}\, e^{-\frac{1}{2}\left(\frac{x-69·7}{1·86}\right)^2} \tag{i}$$

where $\pi$ and $e$ are two well-known mathematical constants.*

If so, we can throw away the bulky table that has led us to this conclusion, and the entire information contained therein is neatly epitomized in equation (i). In this way, like the truly great, we can cast aside the ladder by which we did ascend.

Now equation (i) is only a special case of a very general class of equations obtained by substituting $m = 69 \cdot 7$ and $s = 1 \cdot 86$ in

$$y = \frac{1}{\sqrt{2\pi}\, s}\; e^{-\frac{1}{2}\left(\frac{x-m}{s}\right)^2} \qquad \text{(ii)}†$$

This equation is of very frequent occurrence and a vast majority (though not all) of statistical data can be made to fit an equation of this type. When this happens to be the case a knowledge of the two constants $m, s$ in the equation (ii) alone enables us to calculate the proportion of items having values lying in *any* stated range, whether small or large, by means of the frequency equation (ii). To be sure there are many other types of equations and we have to discover by trial and error the class of frequency curve or equation to which our statistical table conforms best. Once we have discovered the class of frequency curve a knowledge of a few constants like the $m$ and $s$ occurring in equation (ii) enables us to practically reproduce our table and even to create a new one with finer boundaries than the original. This is the reason for introducing frequency curves. They enable us to summarize our tables by means of a few selected parameters like $m$ and $s$. We first use the given table to draw the frequency curve in a rough sort of way. This rough diagram then suggests the class of frequency curve to which it most probably belongs. The class of frequency curve is defined by its equation which involves one or more constants like the constants $m$ and $s$ occurring in equation (ii). The set of values of these constants occurring in the equation of the frequency curve is the complete summary of our table of figures we wanted to summarize. The summary is now perfect, because the entire table can be replaced

---

*$\pi$ is the ratio of the circumference of a circle to its diameter and its value is approximately $3 \cdot 14 \ldots$; $e$ is used in the theory of logarithms and is equal to $2 \cdot 71 \ldots$ See page 42, Chapter 3 also.

†The frequency distribution conforming to this equation is called 'normal' or gaussian distribution. See also page 58, Chapter 3.

by these two (or more) constants practically without any loss of information. The problem of statistical summarization is thus reduced to that of statistical specification, that is, derivation of theoretical distributions required as norms of comparison. We shall deal with it in the next chapter.

## CHAPTER 3

# The Art of Numeracy:
# Statistical Specification

WE have seen how the problem of statistical summarization leads naturally to that of statistical specification, namely, the derivation of a number of theoretical frequency distributions to serve as norms of comparison. To deal with it we need simple elaborations of two main principles. I will call them the principles of the slide-rule and race-course to facilitate future reference. The slide-rule principle is a way of transforming numbers so that multiplication of any 2 of them may be turned into addition of their transforms called logarithms. The device works because by definition if a number $x$ is some power $a$ of another base number $m$, that is, if $x = m^a$, then log $x = a$.* If some other number $y$ is some other power $b$ of the *same* base number $m$, that is, if $y = m^b$, then log $y = b$. But since $xy = m^a$. $m^b = m^{(a+b)}$, by the same tokens log $(xy) = a+b = \log x + \log y$. In other words, the sum of the logarithms of any 2 numbers $x$ and $y$ is the logarithm of their product $xy$.

The second or race-course principle is the punter's rule for evaluating his betting odds. He assesses them according to the formula that while the chance of a 'win' or 'place' is the sum of individual chances of the respective events in question, that of a double or triple tote is their product. These additions and multiplication rules of compounding probabilities suggested by the punter's intuition apply universally to all uncertain events governed by the laws of chance. Consequently they are the basis of the whole of probability calculus on which theories of statistical specification and statistical inference have been reared. It is therefore worth our while to digress a little on the theory of probability and its underlying race-course principle.

*The base number may be any number whatever. But it is usually either 10 for ordinary numerical computations, or $e = 2 \cdot 71$ mentioned earlier at page 40 Chapter 2 for more theoretical investigations.

Although large volumes have been written by learned people just to explain what we ought to understand by the word 'probability', in statistics one can get along well enough with the ordinary common-sense view of probability. All of us have a primitive intuition which enables us to judge in certain cases whether one event is more likely than another. Thus every poker player knows that a 'full' house is less likely than a double pair though more likely than a 'four'. It is this primitive notion of probability that sustains the probability calculus. We may explain it by means of a single example. Suppose we have an urn containing 3 similar balls of which 2 are black and 1 white. If we draw 1 ball at random we may chance to pick any one of the 3. There are thus 3 equally likely ways of picking a ball of which 2 give black balls and 1 white. Hence the probability of drawing a black ball is 2 chances in 3 or $\frac{2}{3}$. Similarly the probability of drawing a white ball is $\frac{1}{3}$. More generally, if there are in all $n$ equally likely ways in which an event can happen of which $m$ are favourable to a certain outcome, then the probability ($p$) of that outcome is $\frac{m}{n}$. Thus, if we had an urn with 6 balls of which 3 are black, 2 white, and 1 red, the probability of drawing a black ball would be 3/6 or $\frac{1}{2}$. For the ball could be drawn in 6 ($n = 6$) possible ways of which only 3 ($m = 3$) are favourable to the emergence of a black ball. Similarly the probability of drawing a white ball would be 2/6 or $\frac{1}{3}$ and that of drawing a red only 1/6. If the number of ways favourable to an outcome ($m$) is equal to the total number of ways ($n$) in which the event can possibly occur, that is, if it is absolutely certain that the event would take place, the probability ($p$) of the event is $\frac{n}{n} = 1$. On the other hand, if the number of ways ($m$) favourable to its outcome is 0, that is, if it is certain that the event cannot take place at all, the probability ($p$) of the outcome is $\frac{0}{n} = 0$. In other words, if it is absolutely certain that the event is impossible, its probability is 0. It follows that the probability $p$ of any event can only take some value between 0 and 1. If the event is absolutely certain (such as tossing 'head' with a spurious coin which has a head imprinted on both sides), $p$ is unity. If, on the other hand, the event is impossible (such as drawing a picture card from a pictureless bridge hand), $p$ is 0. For other events which are neither absolutely certain nor impossible $p$ is some intermediate number between 0 and 1.

With the foregoing definition of probability it is possible to develop a mathematical theory of probability. For this purpose we need only two rules implicit in the race-course principle, namely, the addition and product rules for deriving the probability of compound events composing it. The man who first said, 'Heads I win, tails you lose' was no mere sly author of a deceptive phrase; he was an adept at the addition law of probability. He knew that to calculate the total chance of a win he had to add up the probabilities of each of the several ways in which he could win. In the first place, he would win if the coin turned up 'head'. This has the chance $\frac{1}{2}$. In the second place, you would lose, or he would win, if the coin turned up 'tail' of which the chance is again $\frac{1}{2}$. Adding together the 2 probabilities the chance ($p$) of his winning is $\frac{1}{2}+\frac{1}{2} = 1$. And since an event whose probability is unity is absolutely certain, there is no doubt that the sly phrase-monger would win. To take another example of the addition law, suppose we wanted to find the probability of drawing *either* a black *or* a white ball from an urn containing 3 black, 2 white, and 1 red ball. As there are 3 black and 2 white balls in the urn, there are 5 ways in which the ball drawn will be *either* black *or* white. But there are 6 balls in all in the urn. So the event, viz. drawing a ball, could happen in 6 ways of which 5 ways lead to the emergence of a white *or* black ball. The probability of drawing either a black or a white ball is therefore 5/6. But

$$5/6 = 3/6+2/6.$$

As we have seen, 3/6 is the probability of drawing a black ball and 2/6 that of drawing a white ball. Hence the probability of drawing *either* a white *or* a black ball is the sum of the probability of drawing a black ball *and* that of drawing a white ball. The rule is perfectly general and may be written symbolically:

probability of $E_1$ or $E_2$ = probability of $E_1$+probability of $E_2$.

Product rule is concerned with the conjunction or simultaneous occurrence of 2 events. Suppose $E_1$ is the event of drawing a black ball in the *first* draw. To make the conditions of the second draw identical with those of the first we replace the ball drawn in the first draw and draw another ball a *second* time. Suppose $E_2$ is the event of drawing a white ball in the *second* draw. What is the prob-ability of the simultaneous occurrence of $E_1$ and $E_2$, that is, of drawing a black ball in the first draw *and* a white one in the second? Let us denote the 3 black balls by $B_1$, $B_2$, $B_3$, 2 white balls by $W_1$, $W_2$, and 1 red ball by $R$. We could draw any of the 6 balls

$$B_1, B_2, B_3, W_1, W_2, R$$

in the first draw. Suppose we drew $B_1$ and replaced it after noting its colour before making the second draw. Again we could draw any one of the 6 balls so that our combination of 2 events could be any one of the 6 combinations:

$$B_1 B_1, B_1 B_2, B_1 B_3, B_1 W_1, B_1 W_2, B_1 R.$$

But if we had drawn $B_2$ in the first draw our combination of the 2 events would have been:

$$B_2 B_1, B_2 B_2; B_2 W_3; B_2 W_1, B_2 W_2, B_2 R.$$

Proceeding in this way it is easy to see that our combination of 2 events could take place in any one of the following $6 \times 6 = 36$ ways:

$$
\begin{array}{cccccc}
B_1 B_1, & B_1 B_2, & B_1 B_3, & B_1 W_1, & B_1 W_2, & B_1 R \\
B_2 B_1, & B_2 B_2, & B_2 B_3, & B_2 W_1 & B_2 W_2, & B_2 R \\
B_3 B_1, & B_3 B_2, & B_3 B_3, & B_3 W_1, & B_3 W_2, & B_3 R \\
W_1 B_1, & W_1 B_2, & W_1 B_3, & W_1 W_1, & W_1 W_2, & W_1 R \\
W_2 B_1, & W_2 B_2, & W_2 B_3, & W_2 W_1, & W_2 W_2, & W_2 R \\
R B_1, & R B_2, & R B_3, & R W_1, & R W_2, & R R
\end{array}
$$

Of these 36 ways only the following 6 combinations give a black ball in the *first* draw and a white one in the *second*:

$$
\begin{array}{cc}
B_1 W_1 & B_1 W_2 \\
B_2 W_1 & B_2 W_2 \\
B_3 W_1 & B_3 W_2
\end{array}
$$

Hence the probability ($p$) of drawing a black ball in the *first* draw and a white one in the *second* is:

$$p = \frac{6}{36} = \frac{3 \times 2}{6 \times 6} = \frac{3}{6} \times \frac{2}{6}$$

  = (probability of drawing a black ball in the first draw)

  × (probability of drawing a white ball in the second draw)

  = probability of $E_1$ × probability of $E_2$

Hence probability of $E_1$ and $E_2$ = probability of $E_1$ × probability of $E_2$.

By means of these two rules we can calculate the probability of any combination, however complex, of elementary events, although the actual solution of the problem may present considerable technical difficulties.

Having grasped the two computational rules implicit in the race-course principle we can now proceed to derive one of the most important discrete frequency distributions. It is called the binomial distribution because it follows the pattern of Newton's binomial theorem we learnt at school. It derives its importance from the fact that it arises naturally in many practical problems, where we have to deal with a population in which a fixed proportion $p$ of individuals have a given characteristic. Such, for instance, is the case with any bulk of manufactured goods when the manufacturing process yields a certain fixed proportion, say, 1/5 of defectives. If we sample batches of 10 articles taken at random from the bulk produced it is unlikely that any particular sampled lot will have exactly 2 defectives though it is very likely that the *average* of defectives found in a large number of such samples will converge to 2. Obviously our sampling process, if repeated often enough, will catch a very mixed bag. Some batches will have no defectives, others may have as many as 8 or even more. Indeed, theoretically a batch of 10 articles sampled at random may have any whole number of defectives lying between 0 and 10 in the full range of discrete integers

$$0, 1, 2, 3, 4, 5, 6, 7, 8, 9, 10.$$

Since we assume that the bulk from which we sample has a fixed proportion 1/5 of defectives, the chance or probability of picking a defective article is 1/5. *Per contra*, the chance of picking an acceptable article is 4/5.

Now suppose we draw 1 article from the given lot, which we assume to be quasi-infinite so that drawing an article has little or no effect on the probability of later draws. Since the lot consists of both defective and acceptable articles, the result of a single draw is either a defective *or* an acceptable article. As assumed, the probabilities of the 2 events are 1/5 and 4/5 respectively. Consider now a set of 2 draws. Clearly we can have 1 and only 1 of the following 4 possible ways of drawing 2 articles from the lot where $A$ denotes an acceptable article and $D$ a defective one:

| First draw | Second draw |
|:---:|:---:|
| $(A)$ | $(A)$ |
| $(D)$ | $(A)$ |
| $(A)$ | $(D)$ |
| $(D)$ | $(D)$ |

What is the probability of each of these 4 possible ways of drawing a sample of 2 articles? Since the probability of drawing an acceptable article in each draw is 4/5 and that of a defective one 1/5, the probability of each of the aforementioned 4 ways may easily be calculated by the product rule. Thus the probability of first draw, viz. that of obtaining an acceptable article in both the draws, is $(4/5)(4/5) = (4/5)^2$. Similarly the probability of the second arrangement, viz. a defective or $D$ in the first draw and an acceptable or $A$ in the second, is $(1/5)(4/5)$, and so on for the other 2 alternatives. We can now summarize the probabilities of each possible permutation of 2 draws:

| | *Permutation* | | *Probability* |
|:---|:---:|:---:|:---:|
| | *first draw* | *second draw* | |
| Both acceptable | $(A)$ | $(A)$ | $(4/5)(4/5) = (4/5)^2$ |
| 1 acceptable and } | $(D)$ | $(A)$ | $(1/5)(4/5) = (4/5)(1/5)$ |
| 1 defective } | $(A)$ | $(D)$ | $(4/5)(1/5) = (4/5)(1/5)$ |
| Both defective | $(D)$ | $(D)$ | $(1/5)(1/5) = (1/5)^2$ |

But if we disregard the order in which the acceptable and defective articles actually occur while we draw a sample of 2 since we merely want the probability of obtaining one $A$ and one $D$ in a draw of 2 articles, the probability of such a *combination* is given by the addition rule. For it is produced by either the arrangement $DA$ or $AD$. Its probability is therefore the sum of the probabilities of these 2 permutations, that is:

$$\left(\frac{1}{5}\right)\left(\frac{4}{5}\right)+\left(\frac{4}{5}\right)\left(\frac{1}{5}\right) = 2\left(\frac{4}{5}\right)\left(\frac{1}{5}\right).$$

The probabilities of all the possible 3 *combinations* to which the aforementioned permutations lead, if we disregard the order in which the $A$-and $D$-articles appear in the set of 2 draws, are therefore

| Combination | Probability |
|---|---|
| Both acceptable | $(4/5)^2$ |
| 1 acceptable, 1 defective | $2(4/5)(1/5)$ |
| Both defective | $(1/5)^2$ |

If we add up the 3 probabilities, the sum is 1, as, of course, is natural because we are certain to have one or other of these 3 combinations. In fact, we have

$$(4/5)^2+2(4/5)(1/5)+(1/5)^2 = (4/5+1/5)^2 = 1^2 = 1.$$

It also follows that the probabilities of the 3 possible combinations are the 3 terms of the binomial expansion $(4/5+1/5)^2$.

Consider next a set of 3 draws from the given lot. The number of possible permutations is now 8 instead of 4 and the result of a draw can be 1 and only 1 of them. As before, the probability of each permutation is given by the product rule. All the 8 possible permutations and their corresponding probabilities are as shown below:

| | Permutation | | | Probability |
|---|---|---|---|---|
| | *first draw* | *second draw* | *third draw* | |
| All acceptable | $(A)$ | $(A)$ | $(A)$ | $(4/5)(4/5)(4/5) = (4/5)^3$ |
| 2 acceptable, } | $(A)$ | $(A)$ | $(D)$ | $(4/5)(4/5)(1/5) = (4/5)^2(1/5)$ |
| 1 defective } | $(A)$ | $(D)$ | $(A)$ | $(4/5)(1/5)(4/5) = (4/5)^2(1/5)$ |
| | $(D)$ | $(A)$ | $(A)$ | $(1/5)(4/5)(4/5) = (4/5)^2(1/5)$ |

| 1 acceptable, ⎫ | $(D)$ | $(D)$ | $(A)$ | $(1/5) (1/5) (4/5) = (4/5) (1/5)^2$ |
|---|---|---|---|---|
| 2 defective ⎬ | $(D)$ | $(A)$ | $(D)$ | $(1/5) (4/5) (1/5) = (4/5) (1/5)^2$ |
| ⎭ | $(A)$ | $(D)$ | $(D)$ | $(4/5) (1/5) (1/5) = (4/5) (1/5)^2$ |
| All defective | $(D)$ | $(D)$ | $(D)$ | $(1/5) (1/5) (1/5) = (1/5)^3$ |

Again, if we disregard the order in which the acceptable and defective articles appear in the various permutations and want the probability of a given *combination* of acceptable and defective articles, we find that the 3 permutations $(A) (A) (D)$, $(A) (D) (A)$, $(D) (A) (A)$, for example, lead to a single combination, viz. 1 defective and 2 acceptable articles in a set of 3 draws from the lot. The probability of this combination is therefore the sum of the probabilities of its 3 composite permutations, that is, $3(4/5)^2(1/5)$. Similarly the 3 permutations $(D) (D) (A)$, $(D) (A) (D)$, $(A) (D) (D)$ lead to the combination, 1 acceptable and 2 defective articles, with probability $3(4/5) (1/5)^2$. All the 4 possible combinations in a set of 3 draws have therefore the probabilities:

| Combination | Probability |
|---|---|
| All 3 acceptable | $(4/5)^3$ |
| 2 acceptable, 1 defective | $3 (4/5)^2 (1/5)$ |
| 1 acceptable, 2 defective | $3 (4/5) (1/5)^2$ |
| All 3 defective | $(1/5)^3$ |

Again we may readily verify that the sum of the 4 probabilities is unity, as one or other of these 4 combinations is certain to occur. In fact,

$$(4/5)^3 + 3 (4/5)^2 (1/5) + 3 (4/5) (1/5)^2 + (1/5)^3 = (4/5 + 1/5)^3$$
$$= 1^3$$
$$= 1.$$

This also shows that the 4 probabilities are the terms of the binomial expansion $(4/5 + 1/5)^3$. If we proceed in this manner we can easily show that in a set of $n$ draws there can be only $(n+1)$ possible *combinations* (though $2^n$ permutations) and that the probability of each combination is as shown below:

| Combination | Probability |
|---|---|
| All $n$ acceptable, 0 defective | $(4/5)^n$ |
| $(n-1)$ acceptable, 1 defective | $n(4/5)^{n-1} (1/5)$ |
| $(n-2)$ acceptable, 2 defective | $\dfrac{n(n-1)}{1 \cdot 2} (4/5)^{n-2} (1/5)^2$ |
| . . . . . . . . . . . . . . . . . . . . . . . . . . . . . . . . . . . . . . . . . |  |
| 1 acceptable, $(n-1)$ defective | $n(4/5) (1/5)^{n-1}$ |
| 0 acceptable, all $n$ defective | $(1/5)^n$ |

As before, the probabilities of the various combinations are the terms of the binomial expansions $(4/5+1/5)^n$. Consequently the probability of a combination of $x$ defective and $n-x$ acceptable articles appearing in a sample of $n$ draws is

$$\frac{n(n-1)(n-2)\ldots(n-x+1)}{1.2.3 \qquad \ldots \quad x}(4/5)^{n-x}(1/5)^x$$

or,

$$n_{C_x}(4/5)^{n-x}(1/5)^x$$

where $n_{C_x}$, as usual, is the coefficient of $(4/5)^{n-x}(1/5)^x$ in the binomial expansion $(4/5+1/5)^n$. More generally, if the probability of the defective draw is $p$ instead of $1/5$ and therefore of an acceptable draw $q$ instead of $4/5$ (where $q = 1-p$), the probability of drawing a sample of $n$ articles with $x$ defectives is $n_{C_x}p^xq^{n-x}$. If we agree to denote the product of successive integers from unity onwards, that is, the product $1.2.3.4\ldots x$ by the symbol $x!$ (read factorial $x$), the expression $n_{C_x}p^xq^{n-x}$ can also be written as

$$\frac{n(n-1)(n-2)\ldots(n-x+1)}{1.2.3 \qquad \ldots \quad x}p^xq^{n-x}$$

$$=\frac{n(n-1)(n-2)\ldots(n-x+1)}{1.2.3 \qquad \ldots \quad x}\frac{(n-x)(n-x-1)\ldots3.2.1}{(n-x)(n-x-1)\ldots3.2.1}p^xq^{n-x}$$

$$=\frac{n!}{x!(n-x)!}p^xq^{n-x}.$$

Consequently the probability that a sample of size $n$ drawn from a quasi-infinite lot having a proportion $p$ of defectives contains $x$ defective articles is $n_{C_x}p^xq^{n-x}$. We use this expression to compute the probability of drawing a sample of 10 articles having $x$ defectives where $x$ may have any 1 of the following 11 discrete values:

$$0, 1, 2, 3 \ldots 9, 10.$$

The computed values are shown in Table 4 below:

*Table 4.* Binomial Frequency Distribution. Probability of drawing $x$ defectives in a sample of 10 articles drawn from a bulk having 1/5 defectives.

| Number of defectives | Binomial probability | |
|:---:|:---:|:---:|
| 0 | $\left(\frac{4}{5}\right)^{10}$ | $= 0 \cdot 1074$ |
| 1 | $10 \left(\frac{4}{5}\right)^{9} \left(\frac{1}{5}\right)$ | $= 0 \cdot 2684$ |
| 2 | $45 \left(\frac{4}{5}\right)^{8} \left(\frac{1}{5}\right)^{2}$ | $= 0 \cdot 3020$ |
| 3 | $120 \left(\frac{4}{5}\right)^{7} \left(\frac{1}{5}\right)^{3}$ | $= 0 \cdot 2013$ |
| 4 | $210 \left(\frac{4}{5}\right)^{6} \left(\frac{1}{5}\right)^{4}$ | $= 0 \cdot 0881$ |
| 5 | $252 \left(\frac{4}{5}\right)^{5} \left(\frac{1}{5}\right)^{5}$ | $= 0 \cdot 0264$ |
| 6 | $210 \left(\frac{4}{5}\right)^{4} \left(\frac{1}{5}\right)^{6}$ | $= 0 \cdot 0055$ |
| 7 | $120 \left(\frac{4}{5}\right)^{3} \left(\frac{1}{5}\right)^{7}$ | $= 0 \cdot 0008$ |
| 8 | $45 \left(\frac{4}{5}\right)^{2} \left(\frac{1}{5}\right)^{8}$ | $= 0 \cdot 0001$ |
| 9 | $10 \left(\frac{4}{5}\right)^{1} \left(\frac{1}{5}\right)^{9}$ | $= 0 \cdot 0000$ |
| 10 | $\left(\frac{1}{5}\right)^{10}$ | $= 0 \cdot 0000$ |
| sum | $1 \cdot 00$ | $1 \cdot 0000$ |

Now if we draw a series of 10-article samples and observe the actual number ($x$) of defectives in each, the series will yield us a number array of defectives. We could group the data in a frequency table showing the relative frequencies of samples carrying 0, 1, 2, . . . 9 and 10 defectives. Table 5 shows the grouping that we may obtain from an actual experiment.

A comparison of the actual *relative* frequencies of the occurrence of samples having $x$ defectives where $x$ may be any 1 of the 11 digits 0, 1, 2, 3 . . . and 10 as shown in Table 5 with the computed binomial probabilities recorded in Table 4 will enable us to decide whether or not the samples have been drawn from a bulk having a proportion 1/5 of defectives. It is greatly facilitated by graphing together the actual and computed relative frequencies as in Figure 5, where the former frequencies are denoted by vertical lines

*Table 5.* Frequency distribution of 50 samples of 10 articles each containing $x$ defectives.

| Number of defectives | Frequency or number of samples with $x$ defective | Relative frequency |
|:---:|:---:|:---:|
| 0 | 5 | 0·1000 |
| 1 | 14 | 0·2800 |
| 2 | 15 | 0·3000 |
| 3 | 10 | 0·2000 |
| 4 | 4 | 0·0800 |
| 5 | 1 | 0·0200 |
| 6 | 1 | 0·0200 |
| 7 | 0 | 0·0000 |
| 8 | 0 | 0·0000 |
| 9 | 0 | 0·0000 |
| 10 | 0 | 0·0000 |
| sum | 50 | 1·0000 |

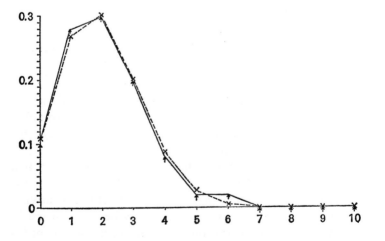

*Figure 5.* Comparison of computed and actual frequencies.

ending in arrows (↑) and the latter by those terminating in crosses (×).

In sum, one way of tackling the specification problem when the variate happens to be discrete is to examine whether the actual frequency distribution yielded by measurements made approximates to some one of the numerous binomial distributions that are available. For to each value of the proportion *p* (which is naturally a positive proper fraction not exceeding unity) of individuals possessing the given characteristic *and* to each value of the sample size *n* (which is always a positive whole number) there corresponds a different binomial-probability table. But all such tables may be readily computed by substituting one at a time the different admissible values of the variate *x* from $0, 1, 2, \ldots$ to *n* in the expression $n_{C_x} p^x q^{n-x}$ we have already deduced. By recourse to it we can generate a whole class of binomial distributions. Only we have to assign to both *n* and *p* specific numerical values to obtain a specific binomial distribution. The binomial distributions are thus a 2-parameter family requiring prior fixation of 2 parameters *p* and *n* to obtain the one we need on any given occasion.

No matter what values we may choose to assign to the 2 parameters *p* and *n*, all binomial distributions behave alike as, indeed, it behoves the members of one family to do. Examine, for the sake of illustration, the binomial frequency distributions for a few typical values of $n = 5, 10, 50, 100$ graphed in Figure 6. It will be seen that as *n* increases the pattern of ordinate lines becomes more and more symmetrical as well as more scattered. This is true not only for the particular values of *n* and *p* pertaining to the distributions of Figure 6 but in all cases. For if we compute the measures of the central tendency as well as scatter of any binomial distribution in the manner previously described we find that the former, that is, the arithmetic mean is *np* and the latter, that is, the standard deviation is $\sqrt{np(1-p)}$. Clearly for any fixed *p*, the larger the *n*, the greater is its arithmetic mean as well as scatter. Since the expressions for the central tendency and scatter of a binomial distribution depend solely on the 2 parameters *n* and *p*, by equating one or both of these measures to their analogues of an actual distribution suspected to be binomial we can determine *n* and *p*

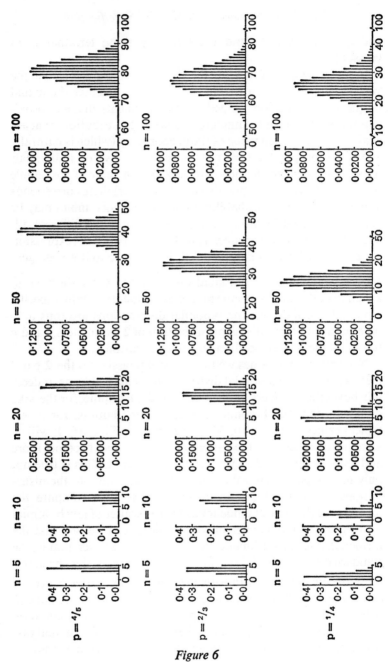

*Figure 6*

needed to confirm or deny the surmise. Consider, for instance, the following frequency distribution:

*Table 6*

| Variate<br>$x$ | Relative frequency<br>(actual) |
|:---:|:---:|
| 0 | 0·01 |
| 1 | 0·09 |
| 2 | 0·39 |
| 3 | 0·51 |
| sum | 1·00 |

Its arithmetic mean is the 'weighted' sum

$$0(0{\cdot}01) + (0{\cdot}09) + 2(0{\cdot}39) + 3(0{\cdot}51) = 2{\cdot}40.$$

Obviously a binomial distribution tailored to approximate an actual one must have at least the same arithmetic mean as the latter. Consequently $np$, the arithmetic mean of the binomial norm, must equal 2·4, the mean of the actual distribution under test. Recalling that the maximum value that the variate can assume is the sample size $n$ itself, it is clear that $n = 3$, whence $p = \dfrac{2{\cdot}4}{3} = 0{\cdot}8$. Table 7 below gives the values of computed binomial probabilities corresponding to $n = 3$ and $p = 0{\cdot}8$ in juxtaposition with the actual relative frequencies:

*Table 7.* Comparison of actual and computed binomial relative frequencies.

| Variate | Relative frequencies<br>(actual) | Binomial probabilities<br>(computed)<br>$n = 3,\qquad p = {\cdot}8$ |
|:---:|:---:|:---:|
| 0 | 0·01 | 0·008 |
| 1 | 0·09 | 0·096 |
| 2 | 0·39 | 0·384 |
| 3 | 0·51 | 0·512 |
| sum | 1·00 | 1·000 |

The agreement between the two is, indeed, very close so that we can identify our actual distribution as binomial. The value of the identification stems from the fact that the whole gamut of frequencies of the given distribution may be derived from a knowledge of only two parameters. We are thus in a manner of speaking able to tell the animal from the single bone, for a mere number pair, viz. ($n$ and $p$), contains almost all the information locked in the original data. Although many other types of discrete frequency distributions can be devised to meet various kinds of special situations we shall not go into them here. For the binomial distribution already described ties into a single statistical enunciation a host of individual cases that occur daily in our industrial and engineering practice. If this protean behaviour of the binomial distribution makes it the *prima donna* of *discrete* distributions, it equally results in marking the 'normal' distribution we encountered earlier at page 40, Chapter 2 as the queen of their *continuous* counterparts. The reason is that when we make the transition from the discrete to the continuous in the usual way already hinted at earlier, the binomial distribution becomes metamorphosed into the normal.* Now the transition from the discrete to the continuous is brought about by indefinitely refining the scale of our measurement. Consider, for example, the case of height measurements of 80 individuals cited earlier. So long as the measurements made were assumed correct to the nearest inch, the continuous variate – height – remained for all practical purposes discrete capable of assuming only integral values in the range 64 to 75. Even when we refine the measurement to make it correct to the nearest $\frac{1}{10}$ in. the variate still remains discrete. For if we replace the original unit of measurement, viz. inch, by $\frac{1}{10}$ in. the measurement becomes discrete again. Only the range of admissible integers now becomes about tenfold wider, extending from 642 to 749. In other words, by adopting a sufficiently small unit of measurement any continuous variate may be turned into discrete. In fact it was by the application of this idea that de Moivre was able to show that the continuous counterpart of a (discrete) binomial distribution is the normal or gaussian distribution. It is also called gaussian after Gauss, who derived it even more simply from considerations that sprang up in trying to grapple with errors of observation.

The theory of errors of observation came to the fore for the

* See page 38 Chapter 2.

first time during the nineteenth century, when astronomers and surveyors were confronted with the problem of deriving the *true* value from a series of observations they made. For if you make an observation, such as the right ascension of a star, it is not likely that each observation will yield you the same measure. In fact, each observation will give a slightly different measure. Since *n* different observations of the same object – a star's position in the case under review – give rise in general to *n* different measures, the question of deciding which of them or their combination is the *true* measure of its position became an important issue in the theory of errors of observation.

Suppose, for the sake of definiteness, the true value of the right ascension of the star or whatever else is under observation is *m* and $0_1$, $0_2$, $0_3$ ... $0_n$ are *n* different observations. Then $(0_1 - m)$, $(0_2 - m)$, $(0_3 - m)$, ... $(0_n - m)$ are the corresponding errors of observation. The theory of errors is really a question concerning the frequency distribution of errors of observation when the observation is repeated a great many times. We can derive it very simply from a few plausible considerations.

To begin with the errors are likely to be distributed symmetrically about the true value. In other words, corresponding to every case of an error $+\epsilon$ arising there must occur another of error $-\epsilon$. The simplest way of ensuring such a symmetry is to require that the frequency *y* of an error of any given magnitude $\epsilon$ is a function of $\epsilon^2$ instead of $\epsilon$. In this way the value of *y* corresponding to $+\epsilon$ will always be the same as for $-\epsilon$. We have next to decide what sort of function *y* must be of $\epsilon^2$. In other words, how does the frequency of error grow (or decay) with the magnitude of the error or rather of its square, $\epsilon^2$? There are a number of growth laws we can make use of. The best known of these is the usual proportionate or linear law you learnt during your arithmetic lessons at school. Thus if 1 yard costs you 1 rupee, then 100 yards will cost you 100 rupees. This is the linear law of growth where the cost increases exactly in proportion to the quantity of cloth purchased. More generally, if any quantity *y* grows linearly with the growth of another variate *x*, then $y = kx$ where *k* is a constant of proportionality. But in real life there are other non-linear laws of growth. The most common of this latter type is the exponential law of growth of human population, which threatens to make our already over-crowded planet even more populous than it already is. The essence of such an exponential growth (or for that matter its reverse decay) is that it is *not* the growing variable $y$ that increases linearly with $x$ but rather its logarithmic transform log $y$.* In other words,

$$\log y = kx, \tag{i}$$

or, alternatively

$$y = e^{kx} \tag{ii}$$

is the general mathematical expression of the law of exponential growth (or decay), where the growth (decay) *rate* of $y$ depends on its *own* magnitude as is the case with population growth.

Now it seems plausible to assume that the frequency $y$ of an error of magnitude $\epsilon^2$ *decays* exponentially. For in a large series of well-conducted observations the bigger the magnitude of error the smaller its frequency. The situation is not unlike that of a very competent marksman firing rifle shots at a bull's-eye. Naturally, in a large number of shots those closer to the bull's-eye will tend to overwhelm those farther away. This is a way of saying that the frequency of deviations from the bull's-eye *decays* exponentially as the magnitude of the deviation increases. The case of errors of observation is no different. It therefore follows that the law of frequency distributions of errors is given by

$$\log y = -k\epsilon^2 \tag{iii}$$

where we have changed the constant $k$ in equation (i) into $-k$ because the frequency *decays* with increasing magnitude of error. But (iii) is only another way of writing

$$y = Ae^{-k\epsilon^2},$$

where $A$ is a constant and $e$ is the base of natural logarithms we have already encountered earlier. But the error $\epsilon = (x-m)$, where $x$ is the observation and $m$ its true value. Consequently the frequency distribution ($y$) of any observation $x$ is

$$y = Ae^{-k(x-m)^2}$$

* Mathematically growth and decay are on a par. Negative growth is decay and vice versa.

The values of two constants $A$ and $k$ may be determined by two further stipulations. First, the arithmetic mean of any number $n$ of observations made should naturally converge to the true value $m$ as the number $n$ of observations is indefinitely increased. Second, the frequencies for all possible values of $x$ should add up to one as required by our normalizing rule mentioned earlier. It can then be shown that $A = \dfrac{1}{\sqrt{2\pi}s}$ and $k = \dfrac{1}{2s^2}$, where $s$ is the standard deviation of the distribution. Consequently the frequency distribution $y$ of any observation $(x)$ is given by the equation

$$y = \frac{1}{s\sqrt{2\pi}}\; e^{-\frac{1}{2}(x-m)^2/2s^2} \tag{iv}$$

where $m$ is the true mean value of the distribution and $s$ its standard deviation. This is the celebrated normal distribution, which crops up in a wide spectrum of numerical data ranging from errors of observations to heights of human beings.

We may, however, explain that the quantity $y$ on the left-hand side of the equation (iv) is the height of the curve at any point along the scale $x$. It measures the *relative* frequency of the variate $x$ when multiplied by an infinitesimal width $dx$ cornered at $x$. For in the case of a continuous distribution the frequency of any value $x$ is measured not by the *length* of the ordinate line but by the *area* of an infinitely thin rectangular strip bounded by the ordinate $y$ and an infinitesimally small width $dx$ at $x$. Consequently the relative frequency of any value $x$ of the normal distribution under consideration is the product $ydx$, or

$$\frac{1}{\sqrt{2\pi}s}\; e^{-(x-m)^2/2s^2}dx$$

$$= \frac{1}{\sqrt{2\pi}}\; e^{-(x-m)^2/2s^2}\, d\left(\frac{x}{s}\right). \tag{v}$$

Although the shape of any particular normal curve must inevitably depend on the values we choose to assign to the two parameters $m$ and $s$, there is a sense in which all of them can be considered as fundamentally alike. A glance at Figure 7, which

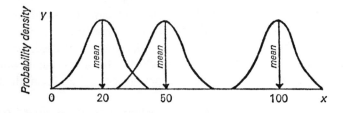

*Figure 7.* Normal distributions with the same standard distribution but different means.

shows the different sorts of normal curves we obtain by assigning different values to $m$ but keeping $s$ fixed, reveals the strong family resemblance that runs through them all. Indeed, they are identical curves located at different points on the scale of $x$. This is why $m$ is not only a measure of its central tendency but of location as well. Likewise, Figure 8 illustrating the variety of shapes of normal curves we obtain by keeping the location parameter $m$ fixed but varying $s$ demonstrates the kinship of normal curves in another dimension. While the central tendency of all the curves is the same, their scatter about it is widely different. As a result each curve has its own summit. The varying heights at the modal or mean value of the variate of the normal curves in Figure 8 is a consequence of the

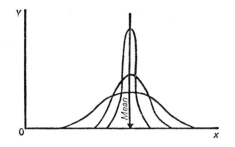

*Figure 8.* Normal distributions with the same mean but different standard deviation.

fact that the area bounded by each must be unity by our normalizing rule fixing the total of all relative frequencies at unity. Since area has to be the same a curve with a larger scatter or spread must have a lower peak and vice versa. We can, however, subsume all the variety of shapes of Figures 7 and 8 under a single typical form by a stratagem whereby all their idiosyncrasies are neatly suppressed without doing any violence to their essential nature. Obviously the vagaries of form stem from the 2 degrees of freedom available to us in the choice of the 2 parameters $m$ and $s$. By a judicious exercise of the choice allowed us we can eliminate the variations of shape on both counts. In the first place, we could choose to measure our variate from any origin. Thus instead of measuring the heights of individuals of our earlier illustration in the usual way, we could measure them by their deviations from the mean. If we do so, the height measurement 74·9 ins. is replaced by its deviation from the mean (69·7 ins.) viz. the difference $(74·9 - 69·7) = +5·2$ ins. Likewise, the height 65·8 ins. is transformed into the deviation $(65·8 - 69·7) = -3·9$ ins. With this convention we can ensure that the mean of our measurements $m$ is always 0. The relative frequency of $x$ is then obtained by substituting $m = 0$ in (v) so that it becomes

$$\frac{1}{\sqrt{2\pi}} \, e^{-x^2/2s^2} \, d\left(\frac{x}{s}\right). \qquad \text{(vi)}$$

Next we can measure the variate on any scale to suit our convenience. If we measure the variate not in terms of the original unit but in terms of the standard deviation $s$ of the distribution, the second parameter $s$ too will no longer appear overtly. For $x$ in original units will be transformed into $\frac{x}{s} = t$ units in the new scale, since $s$ is the new unit of measurement. Consequently the expression (vi) for relative frequency assumes the form

$$\frac{1}{\sqrt{2\pi}} \, e^{-\frac{1}{2}t^2} dt \qquad \text{(vii)}$$

because $\frac{x}{s} = t$ and in the new scale of measurement $s = 1$. This is a way of saying that the ordinate $y$ corresponding to any value $t$ of the transformed variate to yield us its relative frequency by the area $ydt$ of an infinitely thin strip of rectangle cornered at $t$ is given by the equation:

$$y = \frac{1}{\sqrt{2\pi}} e^{-\frac{1}{2}t^2} \qquad \text{(viii)}$$

This is the normal curve in its standard form independent of the vagaries of location as well as units of measurement.

Although as mentioned earlier the normal distribution can be derived as the limiting form of a discrete binomial distribution, it has also been found to be the limiting form of a large miscellany of discrete observations distributed in almost any imaginable way. This fact is grist to the mill of statistical inference as we shall see more clearly in the next chapter. Suffice it to mention here that we cannot devise exact tests of statistical hypotheses based on a limited amount of data without invoking the normality assumption. This is why it is necessary to spotlight the main attributes of normal distribution for future use.

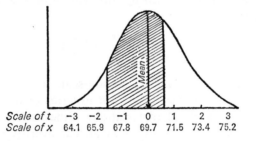

| Scale of $t$ | −3 | −2 | −1 | 0 | 1 | 2 | 3 |
|---|---|---|---|---|---|---|---|
| Scale of $x$ | 64.1 | 65.9 | 67.8 | 69.7 | 71.5 | 73.4 | 75.2 |

*Figure 9.* Values of $x$ denote height measurements of Table 3. Values of $x$ shown under corresponding values of $t$ are derived from the equation $t = \dfrac{x-a}{s}$, where $a$ and $s$ are easily seen to be 69·66 inches and 1·86 inches respectively.

Figure 9 exhibits the shape of the normal curve (viii) in its standard form. It can be shown that the area under this curve is equal to unity. In fact, the constant $\dfrac{1}{\sqrt{2\pi}}$ has been inserted just to ensure that the area under the curve is exactly unity. Since the area under *any* distribution curve between any 2 ordinates measured to the scale $t_1$ and $t_2$ represents the *relative* frequency of the variate ($t$) lying between $t_1$ and $t_2$, the area under the curve between any 2 values $t_1$ and $t_2$, of $t$ represents the probability that any measurement chosen at random from the distribution in question will fall between the values $t_1$ and $t_2$. Thus in Figure 9 the area under the curve between $t_1 = 1$ and $t_2 = 2$ represents the probability that the variate lies between these two values. In general, as a glance at Figure 9 clearly shows, the normal curve extends symmetrically in either direction approaching asymptotically the $t$-axis, although for all practical purposes it may be deemed to terminate at $t = \pm 3$ or at most $t = \pm 4$. For it can be shown mathematically that 99·73 per cent of the area falls between the values $t = -3$ and $t = +3$ and 99·994 per cent between the values $t = -4$ and $t = +4$. In other words, if the distribution of a variate is normal, the probability of $t = \dfrac{x-m}{s}$ lying between $-3$ and $+3$ or $x$ lying between $m-3s$ and $m+3s$, where $m$ is the mean and $s$ the standard deviation of the distribution is 0·997.

The values of the area of the standard normal curve lying between any two specified limits of $t$ have been computed and tabulated in published tables of normal distribution. These tables record the probability $p$ with which the value of a normal variate chosen at random may be expected to lie between $m-ks$ and $m+ks$ where $m$ and $s$ are respectively the mean and standard deviation of the distribution and $k$ is any pre-assigned limiting number like 3 of the earlier illustration. Thus for $k = 2$ a reference to the published normal distribution tables tells us that the probability of the variate lying between $m-2s$ and $m+2s$ is approximately 0·95 or about 95 per cent. Accordingly all the information of any given frequency distribution may be distilled into a mere number pair, that is, its mean and standard deviation provided only it is normal. It is therefore natural that on first encounter with a continuous frequency distribution our main concern should be to devise a normal distribution that could be used as a substitute. To find one we merely follow the earlier precedent of discrete distributions. Just as we picked up a binomial distribution as a norm of comparison by identifying the mean of the actual distribution with $np$, so also in the continuous case we can adopt the normal curve corresponding to the arithmetic mean and standard deviation of the actual distribution as our standard of comparison. This is how many of the wide diversity of continuous frequency distributions we encounter in various fields may be made to conform to some one of the family of normal distributions by a suitable choice of its two parameters, viz. the mean $m$ and standard deviation $s$. When mere visual examination of actual frequencies and those computed from the normal distribution adopted as our norm cannot indicate how good the fit is, more objective criteria of 'goodness of fit' are available and may be applied. If these tests reveal that the conformity or fitment is secured by procrustean violence to the data we must make another bed rather than force the normal one to do duty on all occasions. Indeed, in many cases an appropriate bed is made with surprising ease. All we need do is to transform the original variate $x$ into another by some suitable substitution. The most useful of these normality-generating substitutions is the logarithmic transform, the basis of the slide rule, whereby we replace the original variate $x$ by its logarithm $z = \log x$. For example, when the reaction rate in a chemistry experiment is proportional to the concentration of reacting substances the distribution of rates is not likely to be normal. But the distribution of their logarithms may well be. Replacing $x$ by $z = \sqrt{x}$ is another transform that may produce normality. An easy way to decide whether one of these transformations is likely to yield normality is to make use of special graph papers that are commercially available. Thus log-probability graph paper will do if $z = \log x$ produces normality. There are, however, quite a number of recalcitrant non-normal distributions which cannot be chiselled into normality by any possible transformation of the original variate. The study of these obdurate non-normal forms as well as their theoretical derivation has been particularly active since the turn of the century. It will suffice here to mention that particular statistical problems are found to yield distributions of observations which are not symmetrical on either side of their mean as with the normal curve, but are grouped more closely on one side of the mean than the other. Figure 10 is an illustration of a single-summit distribution that exhibits such a skew tendency. Various problems in probability and sampling lead to curves of the distribution of chances which exhibit the skewness characteristic of groups of statistical observations of certain kinds.

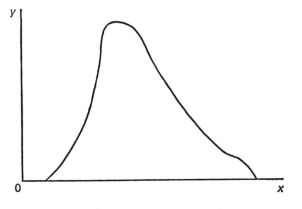

*Figure 10.* Single modal skew distribution.

The great statistician Karl Pearson gave a general method of generating a whole class of such skew as well as symmetrical distributions. He observed that in a certain approximate sense many of the distributions, like the binomial and normal we have already cited, could all be derived from a single differential equation. But though derived from a single source they could all be grouped into a family of four main types of distributions. We will not digress on them here except for a brief mention of two typical distributions that often occur in engineering practice. First is what we may call the 'dromedary' distribution, having two humps in contrast with the 'camel' of a single-humped distribution like the normal (see Figure 11). It arises when the measurements obtained relate not to a distinct homogeneous group but to a mixture of two or more. Such, for instance, is the case when an industrial process is worked by mixed teams of trained operators taking turns with callow fledglings or is fed on a mixed diet of raw materials. In general, it is a pointer that the distribution is made up of two or more groups of different characteristics the members of which have been included within one and the same series of observations. A segregation of the two groups is clearly an important preliminary in deciphering

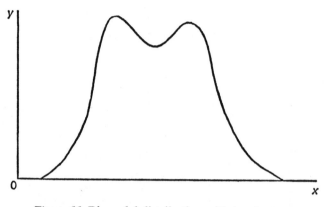

*Figure 11.* Bi-modal distribution with two humps.

the meaning of the measurements made. The second distribution is the rectangular one shown in Figure 12. It is a special type of distribution that is an amalgam of many distributions indicating that the process is a hodge-podge of practices of widely varying quality. In other words, it is a warning that chaos prevails and the process requires investigation.

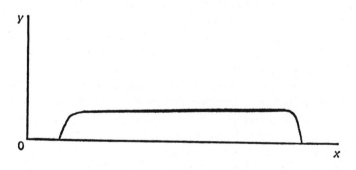

*Figure 12.* Rectangular distribution.

# CHAPTER 4

# The Art of Numeracy:
## Statistical Inference

THE problem of statistical inference is the eternal problem of arguing from the particular to the general, or in statistical lingo, from the sample to the population. Although the problem is old, fierce controversy has raged over its solution ever since the publication in 1763 of Bayes's posthumous memoire entitled *An essay towards solving a problem in the doctrine of chances.*

The problem's difficulty stems from the fact that the population characteristic or parameter we are trying to estimate from the observed sample may have any one of several alternative values so far as the sample can tell. Consider, for example, a very large population of ball-bearings, a proportion ($p$) of which are defective. If we draw a sample of, say, 100 balls at random, we may find that 10 are defective and the remaining 90 right. What can this sample tell us about the proportion ($p$) of defectives in the bulk? Deductive logic provides no answer, for theoretically we could obtain such a sample from a population containing almost any proportion of defective balls. Nevertheless, certain values of the proportion of defectives are more likely to lead to the observed result than others. For example, it can be shown that if $p$ is 1/10, the probability of finding 10 defective balls in 100 draws is about 35 per cent more than that of obtaining the same result if $p$ were 1/12. $p$ is therefore more likely to be 1/10 than 1/12. But in coming to this conclusion we have *tacitly* assumed, as Bayes was the first to point out, that initially before we begin the experiment, that is, draw the sample, the value of $p$ is as likely to be 1/10 as 1/12, or, for that matter any other. There is, however, no warrant for the assumption. For if we do not know anything about the prior probabilities of possible values of $p$ we cannot assume them to be all equal. It could easily happen that unknown to us some values of $p$ are more favoured than others. The situation is analogous to that encountered in tossing a coin. We have no right to presume – as we usually do –

that the prior probabilities of the two alternative outcomes – a head or tail – are equal, because the coin may well be biased. In fact, most coins are, with continual uneven wear. Similarly it could easily happen that some values of $p$ are initially more favoured than others even though we may be unaware of the latent bias. Thus suppose $p = 1/12$ is twice as likely as $p = 1/10$. If so, our confidence in the sampling estimate being $p = 1/10$ on the basis of the same sample would be greatly undermined. Bayes's solution of the estimation problem is thus seen to be based on the *prior* belief that no particular value of $p$ is more heavily loaded than any other. In the absence of any definite information it derives the sampling estimate by simply assuming equal distribution of ignorance – a procedure obviously full of pitfalls.

## POSTULATE OF MAXIMUM LIKELIHOOD

It was, indeed, one of the major services of Sir Ronald A. Fisher to spotlight the tacit arbitrariness in the Bayesian solution of the inference problem and to formulate an alternative approach. He suggested that the inference from sample to population be framed in terms of a new notion he called 'likelihood' of the parameter given the sample in contradistinction to the usual mathematical probability and be based on his postulate of 'maximum likelihood'. Without going into technical details, his postulate requires us to select among all the admissible values of a population parameter, such as the proportion defective, that particular value which maximizes the 'likelihood' of obtaining the sample actually observed. Thus if we hark back to our earlier sample of 100 balls from a quasi-infinite population with proportion $p$ defectives, the probability or rather the 'likelihood' of obtaining the sample with 10 defectives is seen to be $100_{C_{10}} p^{10}(1-p)^{90}$. It is then not difficult to see that the 'likelihood' attains its maximum value when $p = \dfrac{1}{10}$.

The warrant for treating the estimate $p = \dfrac{1}{10}$ as the 'best' is the fact that the 'likelihood' of the given sample is maximal for this value of $p$ and no other.

Although Fisher's maximum likelihood postulate did the job it was designed to perform it was criticized on the ground that on closer examination it too makes, albeit in a disguised way, the same assumption about prior probabilities as Bayes. Accordingly Wald suggested an alternative approach to the problem of statistical inference. In general, the problem is simply this: we are given a set of observations like the proportion $x$ of defectives found in a series of samples of given size drawn from a population. The population itself is specified by a number of *unknown* parameters like the proportion $p$ of defectives. We are required to devise ways and means of using the raw material of observations made to determine the unknown population parameters. The determination may be exact in which case it is called point estimation; or alternatively it may consist of an assessment of the probability with which the parameter may be expected to lie within a pre-assigned range. In the latter case it is called estimation by confidence interval, because we compute the confidence or probability with which the assertion that the parameter in question falls within any given interval $(c, d)$ may be made. Finally we may merely content ourselves with deciding whether or not the parameter in question exceeds some specified value $m$. In the last-mentioned formulation of the problem of statistical inference we have to choose between two decisions: Decision 1 that the parameter exceeds $m$ and Decision 2 that it is less than or equal to $m$. In other words, we have to test the hypothesis that the parameter exceeds $m$ for acceptance or rejection.

Testing of statistical hypotheses is therefore essentially a two-decision problem. It is true that two-decision problems are over-simplifications of real-life situations. For most of them are not dilemmas like Hamlet's 'to-be-or-not-to-be' question but multi-lemmas requiring a choice between a multiplicity of alternatives. Unfortunately, the study of multiple-decision problems has only just begun so that its theory – the theory of games – is still very much in the making. We shall deal with it in greater detail in the sequel. Meanwhile, we may anticipate here that whatever rule of procedure we may adopt to resolve the particular multilemma facing us it must be based on a rational comparison of the consequences of adopting different alternatives open to us. But such a comparison cannot be made unless we have some additional information besides the outcomes of sample checks we make.

To illustrate, consider the problem of a manufacturer who has to decide the disposal of goods he has manufactured. If he has undertaken to guarantee that the proportion $p$ of defectives in the shipments made will not exceed 0·01, his decision will in effect depend on whether or not he accepts the statistical hypothesis that the parameter $p$ exceeds the specified ceiling 0·01. Thus, if he concluded on the basis of certain sample checks made that this proportion $p$ was not more than 0·01, he would decide to release the product for sale at regular price. If, on the other hand, he concluded that $p$ was rather large, exceeding, say, 0·1, he might elect to withhold it altogether. For intermediate values between 0·01 and 0·1 he might choose to sell it at a reduced price. To be able to decide which of these three alternatives he should adopt not only must he know the proportion of defectives in one or more samples of given size but also assess the loss he is likely to incur should he make a wrong decision. For no matter what he did he could never be absolutely sure that his estimate of $p$ was 'true'. Since the risk of making a wrong decision cannot be eliminated altogether, he would incur some loss should the decision happen to be wrong. It is true that estimation of such a loss in case of a wrong decision may often run into difficulties. But we may, at any rate temporarily, evade them by remarking that it is not a statistical problem but a problem of 'values'. Granting the existence of a 'loss' function corresponding to the entire field of possible decisions, we may make the natural assumption that any decision ($D$) is better than another decision ($d$), if the expected value of the loss incurred by adopting $D$ is less than that incurred by adopting $d$. But which among the many possible decisions is the best? Here there is a fairly wide choice of criteria available and it cannot be stated unequivocally that any one of them is superior to others in all circumstances. All we have is a rationalization of our hopes and apprehensions. If we fear that the worst will always befall us, we may play safe by adopting a decision ($D$) which minimizes the *maximum* risk as Wald has suggested. On the other hand, if we believe that we live in the best of all possible worlds we may adopt, following Hurwicz, a decision ($D'$) which minimizes the *minimum* risk.

## MINIMAX AND MINIMIN CRITERIA

To explain the meaning of Wald's minimax or Hurcwiz's minimin criteria, let us imagine a collection of 3 different types of urns,* each of which contains certain known proportions of white and black balls which are otherwise alike (see Figure 13). We first select an urn at random and draw from it one ball after another, replacing each ball before the next draw, so as to make the conditions of draw in each case identical. Suppose we made 100 draws and found 55 white and 45 black balls. What type of urn did we select for drawing our series? Here again, our actual series could, in principle, have arisen from almost any type of urn. But we have to select the most reasonable alternative on given evidence. Now, Bayes in his memoire of 1763 referred to earlier showed that such a problem could not be solved without some additional information. Not only must we know the result of the series of draws and the actual proportions of whites in each type of urn, but we must also know the relative proportions of the various types of urns in our collection of urns.

The proportions of various types of urns may be equal or we may have a preponderance of some types of urns over others. The proportion of an urn of any type to the total number of urns in our collection represents the *initial* chance of its being selected for the purpose of drawing our series. Thus, if our collection had 30 urns of 3 types, 10 of each type as in the first scheme of Figure 13, each type of urn has an equal chance of being selected initially. But if, on the other hand, it had 20 of type *A*, 5 of type *B*, and 5 of type *C*, as in the second scheme, the initial chance of selecting an urn of

---

*To anticipate a possible objection as to the relevance of our urn experiment to the problem of statistical inference we may note that it is indeed remarkable that many practical problems in widely different fields – such as the problems arising in the oxidation of rubber, the genetics of bacteria, fruit fly or human beings, testing the quality of manufactured goods, and many more besides – involve the solution of 'urn-problems' of this and similar kinds. For example, the problem of estimating the proportion *p* of white balls in an urn by observing the proportion of white balls in a series of, say, 100 draws taken from it is similar to that of ascertaining the proportion (*p*) of defectives in a production process as a whole by observing the defective fraction in a sample of, say, 100 articles.

### First Scheme

| | |
|---|---|
| 10 urns of type *A* each containing | 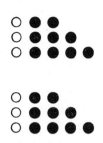 |
| 10 urns of type *B* each containing | |
| 10 urns of type *C* each containing | |

### Second Scheme

| | |
|---|---|
| 20 urns of type *A* each containing | |
| 5 urns of type *B* each containing | |
| 5 urns of type *C* each containing | |

*Figure 13*. Distribution of Urns.

type *A* would be 4 times that of type *B* or *C*. This initial chance is known as its *prior* probability. In the examples just quoted the prior probabilities of the 3 types of urns *A*, *B*, and *C* are all equal, being 1/3 in the former case and 2/3, 1/6, 1/6 respectively in the latter case. Bayes showed that, given the prior probabilities of each type of urn in addition to other information already mentioned, we can work out which of the various alternatives is the most reasonable to adopt. But in the absence of any information about prior probabilities the problem cannot be solved. Nevertheless, Wald's minimax and Hurwicz's minimin criteria already referred to do provide a way out of the impasse and enable us to decide from which of 3 types of urns, *A*, *B*, and *C*, we drew the series. For the sake of simplicity we shall assume that *n* is unity and that the single ball drawn is white. That is, we propose to decide the type of urn selected for making the draw on the basis of a single observation that a ball drawn from it at random is white. Now if we are given the initial chance (or prior probability) of the selection of each type of urn, by means of Bayes's theorem we can calculate the chance that the given series of draws was made from an urn of type *A*, *B*, or *C*. On the basis of these chances we can evaluate the 'loss' that we may expect to incur corresponding to each of the 3 possible decisions that we may adopt. For instance, suppose the initial chance (or prior probability) of the selection of the 3 types of urns was the same for all, that is, 1/3 for all the 3 types *A*, *B*, *C*. On the basis of this assumption we can prove by means of Bayes's theorem that the chance that the urn selected was of type *A* is 20/47, of type *B*, 15/47, and of type *C*, 12/47.

In other words, if we happened to decide that the urn selected

72

was of type *A*, we should expect to be right only about 20 times out of 47 and therefore wrong about 27 times out of 47. Now if we go wrong we incur some 'loss'. Although, as mentioned earlier, the actual estimation of this loss is not a simple matter, yet we may simplify the situation by assuming that every time we make a wrong decision we incur a unit loss, otherwise 0. In other words, the loss that we incur in case we decide in favour of an urn of type *A* is 0 if our decision is right, and 1 if our decision is wrong. But the chance of a right decision in this case is 20/47 and that of a wrong one 27/47. It therefore follows that the *expected* value of the loss in case we decide in favour of an urn of type *A* is $0 \times \left(\dfrac{20}{47}\right) + 1\left(\dfrac{27}{47}\right) = \dfrac{27}{47}$.

Similarly the expected values of loss in case we decide in favour of types *B* and *C* are 32/47 and 35/47 respectively. We note that the minimum of these 3 values is 27/47, corresponding to a decision in favour of type *A*. We may now summarize the results of our discussion as follows:

| Assumed prior probabilities | Values of expected losses corresponding to the 3 possible decisions, *A*, *B*, *C* | | | Minimum loss | Decision corresponding to minimum loss |
|---|---|---|---|---|---|
| | *A* | *B* | *C* | | |
| $\dfrac{1}{3}:\dfrac{1}{3}:\dfrac{1}{3}$ | $\dfrac{27}{47}$ | $\dfrac{32}{47}$ | $\dfrac{35}{47}$ | $\dfrac{27}{47}$ | *A* |

But the assumption that prior probabilities are all equal is arbitrary, for the proportion of urns of various types in our collection is unknown and may well be quite different. If it is, say, $\dfrac{1}{9}:\dfrac{2}{9}:\dfrac{2}{3}$, a similar calculation by means of Bayes's theorem shows that the chances that the urn selected is of type *A*, *B*, or *C* are 10/61, 15/61, and 36/61 respectively. Consequently the 3 values of expected losses are 51/61, 46/61, 25/61, of which the minimum is 25/61. In general, to each set of values of prior probabilities there corresponds a minimum value of the expected loss. Since theoretically the number of sets of values that the unknown prior probabilities can have is infinite and as each set generates its own minimum expected loss, we have an infinite number of such minimum values of expected loss. We may thus construct a table like the one reproduced below showing the minimum loss corresponding to each possible set of values or prior probabilities.

*Minimum Losses*

| Assumed prior probabilities | Values of expected losses corresponding to 3 possible decisions, *A, B, C* | | | Minimum loss | Decision corresponding to minimum loss |
|:---:|:---:|:---:|:---:|:---:|:---:|
| | *A* | *B* | *C* | | |
| $\dfrac{1}{3}:\dfrac{1}{3}:\dfrac{1}{3}$ | $\dfrac{27}{47}$ | $\dfrac{32}{47}$ | $\dfrac{35}{47}$ | $\dfrac{27}{47}$ | *A* |
| $\dfrac{1}{9}:\dfrac{2}{9}:\dfrac{2}{3}$ | $\dfrac{51}{61}$ | $\dfrac{46}{61}$ | $\dfrac{25}{61}$ | $\dfrac{25}{61}$ | *C* |
| $\dfrac{1}{6}:\dfrac{2}{3}:\dfrac{1}{6}$ | $\dfrac{18}{23}$ | $\dfrac{8}{23}$ | $\dfrac{20}{23}$ | $\dfrac{8}{23}$ | *B* |
| .. | .. | .. | .. | .. | .. |
| .. | .. | .. | .. | .. | .. |

Out of this infinity of minimum values of expected loss, each contributed by a possible set of prior probabilities, it is possible that there may be a maximum.* We pick up that decision as the 'best' which corresponds to this *maximum* of the *minimum* losses. Such a solution is known as a *minimax* solution of the decision problem and corresponds to a *least* favourable prior probability of selecting the 3 types of urns. In other words, if we adopt a minimax solution of a decision problem we shall minimize the loss that we stand to suffer even under the *worst* circumstances. *Per contra* we may follow Hurwicz's criterion and look for the *minimum* instead of the infinite set of minimum values of expected loss shown in the

---

* We say 'may' because the set of minima in the third column is infinite. If it were finite, there would certainly be a maximum. But an infinite set need have no maximum belonging to itself.

foregoing table. Such a procedure is called the *minimin* solution of the decision problem. Obviously the Wald–Hurwicz solution of the decision problem is based on the Manichaean heresy that we live in the worst possible world ruled by a malevolent deity, like the God of Blake, or its polar antithesis, namely that ours is the best possible world, like that imagined by Voltaire's Professor Pangloss. Both are unsatisfactory. If one is an unavailing counsel of despair the other is an equally unreasoning riot of euphoria.

Although we have explained the idea of a minimax or minimin solution by means of the notion of prior probability and Bayes's theorem, it must be emphasized that the Wald–Hurwicz approach is actually designed to circumvent the use of prior probabilities. Wald, in particular, has shown that under some very general conditions a minimax solution of a decision problem does exist and that this solution corresponds to Bayes's solution relative to a *least* favourable prior probability of the unknown characteristic of the population (viz. the type of urn from which the series of draws was made in the case under consideration), even though this least favourable prior probability is actually unknown.* By the same token its Hurwicz analogue, the minimin solution, can also be shown to exist and this corresponds to Bayes's solution relative to a *most* favourable prior probability of the unknown characteristic of the population.

However, the main difficulty in applying Wald's theory is three-fold. First, Wald's proof of the existence of a minimax solution of a decision problem is chiefly of heuristic value. It does not enable us to find one in many concrete cases. Second, as we have seen, Wald's principle prescribes in some cases a course of action that would be considered irrational by all reasonable men. Suppose, for instance, a manufacturing process produces articles of which a constant (but unknown) proportion ($p$) is defective. Suppose further the manufacturer wishes to decide between the following two alternative courses of action:

---

*We may remark in passing that there is a close parallel between Wald's theory of decision functions and Neumann's theory of games. Just as we solve a game problem by selecting the maximum of column-minima of the payoff matrix, we solve a decision problem by finding the maximum of the column-minima recorded in the third column of our table. As will be shown later, Wald has developed this parallel still further.

(i) Sell the lot with a double-your-money-back guarantee for each defective article

(ii) Withhold the lot altogether from the market.

Here it can be shown that the minimax solution of the decision problem is in favour of Alternative (ii) so long as the manufacturer considers the possibility $p > \frac{1}{2}$ even remotely possible. Nevertheless, it will be agreed that it would be foolish to junk the lot merely because there is a very slight chance of more than half the lot turning out defective. Third, a rather more serious difficulty arises when Wald's methodology is generalized to cover cases other than those of industrial application. The reason is that in Wald's theory the term 'loss' is not restricted to loss of money which an industrialist may incur by making a wrong decision. It is given a very general meaning and includes 'damage' not necessarily measurable by monetary standard. Thus, if we wanted to estimate the lethal concentration of a certain dosage relative to human beings, and if our estimate was significantly in excess of the 'true' value, our decision would have disastrous consequences. Such a disaster would still be called 'loss' although it could not be measured in money. However, Wald and his followers admit that estimation of 'loss' in general is an unsolved problem but they consider that it is not a statistical one. Consequently they begin by assuming that such an evaluation of 'loss', at least in a simplified and approximate form such as we adopted earlier, is often possible in general even when there is no question of any financial loss.

In spite of these difficulties Wald's theory of statistical decision functions is already a major advance, unifying, as it does, a number of widely different statistical theories. We will dwell on only one of them, namely, the theory of testing hypotheses. Here the question at issue is the acceptance or rejection of a statistical hypothesis $H$. Suppose, for instance, a lot consisting of $N$ units of a manufactured product is submitted with the claim that the proportion ($p$) of defectives in the lot is not more than, say, 0·05 or 5 per cent. The problem is to devise a way of testing the hypothesis ($H$) that $p$ is less than or at most equal to 0·05. The procedure prescribed is to select at random a number ($n$) of articles out of the lot and decide either to accept or reject $H$ on the basis of observations made on the sample. In general, we are given a variate $x$ whose frequency distribution may be one of the two shown in Figure 14, that is, either $f_0(x)$ or $f_1(x)$. What we require is a procedure that enables us to test the hypothesis $H_0$ that the frequency distribution is $f_0(x)$ against the alternative one $H_1$ that it is $f_1(x)$. As before, we select a sample of size $n$ and decide the issue on the

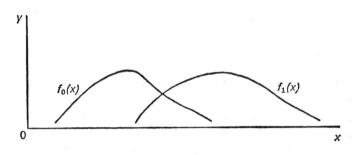

*Figure 14.* $H_0$ is the hypothesis that frequency distribution is $f_0(x)$. $H_1$ is the hypothesis that frequency distribution is $f_1(x)$.

basis of sample measurements made. Since these measurements are the values of the attribute of the $n$ items included in the sample, the sample as a whole may be described by a cluster of $n$ numbers – the values of the variate $x$ pertaining to the $n$ items in the sample.

For the sake of simplicity let us, to start with, assume that the sample size is unity so that a single item drawn from our population constitutes the sample. The sample is thus defined by a single magnitude measuring the particular attribute under study of the selected item. If we take on a straight line a point whose distance from a fixed origin 0 is the single magnitude pertaining to the observed sample, we may represent this single-unit sample by such a point (see Figure 15). If the entire population consists of a finite number of numbers, say, 10,000, it is obvious that the number of samples that can be drawn from it is also finite. In fact, in this case the number of singleton samples that can be drawn from it is the same, viz. 10,000. Consequently the totality of all possible samples that can be drawn may be represented by a set $S$ consisting of 10,000 points on a straight line, each point representing some possible sample, as shown in Figure 15. Such a set $S$ is called sample space as it is a graphic representation in space of the total aggregate of samples that can possibly be drawn. A subclass of samples out of this totality of all possible samples such as, for example, those whose sample magnitudes lie between any two arbitrarily given values will obviously form some subset $s$ of the set $S$ that constitutes our sample space. Naturally this principle of mapping all the totality of samples that can be drawn from a population on an appropriate sample space and then breaking it down into subsets applies even when the sample consists of more than one item. Only in order to represent a sample of size 2 by a point we now require 2-dimensional space and for those of size 3, 3-dimensional space (see Figure 16). In general, a sample of size $n$

*Figure 15.* Set $S$ of singleton sample points. Point $S_1$ represents the singleton sample if the length of the segment $OS_1$ represents the sample measure on an appropriate scale. And so on for other points such as $S_2$, $S_3$, . . . , of the set $S$.

will have $n$ specification numbers, the magnitudes of the attribute of each one of the $n$ items sampled. A simple extension of the graph principle suggests that we can represent such a sample by a 'point' in an imaginary $n$-dimensional space. If our total population consists of $N$ items, an elementary theorem of permutation and combinations shows that there are in all $\dfrac{N!}{n!(N-n)!}$ different ways of selecting a sample of size $n$ out of a lot containing in all $N$ articles. There are thus $S = \dfrac{N!}{n!(N-n)!}$ different samples that could be picked. As before, we could represent them by a set $S$ of points $S_1$, $S_2$, $S_3$, . . . $S_{999}$, . . . in an $n$-dimensional space. Now each sample, whether it consists of one item or more, has a probability of its occurrence depending on the method of drawing the sample and the constitution of the population. For example, under the hypothesis $H_0$, that is, under the assumption that the distribution of the variate $x$ is $f_0(x)$, the probability of a singleton sample represented by the point $S_1$ in 1-dimensional sample space is $f_0(x_1)$. Likewise, the probability of a sample of 2 items $x_1$, $x_2$, represented by the point $S_1$ in 2-dimensional sample space is by the race-course principle $f_0(x_1) f_0(x_2)$, and so on for samples of bigger size. Hence to each sample 'point' of the aggregate of all possible sample points, that is, the entire sample space $S$, there corresponds

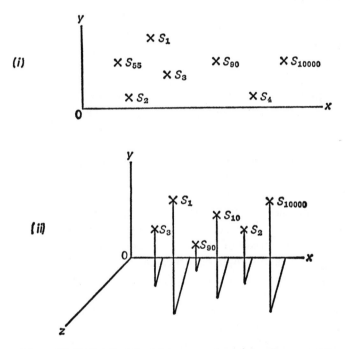

*Figure 16.* (i) Set $S$ of doubleton sample points. $S_1$ represents the doubleton sample point where the abscissa measures the value of the first item and the ordinate that of the second item included in the sample. And so on for other points $S_2$, $S_3$, ..., of the set $S$.

(ii) Set $S$ of tripleton sample points. $S_1$ represents the tripleton sample point whose 3 coordinates represent the measures of 3 items included in the sample. And so on for other points $S_2$, $S_3$, ..., of the set $S$.

its probability of selection. While the sum of the probabilities associated with each sample point is naturally one – because some one of the entire totality $S$ is certain to be selected – the sum of the probabilities associated with sample points of any given part or subset of the sample space will naturally be less than 1. It measures the chance that the 'point' corresponding to the sample selected belongs to the chosen subset. Now a test procedure is merely a method of dividing the entire sample space, that is, the totality $(S)$ of all possible samples of size $n$ into 2 complementary subsets, say, $s$ and $s^*$ together with the statement of a rule prescribing the rejection or acceptance of the hypothesis $(H_0)$ under test according as the sample selected belongs to the subset $s$ or $s^*$. The subset $s$ of the set $S$ of all possible samples is known as the *critical* region. There are in general infinitely many ways of choosing a critical region, that is, a subset $s$ of the set $S$ of all possible samples. Not all such ways are equally good and Neyman and Pearson have suggested certain principles for the proper choice of the critical region, that is, the subset $s$.

They point out that in accepting or rejecting any hypothesis $H_0$ we may commit errors of two kinds:

(i) we may reject $H_0$ when it is, in fact, true;

(ii) we may accept $H_0$ when it is, in fact, false.

They then calculate the probabilities of committing these two kinds of error on the basis of our knowledge of the probability associated with each sample or rather its *locum tenens*, the sample 'point'. The probability $\alpha$ of the former is really the probability determined on the assumption that $H_0$ is true, that the observed sample belongs to the subset $s$ or the critical region. The probability $\beta$ of the latter is really the probability determined on the assumption that $H_0$ is false, that the observed sample belongs to subset $s^*$, that is, falls outside the critical region. The probabilities $\alpha$ and $\beta$ therefore simply mean this. Suppose we draw a large number $(M)$ of samples of size $n$. If we follow the rule of rejecting $H_0$ when any one of the $M$ samples belongs to $s$ and accepting it when the sample belongs to $s^*$, we shall make $M$ statements of rejection or acceptance of $H_0$. Some of these statements will be wrong. If $H_0$ is true and $M$ large, it is practically certain that the proportion of wrong statements will be approximately $\alpha$. Likewise, if $H_0$ is false and $M$ large, it is practically certain that the proportion of wrong statements will be approximately $\beta$. Naturally the choice of critical region or subset $s$ should be such as to minimize both $\alpha$, $\beta$, that is, the proportion of wrong statements whether $H_0$ is true or false. Now it is quite easy to select a critical region for which *either* $\alpha$ or $\beta$ is arbitrarily small. But it is impossible to make both $\alpha$ and $\beta$ arbitrarily small at the same time for a fixed value of sample size $n$. Consequently all we can do is first to fix the probability $\alpha$ of making type (i) error arbitrarily, say, $\alpha = 0.05$, for example, and then to choose the critical region so as to minimize the probability $(\beta)$ of type (ii) error or maximize the power $(1 - \beta)$ of the test. Ideally our choice of the critical region should be such as to make $\beta = 0$. But in practice we can never make such a choice. It therefore results that we cannot devise a test of optimal power unity having to balance the swings of one type of error against the round-abouts of the other in choosing a critical region. How we do such balancing depends on the specific problem in hand. Thus if we are testing the hypothesis $H_0$ that a proposed new manufacturing process is superior, we will not want to incur the expense of changing the existing process unless we are certain of its supposed superiority. Our test procedure must therefore be tailored to yield a *low* probability of type (ii) error, that is, acceptance of the superiority claim when it is *not* true even if we are a little less stringent about the conjugate type (i) error, that is, rejection of the claim when it is true.

## STUDENT'S t-TEST

An interesting application of the aforementioned Neyman–Pearson theory of critical regions is the celebrated $t$-test of 'Student' designed to solve a very common practical problem of everyday administration, viz. deciding whether or not the mean value of a given set of measurements can be said to belong to a normal population having a specified mean. Suppose we have a sample of $n$ measurements $x_1, x_2 \ldots x_n$ of a variate $x$, such as the diameters of ball-bearings turned out by a machine. If we assume that the distribution of the variate $x$ is normal with mean $a$ and standard deviation $s$, we can determine the frequency distribution of mean $z = \dfrac{x_1 + x_2 \ldots + x_n}{n}$ of the $n$ sampled measurements. In fact, it can be shown that for sufficiently large $n$ the frequency distribution of sample means ($z$) drawn from a normal population is itself normal. The two parameters – mean and standard deviation – of the normal distribution of sample means ($z$) are related to their corresponding analogues, $a$ and $s$, of the parent normal distribution of the variate ($x$) in a simple way. While the average of the sample means ($z$) converges to the mean $a$ of the parent population, the standard deviation of the sample means is much less than that of the original population being only $\dfrac{s}{\sqrt{n}}$. In other words, the frequency distribution $y$ of the sample means ($z$) is the normal equation

$$y = \frac{\sqrt{n}}{\sqrt{2\pi}\, s}\, e^{-\frac{1}{2}n(z-a)^2/s^2}\, dz$$

Substituting $t = \dfrac{(z-a)\sqrt{n}}{s}$ \hfill (i)

$$y = \frac{1}{\sqrt{2\pi}}\, e^{-\frac{1}{2}t^2}\, dt,$$

which is the standard normal form. The result is not unexpected. It is natural that means of different samples that we may pick up will not be all alike even though the sample size remains the same. Thus, for instance, 5 samples of 50 picked up from a large lot of ball-bearings may have the following mean diameters: 0·211, 0·199 0·203, 0·198, 0·208 inches. These different sample means have their own mean as well as standard deviation quite distinct from the analogous parameters of the parent lot from which the samples have been drawn. But despite the distinction it is intuitively clear that as the sample size increases and approaches in the limit that of the quasi-infinite parent population, the sample and population means will ultimately coincide. For the average of, say, 100 sample means each of size $n$ is the same as that of a larger sample of size $100\, n$. It therefore follows that the mean of a large number ($m$) of samples each of size $n$ will converge to the population mean $a$ as $m$ tends to infinity. For the same reason the scatter of the sample means about their own average also diminishes as the sample size $n$ increases. Thus if $n$ is infinity, that is, if the sample consists of the entire aggregate of the parent population, there is only one sample mean, $a$, itself so that its scatter is 0. On the other hand, if sample size is unity, the sample mean is the same as the measurement of the singleton individual sampled. Consequently the scatter of sample means is exactly the same as that of the given population. These intuitive anticipations of the behaviour of the sample means are corroborated by the aforementioned theorem with its corollary that the standard deviation of sample means is simply $\dfrac{s}{\sqrt{n}}$.

Among the various uses to which the theorem has been put is the selection of a critical region tailored to give any desired probability $\alpha$ of rejecting $H_0$ the hypothesis that the sample measurements $x_1, x_2 \ldots x_n$ emanate from a normal population when it is true. All we need do is to cut a slice $E$ of sample space such that the sum of the probabilities ($P$) associated with each sample 'point' of the slice $E$ is $\alpha$. The slice or subset $E$ of the sample space is therefore the critical region we require. For if we decide to reject $H_0$ when the sample point belongs to $E$, the chance of making type (i) error will be only $\alpha$. Since the computation of the probabilities involved depends on the ratio $t = \dfrac{(z-a)\sqrt{n}}{s}$ we have employed earlier in reducing the frequency distribution of sample means ($z$) to its standard normal form, the test procedure is called $t$-test. It can be shown that it may be carried out in a routine of four easy steps.

First, we compute the mean $z$ of the $n$ sampled measurements $x_1, x_2 \ldots x_n$. Obviously, $z = \dfrac{x_1 + x_2 + \ldots x_n}{n}$.

Second, we compute the ratio $= \dfrac{|z-a|\sqrt{n}}{s}$, where $1z-a1$ denotes the absolute magnitude of the difference between the sample mean $z$ and population mean $a$, stripped of its sign if negative.

Third, if we do not happen to know $s$, the standard deviation of the population, we substitute for it its sample estimate, that is, the sample standard deviation $s'$, but to compensate for the error entailed by the substitution we replace $n$ by $(n-1)$. This yields us the amended ratio:

$$t = \frac{|z-a|\ \sqrt{(n-1)}}{s'}.$$

Fourth, we consult published tables of $t$-distribution which have been drawn up to show the probability of the ratio $t$ reaching and exceeding any given values. Following the aforementioned four steps we can decide whether or not any sample mean $z$ differs significantly from the population mean $a$ specified by the hypothesis $H_0$ under examination.

To illustrate, consider the following 10 measurements $x_1, x_2, x_3,$ ... $x_9, x_{10}$ (in inches) for ball-bearings of the same type:

| | |
|---|---|
| 0·2021 | 0·2001 |
| 0·2005 | 0·1990 |
| 0·2009 | 0·1987 |
| 0·2002 | 0·1983 |
| 0·1990 | 0·1998 |

We have to test the hypothesis $H_0$ that the sample belongs to a normal population whose mean is 0·2000 ins. The sample mean $z$ is clearly 0·1998667 ins. and $a$ is 0·20000 ins. The standard deviation $s$ of the population being unknown we compute the sample standard deviation $s'$. It may be shown to be 0·001222. It therefore follows that

$$t = \frac{|z-a|\ \sqrt{n-1}}{s'} = \frac{(0 \cdot 000133)\ \sqrt{9}}{0 \cdot 001222} = 0 \cdot 327.$$

To decide whether a value of $t$ as great as or greater than 0·327 could arise by sampling fluctuations and, if so, with what probability we need a table of $t$-distribution. But the three curves shown in Figure 17 will do as well. For they show the value of $t$ which will be reached or exceeded by chance with probabilities 0·05, 0·01, and 0·001 respectively. If the calculated value of $t$ exceeds the ordinate value given by 0·05 probability-level curve for the *number of degrees* of freedom in question, we conclude that the difference between the sample and population means is *probably* significant.* If the ordinate value of the 0·01 probability level curve is exceeded, we conclude that the difference is *definitely* significant. But if the ordinate value of the third, the 0·001 level probability curve is exceeded, it is *almost certainly* significant. For it means that while there are 5 chances in 100 in the first case, there is only 1 chance in 100 in the second and 1 in 1,000 in the third case for *t*-ratio being as high as or higher than the one actually obtained.

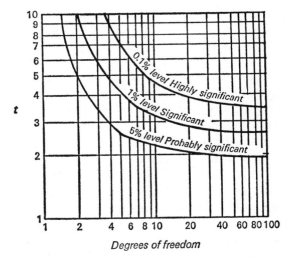

*Figure 17*. Graph of Student's *t* for 5 per cent, 1 per cent, and 0·1 per cent significance levels. If the calculated value for *t* is greater than the value shown above for the appropriate number of degrees of freedom, the indicated level of significance is reached.

A glance at Figure 17 will show that at the 0·05 probability level the value of the curve corresponding to 9 degrees of freedom exceeds 2 by a comfortable margin. The actual value of $t = 0·327$ obtained in the case under review is therefore much too small to be significant at the 0·05 probability level. *Mutatis mutandis*, it is even less significant at the more stringent probability levels of 0·01 and 0·001 because the values of the corresponding curves at the

*For a single sample of *n* measurements, the number of degrees of freedom is $(n-1)$. In our illustration it is easily seen to be $10-1 = 9$.

same degree of freedom are even higher. It therefore follows that there is no case for rejecting $H_0$ and the difference between the sample and population means is *not* significant.

The Neyman–Pearson theory of critical regions is thus able to subsume within the ambit of its sweep Student's *t*-test described above, as, indeed, all other kinds of tests of hypotheses that have been devised. But their theory in turn is only a special case of Wald's decision-function theory that we outlined at the outset. As we shall see more clearly in the sequel, it is possible to interpret a statistical decision problem as posed by Wald as a zero-sum two-person game in the sense defined by von Neumann.*

To summarize, we observe that the art of numeracy has two strings to its bow. On the one hand, it is an exercise in probability calculus aimed at tailoring theoretical frequency distributions to fit pre-assigned operating conditions or to meet specified situations. On the other, it is an attempt to infer the operating conditions or situations given the frequency distributions to which they lead. Obviously these two aspects of the art of numeracy are related like a theorem to its converse. Only the inverse problem, that of statistical inference, is very much harder to solve. For while the two rules of the race-course principle suffice at least in principle to solve the specification problem, we often lack the data required to tackle the other. The nearest approach to a complete solution is Wald's theory of decision functions. As we have seen, it is often of only heuristic value, merely proving the existence of an optimal solution without being able to actually produce one. But the several specific techniques like the Neyman–Pearson theory of testing of hypotheses, Fisher's Principle of maximum likelihood, or Students' *t*-test we have described often suffice to cash in practice the promise of Wald's demonstration.

*See page 150.

# CHAPTER 5

# Network Analysis

WE have described in the preceding three chapters some of the more important statistical techniques a manager requires to reduce to order the chaos of numbers let loose on him by his environment. But the chaos of numbers is only one of the several managerial maladies he has to cure. Another, even more serious, is the confusion caused by the plethora of activities of diverse kinds involved in managing any present-day industrial operation. If he is to survive the confusion he will need some system or way of keeping track of the multitude of activities he has to plan and pilot. Indeed, such a system, if it could be devised, would be the heart of operations research.

For operations research, as the name suggests, is *research* on operations. It is therefore naturally a quest for a general method of orchestrating the diverse activities that must be performed to successfully accomplish them. They need to be orchestrated if only for the reason that every operation or task – be it as simple as repairing a punctured tyre or as complex as a Normandy landing – is only an *organized* way of completing a number of diverse but interlinked activities. Consequently any such task may be resolved into a network of closely dovetailed activities whose ordered completion culminates in its execution. It is true that the resolution of the task, operation, project, or what have you, into its component activities may in turn be divided into its own sub-activities and each of the latter into their own subsidiaries and so on in a virtually unending chain like the fleas of fleas in the well-known doggerel:

> Big operations have little ones
> In a network that binds 'em.
> The little ones have lesser ones
> And so *ad infinitum.*

Nevertheless, in most cases common sense suggests the stage at which a component activity of any specific operation need not be split further and treated as an indivisible whole like atoms in chemistry.

Consider, for example, the simple operation of reaching your office or place of work at the appointed time. Since its daily performance has become a conditioned reflex, you are not conscious of the chain of activities like shaving, bathing, dressing, driving, parking, whose performance in an appropriate sequence leads to your punctual turn-out. However, even a conditioned reflex is an operation. Consequently for purposes of researching it the component activities enumerated above may be treated as atomic, although any particular component like shaving may be further broken into soaping, razoring, wiping, and so on. The reason why we do not actually research such an operation is that the whole process is an automatic routine requiring no elaborate analysis for its performance.* But such is by no means the case when we undertake more difficult and complex tasks like building an office, overhauling a locomotive in a railway workshop or a unit in an oil refinery. We cannot expect to accomplish them at any rate on time without a constant vigil on the progress of diverse activities required in their execution. Since the more complex the task the more numerous its composite activities, the requisite watch is virtually impossible without some technique or tool enabling the manager to represent the components *graphically* in order to give him a total view of the situation from start to finish. Such a *graphic* representation of the composite activities of an operation is given by the recent innovation called Network Analysis or P E R T, which is only an acronym for Programme Evaluation and Review Technique. A graph or chart, in short, is to the industrial manager what a musical score is to the *chef d'orchestre*. It gives the over-all drift of the operation to all the participants and its command and direction to the *maestro*.

Just as music scores are based on a notation – the set of conventional symbols representing musical notes – so also P E R T charts depend on a symbolism of their own. This symbolism, however, is not entirely arbitrary. It derives its validity from the simple fact already mentioned, that any operation may be viewed as a net-

---

*Sometimes we do; when getting up late we have to think out some way of hurrying up these chores.

work of atomic activities, which are linked with one another by what may be called significant milestones. These are events which mark the beginning or end of an atomic activity. Thus if the operation in question is one of going to the office, the milestones are events like shaving *started*, bathing *finished*, parking *commenced* and so on. Because of the importance of these terminal events of an activity, namely its start and finish, an activity is symbolically represented by an arrowed line linking two circles to denote its beginning and end as in Figure 18.

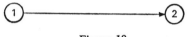

*Figure 18*

As will be observed, event 1, the beginning of activity *A*, is joined by an arrowed line to event 2, the end of activity *A*. In this symbolism events are denoted by numbers whereas activities are given alphabetic labels like *A*, *B*, *C*, etc.

Having adopted a symbolism to represent an atomic activity and its two terminal events, sometimes called its tail and head, our next task is to resolve the total operation into its component atomic activities. Each atomic activity is then labelled by a letter and the whole complex organized in a network to show the sequence in which they need to be performed. To fix the position of any given activity in such a network we have only to inquire which activities precede it and which run concurrently with it. In particular, we have to decide what controls its start and finish.

Consider, for the sake of definiteness, the operation of staging a play. The activities in such an operation could be multiplied depending on the amount of detail the producer-director of the play wanted to control. But for our present purpose of illustrating the network technique the atomic activities listed in Table 8 below should suffice.

Obviously the aforementioned activities cannot be undertaken in any haphazard manner. They must be performed in a certain sequence prescribed by the logic of the play-producing operation. This sequence determines the way the activities are linked with one another. Thus, the writing of the play must obviously precede all other activities exactly as the opening of the show must follow the rest. The logic of the operation further requires that once the play has been written we can commence cast selection and scenery concurrently. After selection of cast we can start acoustics and audition, rehearsal and organizing advertisement simultaneously,

*Table 8*

| Activity code | Description of activity |
|:---:|:---|
| A | Writing of play |
| B | Rehearsal |
| C | Organizing advertisement |
| D | Cast selection |
| E | Acoustics and audition arrangements |
| F | Scenery |
| G | Advance sale of tickets |
| H | Opening of the show |

but not advance sale of tickets which can commence only after advertisement has been organized. In this way, following the logic of the play-staging operation we find that the diverse activities can be sequentially related to one another as shown in the line graph at Figure 19. It may be mentioned that the lengths of the lines, which represent the activities, have no relation to the durations of the activities.

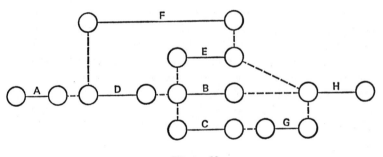

*Figure 19*

This graph shows at a glance that while *A* must precede all other activities, activities *D* and *F* can proceed in parallel or concurrently. Further, *B, C,* and *E* can proceed in parallel after *D* has been completed. *F*, which can commence simultaneously with *D*, can continue in parallel with *B*, *C*, and *E*. *G* cannot start before *C*. *H* can commence only after all the other activities have been completed.

The graph can now be converted into a formal network as shown at Figure 20, in which each event is allocated an identifying number.

It will be noted that event 4 is linked with event 6 by a dotted arrow. This is termed a dummy arrow or dummy activity, the function of which is simply to indicate the sequence of events. A

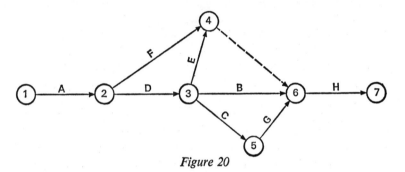

*Figure 20*

dummy activity takes 0 time. The sole implication, in our example, is that although no specific task is performed between event 4 and 6, event 6 must necessarily follow event 4. In other words, activity *H* cannot commence before event 4 is attained.

Although drawing a PERT network demands nothing more than an understanding of the inherent logic of the operation in question one must nevertheless guard against two logical errors that sometime occur when drawing very complicated networks. They are known as *looping* and *dangling*.

Looping, as the name indicates, is the occurrence of a loop somewhere in the network, like the one shown in Figure 21. Such a relationship between events is obviously impossible. For if event 5 occurs *after* event 4 and event 6 in turn *after* event 5, then event 6 must necessarily occur *after* event 4 and *not* before, as the network mistakenly suggests.

Similarly, dangling occurs when an *intermediate* activity dangles

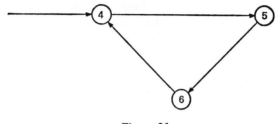

*Figure 21*

in mid-air, as in Figure 22. Obviously the activity represented by the dangling arrow 5–6 is at fault as it is undertaken with no result. We can avoid dangling arrows if we follow two rules:

(i) all events *except* the first and last must have at least one activity entering and one activity leaving them

(ii) all activities must start and finish with an event

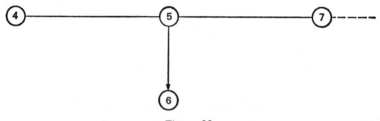

*Figure 22*

The dangling arrow 5–6 in Figure 22 infringes rule (i) in that event 6, which is neither the first nor the last event of the network, has no activity leaving it.

After debugging the network in the light of the aforementioned ground rules we have next to assess the performance time of each activity. It is true that assessment of the time required to perform the activities is in most cases no simple matter.* But assuming that sufficiently reliable estimates of durations of diverse activities are

---

*We will not dwell on this complication here except to remark that it is usual to make three estimates of each activity; optimistic time (*a*), pessimistic time (*b*), and most likely time (*m*). The time adopted for network analysis is then the average time $\dfrac{a+4m+b}{6}$.

available we may proceed to show how to analyse the network and isolate thereon its most important sequence of events, the so-called *critical path.*

To illustrate, let us revert to the operation of staging a play whose network was shown in Figure 20. Figure 23 is the same network re-drawn indicating the duration of each activity in days on the corresponding arrow itself. If we start from event 1 and

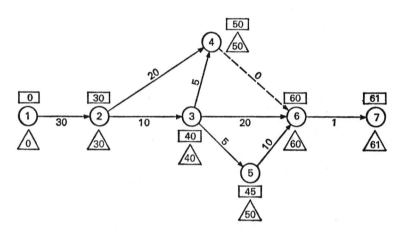

*Figure 23*

assign it 0 time, its next successor event 2 will occur at the earliest in 30 days and event 3 in 40 days. Proceeding in this way we can assign to each event the earliest time it can occur. If several chains of activities lead into an event, the earliest time is naturally fixed by the longest chain, because an event can be treated as attained only when *all* the activities preceding it are accomplished. For instance, event 4 has 2 chains leading into it.

(i)  1–2–4     (30+20 = 50 days)
(ii) 1–2–3–4   (30+10+5 =  45 days)

The earliest time for event 4 is determined by the longer chain (i) which takes 50 days. Similarly, we can easily compute the earliest time (*TE*) for each of the 7 events in the aforementioned network. They are shown enclosed in rectangles for each event on the network, and are also tabulated below.

*Table 9*

| Event | Earliest time in days |
|:---:|:---:|
| 1 | 0 |
| 2 | 30 |
| 3 | 40 |
| 4 | 50 |
| 5 | 45 |
| 6 | 60 |
| 7 | 61 |

Clearly the total time the operation will take is given by the earliest time of the final event 7. Since there are 4 chains of events that lead into it, the earliest time of completion will be the longest of these 4 chains of events:

> (i)  1–2–4–6–7 taking 51 days
> (ii)  1–2–3–4–6–7 taking 46 days
> (iii) 1–2–3–6–7 taking 61 days
> (iv) 1–2–3–5–6–7 taking 56 days

The longest chain (iii) is the *critical path* because any delay in the completion of any activity of this chain will delay the over-all operation. Moreover, its duration – 61 days – is the earliest time for the final event 7. It is, therefore, the total time that the over-all operation will take from start to finish.

We also observe that the chain of activities labelled (i) has a *slack* time of $61 - 51 = 10$ days. Similarly chains (ii) and (iv) have slack times of 15 days and 5 days respectively. We call these time differences between the longest chain and the alternative chains *slack* times because any of the activities in these alternative chains, except those shared with the longest chain, can suffer a delay of 10 days, 15 days, and 5 days respectively *without* affecting the over-all time.

Because of the possible existence of slack in a chain leading into any given event which need not necessarily be the final event of the ⋅

94

network we can also compute the *latest* time by which it must be completed without affecting the over-all time of completion of the operation. To compute it we proceed in the reverse order from the last event of the network backwards, exactly as in computing the earliest time we proceeded forward from the first event. Thus, proceeding from the last event 7, its immediate predecessor is event 6. Since the total time to event 7 by the longest chain is 61 days, and activity 6–7 takes 1 day, the latest time *TL* by which event 6 must be attained is $61-1 = 60$ days. Similarly, *TL* of event 5 is $60-10 = 50$ days. If, however, more than one activity branch out from an event the lowest figure arrived at by each alternative route is adopted. For example, 3 activities emanate from event 3, namely, 3–4, 3–5, and 3–6. The latest times for event 3 via these routes are 55 (60–5), 45 (50–5), and 40 (60–20) days respectively. The lowest of these 3 figures, namely 40 days, is adopted as the latest time of event 3. The rationale of this is obvious, since adoption of the higher figure will delay the completion of the project via the longest chain. Proceeding in this way we have the following latest times of events 1 to 7.

*Table 10*

| Event number | Latest time of completion in days |
|:---:|:---:|
| | *TL* |
| 1 | 0 |
| 2 | 30 |
| 3 | 40 |
| 4 | 60 |
| 5 | 50 |
| 6 | 60 |
| 7 | 61 |

The latest event times are shown enclosed in triangles for each event on the network at Figure 23.

Table 11 below shows the combined upshot of the two computations we have made of the earliest and latest times of completion of each event in our network. The last column of the table records their slack time. It is merely the difference $(TL-TE)$ between the earliest and latest times of completion of the event in question.

*Table 11*

| Event number | Earliest time in days $TE$ | Latest time in days $TL$ | Slack time in days |
|:---:|:---:|:---:|:---:|
| 1 | 0 | 0 | 0 |
| 2 | 30 | 30 | 0 |
| 3 | 40 | 40 | 0 |
| 4 | 50 | 60 | 10 |
| 5 | 45 | 50 | 5 |
| 6 | 60 | 60 | 0 |
| 7 | 61 | 61 | 0 |

The object of the above calculation is to segregate the events with slack from those with none. As will be observed from Table 11 only 2 of the 7 events in our network, namely 4 and 5, have slack times of 10 and 5 days respectively. They could, therefore, be deferred by as many (or fewer) days, if required. But none of the others can brook any delay without correspondingly putting off the over-all operation. They are, therefore, more critical events than 4 and 5.

In order to show more clearly the relative criticality of events with nil slack *vis-à-vis* those with positive slack, we may re-draw our network in a slightly different way with a time scale as in Figure 24. The double-arrowed dotted line covering a duration of 5 days shows the span within which event 5, in a manner of speaking, is free to float.

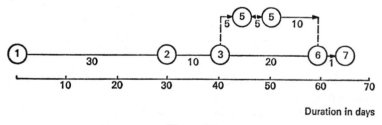

Duration in days

*Figure 24*

Thus, if required, the activity 3–5 may be stretched from its normal duration of 5 days to $5+5 = 10$ days without affecting the over-all operation. Alternatively, the start of its successor activity

96

5–6 can be advanced by 5 days in case we find that it is likely to take longer than expected. In other words, the existence of slack time at event 5 enables us *either* to defer completion of activity 3–5 *or* advance the *start* of activity 5–6 by 5 days. But we cannot do both. If the start of activity 5–6 were to be advanced by 5 days, it would merge on the preceding activity 3–5, reducing its slack or float to 0.

Although in the example considered the total slack or float of an event is available to either of the two activities linked by it, there are cases where the total slack may not be *freely* available on account of the interlocking between adjacent activities. A case in point is the segment of the network in Figure 25.

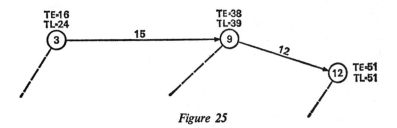

*Figure 25*

Consider the activity 3–9. Since the earliest possible time of its start – $TE$ of its tail event 3 – is day 16 while the latest possible time of its completion – $TL$ of its head event 9 – is day 39, we have a span of $39 - 16 = 23$ days to complete it. But the activity itself takes 15 days. It therefore follows that it has a total slack time or float of $23 - 15 = 8$ days. If we now examine its successor activity 9–12 in the same way we find that its total slack or float is:

$TL$ of event $12 - TE$ of event $9 -$ duration of activity 9–12
$= 51 - 38 - 12$
$= 1$ day.

However, if we allow activity 3–9 to absorb all its slack of 8 days event 9 will be reached by $(16 + 15 + 8) =$ day 39. Consequently the following activity 9–12 cannot possibly start until day 39 so that available time is $51 - 39 = 12$ days. Since 12 days is also the necessary time, there is really now no slack whatever. It follows that if the earlier activity 3–9 absorbs *all* its slack of 8 days the successor activity has no slack at all. But if the earlier activity absorbs only 7 days out of its total slack of 8 days, the next activity 9–12 will retain its slack of 1 day. Thus while activity 3–9 does have a *total* slack of 8 days, only 7 days can be used without reducing the slack in any succeeding activity. In other words, the *free* slack available to it is only 7 days out of its *total* slack of 8.

In general, free slack is the time by which an activity can expand without affecting any subsequent activity. There is also another type of slack called *independent* slack. It is the time by which an activity can expand without affecting any other activity either previous or subsequent. They may all be computed by a simple arithmetical routine or algorithm. The algorithm is based on the fact that any activity in the network has only two milestones, the tail and head event. As tail event of the activity it has two times of *start*, the earliest and the latest times, which we label as EST and LST respectively. Likewise, as *head* event it has two times of completion: the earliest and latest finish times. We may call them EFT and LFT. In other words, corresponding to each activity we have now four times. These four times and the duration D of the activity in question enable us to compute the various kinds of slacks or floats associated with it by following three simple rules:

(i)   Total slack           = LFT–EST–D
(ii)  Free slack            = EFT–EST–D
(iii) Independent slack = EFT–LST–D

The computation of slacks or floats in a network is important in many ways. Above all it isolates the group of activities which have an excess of resources of manpower and/or materials and enables us to rank them in order of this excess. For the magnitude of slack associated with an event determines how critical that event may become. The less the slack the more critical the event becomes. In a project or operation of any consequence there are many paths which lead from the initial event of the network to its last. All of them are not of equal importance to the final upshot of the project. Some of them are more critical than others – the criticality of each path varying *inversely* with the slack of the events on the path. But there will always be *at least* one which is more critical than all others having some positive slack. It is called the critical path and will naturally command the maximum attention.

Network analysis is therefore a manager's filter that vastly improves his signal-to-noise ratio. In the welter of information at his disposal it tells him what precisely to choose and what to ignore in order to achieve his goal of timely completion of the project or operation with optimal use of the available resources. Its utility lies in the fact that it sifts the relevant information without the manager having to concern himself with the manual computations involved therein. These computations may be done by a computer though in case of shorter networks involving no more than a few hundred activities it is usually more economical and quicker to have the slack-time computations performed manually by an individual trained in the use of desk calculator. Such an individual can manually process 200 activities in less than a working day, so that smaller networks can be prepared manually in time. But in whatever way the manager chooses to have the slack times computed all he needs is a table of slack times of all the events of the network. It is usual to begin the table with events having negative slack followed by those with zero and positive slacks. It may seem odd for events to have a negative slack. But such events do arise when one or more activity takes longer than the over-all schedule of the project can possibly allow. In fact, emergence of negative slack in the network is a warning that the final event will *not* be completed on schedule with the *existing* plan. The plan must therefore be reviewed and suitably altered. This is why events with negative slack are sometimes called hypercritical. They require virtual *reformulation* of the network.

*Part II*

# STANDARD TECHNIQUES

# CHAPTER 6

## Linear Programming

IF a manager's problem is concerned with an activity that has some quantifiable or measurable input, that is, consumes some valuable resource such as money, machines, or materials and in turn has some valuable output that can be measured, he may seek one of the following:

(i) to minimize input, that is, the value required to achieve a pre-assigned output

(ii) to maximize output, that is, the value created from a specified input

(iii) to maximize some functions of input and output values, e.g. their difference (profit) or their ratio (return on investment).

Such optimization problems, that is, those dealing with maximization or minimization, can often be solved by what are called programming techniques. The most widely used of them is that of *linear* programming (or L P) because of the extreme simplicity of the constraints to which the input (output) variables conform. For it is assumed that all of them can be expressed mathematically in the form of first-degree equations or inequalities.

Consider, for example, a simple process whereby an entrepreneur, by a suitable combination of two kinds of resources $(R_1, R_2)$ at his command, can produce a pair of commodities $(C_1, C_2)$. If we assume that the total quantities of each resource used and the total return are linear functions of the quantities of the two kinds of commodities produced, we can by recourse to linear-programming technique determine the particular mixture of commodity yields that will maximize the total return. Suppose, for the sake of definiteness, that the return or profit per unit of commodity $C_1$ manufactured is two dollars and that of commodity $C_2$ three dollars. Obviously the total return or profit $(p)$ will be $2x+3y$, where $x$ and $y$ are the numbers of units $C_1$ and $C_2$ manufactured. The choice of $x$ and $y$, or the number of units of $C_1$ and $C_2$ manu-

103

factured, is not arbitrary. It is limited by the availability of resources $R_1$ and $R_2$. Clearly $R_1$ and $R_2$ cannot exceed their respective ceilings, which we may take to be 7 and 10 units respectively. Suppose further a unit of $C_1$ consumes 3 units of $R_1$ and 2 units of $R_2$, and a unit of $C_2$ consumes 2 of $R_1$ and 4 of $R_2$, as shown in Table 12.

*Table 12*

|  | Units of resource consumed | |
|---|---|---|
|  | $(R_1)$ | $(R_2)$ |
| Input per unit of commodity $C_1$ | 3 | 2 |
| Input per unit of commodity $C_2$ | 2 | 4 |
| Total resource input for $x$ units of $C_1$ and $y$ units of $C_2$ | $3x+2y$ | $2x+4y$ |

A glance at Table 12 shows that $x$ units of $C_1$ and $y$ units of $C_2$ will consume $(3x+2y)$ units of $R_1$ and $(2x+4y)$ units of $R_2$. It therefore follows that the total input of $R_1$, namely, $(3x+2y)$, cannot exceed 7, the ceiling of $R_1$. Likewise, the total input of $R_2$, namely $(2x+4y)$, cannot exceed 10. The problem then is simply what pair of values of $x$ and $y$ will maximize the profit or objective function

$$p = 2x+3y, \tag{i}$$

where $x$ and $y$ conform to the following constraints:

| (a) | | $3x+2y \leqslant 7$ | ⎫ | |
|---|---|---|---|---|
| (b) | | $2x+4y \leqslant 10$ | ⎬ | (ii) |
| (c) | | $x, y \geqslant 0.$ | ⎭ | |

Now, invoking the chart-room principle described in Part I, any pair of numbers $(x, y)$ may be represented as a point on a chart or graph paper. Since we are interested only in those pairs of values of $(x, y)$ which conform to the process constraints mathematically expressed as inequalities (ii), it is obvious that the only admissible combinations of $x$ and $y$ are those which lie in the shaded area of Figure 26. For the conditions (ii) require that the admissible combinations of $x$ and $y$ be represented by points lying simultaneously between the line $3x+2y = 7$ and the coordinate axes, on the one hand, and the line $2x+4y = 10$ and the coordinate axes, on the other. Thus the set of admissible combinations of $x$ and $y$ is represented by those points which lie in the shaded portion of Figure 26 including its boundaries, that is, the quadrilateral $OABC$. The problem is to select those of the admissible points which maximize the profit or objective function $p$. Now $p$ too is a

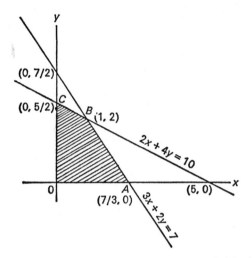

*Figure 26.* Admissible points lie in the shaded region.

linear function of $x$ and $y$. It therefore results that for any given constant value of $p$, the objective function equation (i) will represent a straight line, the line of equiprofit. For any combination of $(x, y)$ represented by a point of the equiprofit line, $p$ remains constant. But for varying values of $p$ the lines of equiprofit form a set of contours like isothermal lines of constant temperature in meteorological charts. In this case, however, the lines of equiprofit form a family of parallel lines, as shown dotted in Figure 27. If we superpose this family of dotted parallel lines of equiprofit on Figure 26, the picture that emerges is shown in Figure 28. A glance at Figure 28 will show that the line $l$ of maximum profit is the one that is farthest away from the origin, subject to the condition that it passes through at least one point of the shaded region to conform to the prescribed constraints of the process. Thus the line $l$ must pass through the corner $B$ of the shaded region which is farthest from the origin. Any other parallel line even a little further away from the

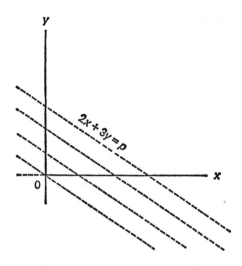

*Figure 27.* Family of equiprofit lines. $p = 2x+3y$.

origin will be too far away to have any point of the admissible region. Indeed, it is intuitively clear that in all cases the line of maximum profit must pass through one or the other of the corners of the shaded region containing all the admissible points. To optimize $p$, we therefore pick that particular line of the family of parallel equiprofit lines that is most distant from the origin and yet passes through at least one of the corners of the admissible region. In this case it is the line $l$ passing through the point $B$ with co-ordinates $(x = 1, y = 2)$. In other words, the maximum profit will accrue if it is decided to produce $x = 1$ unit of commodity $C_1$ and $y = 2$ units of $C_2$, the maximum profit being $p = 2(1)+3(2) = 8$. Any other combination of $x$ and $y$ will lessen the profit.

The foregoing illustration shows that to optimize the objective or profit function in any given case we may merely follow the routine described below:

(i) Demarcate the region or space containing only the admissible points, that is, points conforming to the prescribed constraints. In the present case, as we have seen, the region is the quadrilateral with vertices $O$, $A$, $B$, $C$ whose respective coordinates are $(0, 0)$, $(7/3, 0)$, $(1, 2)$, $(0, 5/2)$.

106

(ii) Since the profit or objective function is maximum only at some one of the vertices or corners of the admissible region, we evaluate the profit function at each of these corners. Thus, starting from the corner $O$ (0, 0), we find that $p$ is 0 at $O$. We then proceed to the next corner $A$ (7/3, 0) and evaluate $p$ there. We find it is 14/3. Since it has increased from 0 to 14/3, we proceed to the next vertex $B$ (1, 2) and find that the value of $p$ at $B$ is 8. Since it has increased again from 14/3 to 8, we proceed to the next corner $C$ (0, 5/2), where the value of $p$ is 15/2. As it is lower than that at $B$, p is maximal at $B$.

In sum, we evaluate $p$ successively at the corners of the admissible region only, proceeding successively from one to the other. We continue this process so long as the value of $p$ increases from one corner to another and stop only when it begins to fall. The value at the penultimate corner will then be maximal.

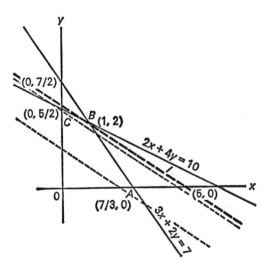

*Figure 28.* Equiprofit line *l* through $B$ is the line of maximum profit with at least one point ($B$) of the admissible region.

We have explained the linear-programming technique by means of an oversimplified illustration wherein only two commodities are produced, subject to only two constraints or resource limitations.

The method, however, applies equally when there are more than two input resources and hence more than two resource limitations – except that the admissible region will now be bounded in the upper-right-hand quadrant of the coordinate axes by as many straight lines as there are constraints instead of only two as in the earlier case. We evaluate the profit function $2x+3y$ at each of the corners of the new polygon and pick the one where it is the greatest. To be more specific, let us assume that there are 4 resources, $R_1$, $R_2$, $R_3$, $R_4$, that have to be utilized to produce 2 commodities, $C_1$, $C_2$. Let the consumption per unit commodity of each resource be as shown in Table 13.

*Table 13*

| Commodity produced | Units of resource consumed per unit of commodity | | | |
| --- | --- | --- | --- | --- |
| | $R_1$ | $R_2$ | $R_3$ | $R_4$ |
| $C_1$ | 3 | 2 | 1 | 3 |
| $C_2$ | 2 | 4 | 3 | 2 |
| Total resource input for $x$ units of $C_1$ and $y$ units of $C_2$ | $3x+2y$ | $2x+4y$ | $x+3y$ | $3x+2y$ |

If the ceilings of the new resources ($R_3$, $R_4$) now added are 3 and 6 respectively, the new constraints will be

$$3x+2y \leqslant 7,$$
$$2x+4y \leqslant 10,$$

and

$$x, y \geqslant 0$$

as before, *plus* the following two conditions:

$$x+3y \leqslant 3,$$

and

$$3x+2y \leqslant 6.$$

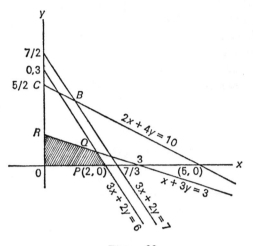

*Figure 29*

It is clear that the admissible region will now be the shaded area shown in Figure 29, which is the overlap bounded by the lines:

$$3x + 2y = 7$$
$$2x + 4y = 10$$
$$x + 3y = 3$$

and

$$3x + 2y = 6.$$

We can find by trial at which of the 4 corners, $O, P, Q, R$, the profit function $2x + 3y$ is maximum or minimum. We may summarize the data of any such problem as in Table 14.

*Table 14*

| Commodity | Resources | | | | Profit function coefficients |
|---|---|---|---|---|---|
| | $R_1$ | $R_2$ | $R_3$ | $R_4$ | |
| $x$ | 3 | 2 | 1 | 3 | 2 |
| $y$ | 2 | 4 | 3 | 2 | 3 |
| $\leqslant$ Ceilings of $R$'s | 7 | 10 | 3 | 6 | |

109

Here each vertical column headed $R$ is an expression of some resource limitation, such as $3x+2y\leqslant7$ in the first or $2x+4y\leqslant10$ in the second. The last column headed 'profit function coefficients' gives the objective function $2x+3y$ to be maximized or minimized. By interchanging the rows and columns of Table 14 we have the elements of *another* related problem. Such an interchange leads to the scheme of numbers shown in Table 15.

*Table 15*

| Commodity | Resources | | Profit function coefficients |
|:---:|:---:|:---:|:---:|
| | $r_1$ | $r_2$ | |
| $p$ | 3 | 2 | 7 |
| $q$ | 2 | 4 | 10 |
| $r$ | 1 | 3 | 3 |
| $s$ | 3 | 2 | 6 |
| $\geqq$ Floors of $r$'s | 2 | 3 | |

As before, if columns denote resources $r_1, r_2$ and rows commodities, we have here a case of 4 commodities ($p, q, s, t$) being produced under 2 resource limitations, namely:

$$3p+2q+\ s+3t\geqslant2$$
$$2p+4q+3s+2t\geqslant3.$$

The objective function now is

$$7p+10q+3s+6t.$$

To the *maximal* solution of the objective function, $3x+2y$, in the first problem there corresponds the *minimal* solution of the objective function, $7p+10q+15s+6t$, in the second, and vice versa. The two related problems are shown in juxtaposition.

A *maximal* solution of problem 1 is a *minimal* solution of problem 2, its dual, and vice versa. Thanks to this duality, we can transform a linear-programming problem involving *any* number of commodities subject only to 2 constraints to its dual, where we have to make do with only 2 commodities. As a result we can readily employ the graphic method already described. The case of 3 commodities

### Table 16

| | Problem 1 | | | | | | Problem 2 | | |
|---|---|---|---|---|---|---|---|---|---|
| Com-modities | Resources | | | | Objective function coefficients | Com-modities | Resources | | Objective function coefficients |
| | $R_1$ | $R_2$ | $R_3$ | $R_4$ | | | $r_1$ | $r_2$ | |
| $x$ | 3 | 2 | 1 | 3 | 2 | $p$ | 3 | 2 | 7 |
| $y$ | 2 | 4 | 3 | 2 | 3 | $q$ | 2 | 4 | 10 |
| | | | | | | $s$ | 1 | 3 | 3 |
| | | | | | | $t$ | 3 | 2 | 6 |
| $\leqslant$ Ceilings of $R$'s | 7 | 10 | 3 | 6 | Maximal | $\geqslant$ Floors of $r$'s | 2 | 3 | Minimal |
| | | | | | Minimal | | | | Maximal |

4 constraints are
$$3x + 2y \leqslant 7,$$
$$2x + 4y \leqslant 10,$$
$$x + 3y \leqslant 3,$$
and $\quad 3x + 2y \leqslant 6.$

Objective function of 2 variables is

$$2x + 3y.$$

2 constraints are
$$3p + 2q + s + 3t \geqslant 2,$$
and $2p + 4q + 3s + 2t \geqslant 3.$

Objective function of 4 variables is
$$7p + 10q + s + 6t.$$

is also amenable to graphic methods, provided we can visualize 3-dimensional graphs in space. The family of parallel lines of equiprofit of the 2-commodity case becomes a family of parallel planes of equiprofit in space. But otherwise the procedure is exactly the same. Again, because of the duality relation, a problem involving *any* number of commodities but subject only to 3 constraints may be solved by graphic methods, though the 'graphs' have to be drawn in space instead of on paper. The case of 4 or more resource limitations with 4 or more commodities to produce is, however, more difficult to handle by graphic methods. And yet almost all actual cases are of this type. The number of resources available, as well as commodities to be produced, is very much larger than 3, so that the graphic representation we have adopted to solve the problem is no longer possible. Nevertheless, this proliferation of resources and commodities in any actual case is no great handicap to the mathematician. He can by extension of our chart-room principle take in his stride all such more complicated cases involving many variables. The 'points', however, will no longer be number pairs as in our illustration. They will now be constellations of many numbers. Every such number constellation can be represented as a 'point' in some multi-dimensional hyperspace. Even though the graphic picture can no longer be readily visualized the principle of the method underlying the 2-dimensional case still applies. We first carve out the admissible region in this hyperspace, having regard for the prescribed constraints. As before, this is a region with a finite number of 'corners' where alone the objective function can be optimal. We begin by evaluating the objective function at any one of these 'corners' and proceed to the next. If the value at the next 'corner' exceeds that at the preceding one we proceed to the succeeding one. If its value there exceeds that at the earlier one we continue the search till we reach a 'corner' where its value is lower than that at the preceding one. In that case the penultimate value is the optimal one.

The procedure outlined above is in essence the *simplex* method of solving a linear-programming problem. It is merely a routine whose iteration is guaranteed to lead to the required solution in a finite number of steps. It is an instance of those convergent iterative routines that are increasingly being devised for computer solution of a problem. Consequently, it is a procedure that is almost tailor-made for the computer. It is lucky that a computer can readily be programmed to execute the simplex routine. For all real problems inevitably involve a large number of variables and an equally numerous set of constraints requiring a computer solution of the problem, if it is to be obtained in time for implementation. Take, for instance, the standard transportation problem, the problem of distributing a specified number of wagons or tonnage of merchandise from given sources or origins to pre-assigned destinations. Although the problem is readily amenable to linear programming a pencil-and-paper solution is often outdated by the time it is obtained. One has therefore to resort to the computer to obtain a solution. One can get a fair idea of the sheer bulk of computation work in simplex method even from a description of the following greatly oversimplified illustration.

Consider, for the sake of definiteness, the problem of moving 2, 6, and 7 tons of materials originating respectively at 3 sources $(S_1, S_2, S_3)$ to 4 destinations $(D_1, D_2, D_3, D_4)$ in such a way that

$D_1$ and $D_2$ receive 3 tons each, $D_3$ 4 tons, and $D_4$ 5 tons. A graphic way of defining the problem is to exhibit the quantities originating from the 3 sources at the bottom of 3 columns and those to be delivered at the 4 destinations at the end of 4 rows, as in Table 17.

*Table 17*

| Destinations | Sources | | | Requirements or row totals |
|:---:|:---:|:---:|:---:|:---:|
| | $S_1$ | $S_2$ | $S_3$ | |
| $D_1$ | ? | ? | ? | 3 |
| $D_2$ | ? | ? | ? | 3 |
| $D_3$ | ? | ? | ? | 4 |
| $D_4$ | ? | ? | ? | 5 |
| Availabilities or column totals | 2 | 6 | 7 | ⑮ |

The problem is to determine the number of tons that ought to be moved from each source to each destination in some optimal way. That is, we require to replace the marks of interrogation [?] in Table 17 with a set of numbers whose row and column totals are as shown there. There are obviously many ways of doing this. But all of them will not be equally efficient or profitable. To select the most efficient or profitable way of distribution we must define what objective function we wish to optimize. We may, for example decide to minimize the total cost of haulage. If so, we need to know the haulage cost per ton from each source to each destination. Suppose these costs are as shown in Table 18.

Thus the haulage cost per ton of moving from source $S_1$ to destination $D_1$ is 13; from $S_1$ to $D_2$, 11; from $S_2$ to $D_2$, 14, and so on – the cost from any source to any destination being given at the intersection of the corresponding column and row as shown in Table 18. If now we assume that

$x_{11}, x_{12}, x_{13}, x_{14}$ tons move from $S_1$ to $D_1, D_2, D_3, D_4$ respectively
$x_{21}, x_{22}, x_{23}, x_{24}$ tons move from $S_2$ to $D_1, D_2, D_3, D_4$ respectively
$x_{31}, x_{32}, x_{33}, x_{34}$ tons move from $S_3$ to $D_1, D_2, D_3, D_4$ respectively,

113

*Table 18*

| Destinations | Sources | | | Requirements or row totals |
|---|---|---|---|---|
| | $S_1$ | $S_2$ | $S_3$ | |
| $D_1$ | (13) ? | (17) ? | (18) ? | 3 |
| $D_2$ | (11) ? | (14) ? | (18) ? | 3 |
| $D_3$ | (15) ? | (12) ? | (15) ? | 4 |
| $D_4$ | (20) ? | (13) ? | (12) ? | 5 |
| Availabilities or column totals | 2 | 6 | 7 | |

then obviously we need to minimize the total haulage cost of the operation, namely,

$$\left.\begin{array}{l} 13x_{11}+11x_{12}+15x_{13}+20x_{14} \\ +17x_{21}+14x_{22}+12x_{23}+13x_{24} \\ +18x_{31}+18x_{32}+15x_{33}+12x_{34} \end{array}\right\} \qquad \text{(i)}$$

with the restraining conditions that column totals are as shown in Table 17, that is,

$$\left.\begin{array}{l} x_{11}+x_{12}+x_{13}+x_{14} = 2 = \text{total tons from source } S_1 \\ x_{21}+x_{22}+x_{23}+x_{24} = 6 = \text{total tons from source } S_2 \\ x_{31}+x_{32}+x_{34}+x_{34} = 7 = \text{total tons from source } S_3 \end{array}\right\} \qquad \text{(ii)}$$

and row totals are as shown in Table 17:

$$\left.\begin{array}{l} x_{11}+x_{21}+x_{31} = 3 = \text{total tons required at } D_1 \\ x_{12}+x_{22}+x_{32} = 3 = \text{total tons required at } D_2 \\ x_{13}+x_{23}+x_{33} = 4 = \text{total tons required at } D_3 \\ x_{14}+x_{24}+x_{34} = 5 = \text{total tons required at } D_4 \end{array}\right\} \qquad \text{(iii)}$$

All the aforementioned features of the problem can be expressed in a single table (Table 19) by superposing the haulage costs shown in Table 18 on Table 17 and substituting $x_{11}, x_{12}, x_{13}$, and so on, for the interrogation marks [?] in Table 18.

*Table 19*

| Destinations | Sources | | | Requirements or row totals |
|---|---|---|---|---|
| | $S_1$ | $S_2$ | $S_3$ | |
| $D_1$ | (13) $x_{11}$ | (17) $x_{21}$ | (18) $x_{31}$ | 3 |
| $D_2$ | (11) $x_{12}$ | (14) $x_{22}$ | (18) $x_{32}$ | 3 |
| $D_3$ | (15) $x_{13}$ | (12) $x_{23}$ | (15) $x_{33}$ | 4 |
| $D_4$ | (20) $x_{14}$ | (13) $x_{24}$ | (12) $x_{34}$ | 5 |
| Availabilities or column totals | 2 | 6 | 7 | |

The objective function to be optimized is then given by adding the product of each $x$ by the cost coefficient shown in its own box (e.g. $x_{11}$ by 13 and $x_{21}$ by 17, and so on). The constraint equations are obtained by adding all the $x$'s in any column (row) and equating the sum to the number at the end of the corresponding column (row). The problem is solved by applying the simplex method whose theory has already been described. Applying this method we find that the values of $x$'s as shown in Table 20 will minimize the total haulage cost. If we multiply each of the values of $x$'s shown in Table 20 by its corresponding cost coefficient (the numbers in parentheses directly above it) we find that the total cost of haulage will be

$$1(13)+0(17)+2(18)$$
$$+1(11)+2(14)+0(18)$$
$$+0(15)+4(12)+0(15)$$
$$+0(20)+0(13)+5(12) = 196.$$

No other way of dispatching materials in accordance with the prescribed constraints will cost less than 196. If the numbers in parentheses shown in Table 18 had represented the *return* per ton of the hauler instead of his cost, he would naturally have desired to

115

*Table 20*

| Destinations | Sources | | | Requirements or row totals |
|---|---|---|---|---|
| | $S_1$ | $S_2$ | $S_3$ | |
| $D_1$ | (13) 1 | (17) 0 | (18) 2 | 3 |
| $D_2$ | (11) 1 | (14) 2 | (18) 0 | 3 |
| $D_3$ | (15) 0 | (12) 4 | (15) 0 | 4 |
| $D_4$ | (20) 0 | (13) 0 | (12) 5 | 5 |
| Availabilities or column totals | 2 | 6 | 7 | |

maximize the same objective function instead of minimizing it. A similar application of the simplex method will show that the values of $x$ for maximizing the objective function would have to be as shown in Table 21.

*Table 21*

| Destinations | Sources | | | Requirements or row totals |
|---|---|---|---|---|
| | $S_1$ | $S_2$ | $S_3$ | |
| $D_1$ | (13) 0 | (17) 3 | (18) 0 | 3 |
| $D_2$ | (11) 0 | (14) 0 | (18) 3 | 3 |
| $D_3$ | (15) 0 | (12) 0 | (15) 4 | 4 |
| $D_4$ | (20) 2 | (13) 3 | (12) 0 | 5 |
| Availabilities or column totals | 2 | 6 | 7 | |

The maximum return is then the sum of the products of each value
of $x$ shown in Table 22 by its corresponding return, namely,

$$0(13)+3(17)+0(18)$$
$$+0(11)+0(14)+3(18)$$
$$+0(15)+0(12)+4(15)$$
$$+2(20)+3(13)+0(12) = 244.$$

No other way of dispatching the materials will make the return
larger than 244.

In short, linear programming is a way of optimizing a linear
function (like the haulage cost of the aforementioned transportation problem) subject to linear constraints. Despite the great
simplicity of its mathematical structure, it is sufficiently powerful
to take in its stride a wide range of applications. For example, it is
as readily applicable to the optimum deployment of aircraft to
maximize a country's chance of winning a war as with the product-
mix that a refinery ought to produce to maximize its profits. Here is
a small sample of fields to which linear programming has been
successfully applied:

*Agricultural applications.* These are of two kinds. In one case we
consider agricultural economics in the large, i.e. as related to the
economy of the nation or region as a whole. In the other we deal
with the problems of the individual farm. A typical farm-manage-
ment problem of the latter category is that of allocating resources
such as acreage, labour, water supply, or working capital in such a
way as to maximize net revenue. The problem is to choose simultaneously the particular crop or crops to be grown in the following
period, the number of acres of land to be allotted to each of these
crops and the particular method to use in their production.
Another example of the same type is the selection of the optimal
crop-rotation plan by the individual farmer.

*Contract awards.* Tenders or bids often include complicated
stipulations so that it is often not readily apparent which one of
several bids made is the cheapest. Evaluation of bids by recourse to
linear-programming technique guarantees that the awards are, in
fact, made in the cheapest way. What is even more important is
that use of the technique proves objectively that this has been done.
Chief auditors and financial advisers might well beware, as wide-
spread use of linear programming might make them redundant!

*Industrial applications.* Applications in industry are of the most diverse kind. We have already described the transportation model particularly suited to solving the problem of coal distribution, or for that matter distribution of any sort of merchandise. Its structure is as readily adaptable to problems of production and inventory control. For example, linear programming has been used to discover the optimal scheduling of 25 machines of varying capacities used in electrochemical formation of aluminum oxide films on etched aluminum foil. The foil comes in about 45 combinations of voltage capacity and width, each with its corresponding current requirements. The total current load is limited by the company's power-distribution facilities. The scheduling problem turns out to be a straightforward linear-programming problem which involves the capacities, power limitations, and other constraints.

In the communications industry linear programming has been employed to evolve optimal design and utilization of communication networks, including problems involving facilities for transmission, switching, and relaying. In the steel industry minimum-cost steel-production programmes have been derived from a linear-programming model which has been used to determine the optimum monthly plan of the open hearth, the rate of hot-metal production by the blast-furnace department, and the amount and type of steel scrap to be purchased.

In the paper industry linear programming has been applied to reducing trimming losses to a minimum. The rolls of newsprint paper have to conform to customers' specifications as to width and diameter. In cutting these rolls from larger reels of paper trim losses are incurred. Linear programming helped determine on which machines and in what combinations the orders should be cut to cause a minimum over-all trim loss. The saving made was equivalent to an increase in production of over 15 tons per day.

The foregoing list of applications, brief though it is, could be extended almost indefinitely. But the examples enumerated will suffice to indicate the range, power, and versatility of linear-programming technique. This is not to say that it is a panacea for all our management, industrial, or agricultural problems. It is not. To mention only one difficulty, the assumption of linearity can be a serious handicap. For in most economic situations sooner or later the law of diminishing returns begins to tell. For example, by doubling *all* our inputs we may increase our profits by only 40 per cent, if even by that. The reason may be either because the physical outputs fail to keep pace with additional inputs or because of increasing consumer resistance to the sale of additional outputs. It is therefore natural that attempts be made to develop programming techniques in which the linearity condition is abandoned or greatly relaxed. Such non-linear programming techniques, which may be described as the analysis of constrained optimization problems in the presence of diminishing or increasing scale effects, have been difficult to formulate. Results of proved practical value are as yet few.

CHAPTER 7

# Theory of Games:
## The Logic of Rational Decisions

### PAY-OFF MATRIX

THE chief problem of an administrator or manager of an undertaking is to pinpoint both favourable and unfavourable consequences of each of several courses of action open to him. He frequently makes a balance sheet of pros and cons of each alternative in order to find rational criteria for choosing one of them. Very often the consequence of each alternative can be reduced to a single pay-off number, such as the dollar profit or consumption of some value or utility-per-unit output. Mathematicians have devised a neat way of summarizing such pay-off numbers measuring the consequences of various alternatives available. Suppose, for the sake of definiteness, we have certain funds to invest. Suppose further we can make only one of three possible investments: speculative stocks, high-grade stocks, or bonds. The consequences of each choice open to us will naturally depend on a future state of nature (or history) beyond our control. Thus if war breaks out the speculative stocks will appreciate greatly; but if peace prevails the return may be small. If we further assume that only 4 states of nature can occur – war, cold war, peace, and depression – each mode of investment will have 4 consequential returns or pay-offs. Since there are in all only 3 modes of investments or alternatives for action available to us, there will be $3 \times 4$ consequential pay-offs, each alternative or mode of investment having 4 consequences corresponding to each of the 4 possible states of nature. These $3 \times 4$ pay-offs can be arranged in a tabular form consisting of 3 rows and 4 columns, where each row indicates the 4 consequences of each of the 3 modes of investment, and each column, for each of the 4 states of nature, the consequences of each of our 3 modes of investment. Such a tabular arrangement is called a pay-off matrix. It is simply a 2-dimensional array of pay-off numbers in rows and columns as shown in Table 22.

*Table 22.* $3 \times 4$ pay-off matrix with 3 alternatives and 4 states of nature.

| Mode of investment or alternative available | Percentage return on capital for four states of nature | | | |
| --- | --- | --- | --- | --- |
| | War | Cold war | Peace | Depression |
| | $(N_1)$ | $(N_2)$ | $(N_3)$ | $(N_4)$ |
| Speculative stocks (alternative $S_1$) | 20 | 10 | 2 | $-5$ |
| High-grade stocks (alternative $S_2$) | 12 | 9 | 5 | 0 |
| Bonds (alternative $S_3$) | 3 | 3 | 3 | 3 |

This $3 \times 4$ matrix shows the likely returns on capital or pay-offs corresponding to each mode of investment and state of nature. Thus, if we invest in speculative stocks, alternative $S_1$, we may expect to gain 20 per cent in case of war or lose 5 per cent in case of depression. The number at the intersection of each row and column is the pay-off expected, if we adopt the alternative corresponding to the row under the state of nature corresponding to the column.

Having expressed the consequences of various alternatives in matrix form our next problem is to formulate criteria for choice of an optimal course of action. Unfortunately no such criteria exist – only more or less plausible rationalizations of our own moods. If we wish to play safe we shall, anxious to guard ourselves against the worst possible contingency, adopt what Abraham Wald called the *maximin* criterion. That is, we shall select the maximum of the row minima, hence the name *maximin*. The underlying rationale of the criterion is this: suppose we adopt the first alternative, $S_1$. In that case, if the worst happens, we shall have a return of $-5$, which is the minimum of the pay-offs in the first row. Similarly, under the second alternative, $S_2$, our worst pay-off will be the minimum of the numbers in the second row, which is 0. Finally, with the third alternative, $S_3$, we may expect at worst the minimum of the pay-offs in the third row, namely, 3. We summarize these conclusions in Table 23.

*Table 23*

| Alternative or mode of investment adopted | Worst or minimum pay-off |
|:---:|:---:|
| $S_1$ | −5 |
| $S_2$ | 0 |
| $S_3$ | 3 |

Following Wald's suggestion of caution at any cost, and therefore assuming that nature will always be malevolent even though it is actually quite indifferent to our hopes and desires, the best we can do is to select the alternative which has the largest such minimum pay-off, that is, the maximum of the 3-row minima shown in Table 23. This is the maximin criterion of Wald, which tells us to select alternative $S_3$, that is, invest in bonds. However, since nature acts independently of our wishes the underlying assumption of Wald's criterion – that the worst will happen – is not always justified. This has led Hurwicz to jump to the other extreme. Like Voltaire's Candide, he assumes that we might as well hope for the best. We may therefore select the maximum pay-off corresponding to each alternative, instead of the minimum as we did under the Wald criterion. Thus, if we adopt the alternative $S_1$, we may hope (dismal thought) for the maximum pay-off, which is 20. Similarly, for alternatives $S_2$ and $S_3$ the maximum pay-offs are 12 and 3, respectively. These conclusions may be summarized as in Table 24.

*Table 24*

| Alternative or mode of investment | Best or maximum pay-off |
|:---:|:---:|
| $S_1$ | 20 |
| $S_2$ | 12 |
| $S_3$ | 3 |

And since now we are in an optimistic mood, we will naturally select the mode of investment with the largest of these maxima, that is, the maximum of maxima, usually abbreviated the *maximax*

The maximax pay-off in the case under review is obviously 20, corresponding to alternative $S_1$.

Between the two extremes of maximin and maximax criteria there are any number of half-way houses according to our judgement about the shape of things to come. If we assume that any one of the possible 4 states of nature is as likely to occur as any other the probability of each of the 4 alternative states of nature $S_1, S_2, S_3, S_4$ will naturally be 1/4. The expected pay-off then is merely the weighted average of the row pay-offs, each pay-off being weighted by the probability of the state of nature to which it corresponds. It is therefore

$$20(1/4) + 10(1/4) + 2(1/4) - 5(1/4) = 27/4 = 6 \cdot 75.$$

Proceeding in this manner we can calculate the weighted pay-off of the other 2 alternatives and choose the one with the greatest expected pay-off.

*Table 25*

| Alternative or mode of investment | Expected pay-off |
|:---:|:---:|
| $S_1$ | 6·75* |
| $S_2$ | 6·50 |
| $S_3$ | 3·00 |

∴ Choice made: $S_1$, as it yields the maximum expected pay-off.

If, on the other hand, having faith in human sanity, we consider war unlikely, we may assign it lower probability. Thus, we may consider that the probabilities of the 4 states of nature (war, cold war, peace, and depression) are respectively 1/100, 4/10, 5/10 9/100 – the total naturally adding to 1. In that case the expected pay-offs will be different and so also will be the choice of action (see Table 26).

All these criteria are in reality only mathematical rationalizations of our hopes and fears concerning what nature is likely to have in store for us. The question then arises as to how they are any better than the mere gusts of emotion or flashes of intuition that usually inspire our investment decisions, when any alternative may be justified by an appropriate constellation of probability numbers

*Table 26*

| Alternative or mode of investment | Weighted pay-off |
|---|---|
| $S_1$ | $20(1/100) + 10(4/10) + 2(5/10) - 5(9/100) = \dfrac{47 \cdot 5}{10} = 4 \cdot 75$ |
| $S_2$ | $12(1/100) + 9(4/10) + 5(5/10) + 0(9/100) = \dfrac{62 \cdot 2}{10} = 6 \cdot 22^*$ |
| $S_3$ | $3(1/100) + 3(4/10) + 3(5/10) + 3(9/100) = \dfrac{30 \cdot 0}{10} = 3 \cdot 00$ |

$\therefore$ Choice made: $S_2$, as it yields the maximum expected pay-off.

such as (1/4, 1/4, 1/4, 1/4) or (1/100, 4/10, 5/10, 9/100). The answer is that, by putting in sharp focus the motives of our conduct we are compelled to correct our biases in the light of more reasoned anticipations of what the future is likely to bring us. But we can certainly be much less arbitrary in our decisions when we face not impersonal nature (which is consciously neither benevolent nor malevolent towards us) but an intelligent opponent or competitor, as in war or a game. In such a conflict situation we may depend on our adversary, if he is as rational and intelligent as ourselves, to take counter-steps to thwart our efforts to make a profit at his expense. Such a situation, where we are up against a rational opponent whose behavioural motives we can foresee, provides a firmer basis for decision than the earlier one, in which there is but one decision-maker, namely, ourselves trying blindly to guess what the state of nature is likely to be.

Von Neumann and Morgenstern, in an attempt to provide a new approach to economic questions as yet unsettled, were the first to suggest a method for handling conflict situations of this type. As they rightly point out, classical economics left out of consideration a vital element of political economy, that is, group rivalries and clashes of interests. Of old, it had been known that whereas some economic policies might benefit everybody in greater or lesser degree, certain policies would benefit one or more groups only at the cost of others. In spite of this conflict of various group interests classical economics was dominated by the idea that if an individual were free to pursue his own good he in some mysterious manner promoted the good of everyone else at the same time. Hence its advocacy of the Benthamite formula: the promotion of 'the greatest good of the greatest number'.

In an economy of the isolated Robinson Crusoe type it is, no doubt, possible for an individual (that is, Crusoe) to implement this formula, at least in principle, and direct his economic effort to maximizing his own good. But even a Crusoe begins to be disturbed when he sees signs of another will intruding on his domain, as Crusoe did when he saw strange footsteps on the beach. Consequently, the Benthamite formula is practical economics for an isolated Crusoe but not for a participant in a real economy. For, while the former faces merely physical impedimenta, that is, 'dead data', or the unalterable physical background of the situation, the latter has to face, in addition, 'living data' – that is, the actions of other participants which he can no longer control and whose interests often run counter to his own.

## GAMES OF STRATEGY

The above consideration introduces a difficulty hitherto ignored by classical economics. It is with a view to overcoming it that von Neumann and Morgenstern have developed the mathematical theory of 'games of strategy', their object being the creation of theoretical models designed to play the same role in economic theory as the various geometrico-mathematical models have played in physical theory. Admittedly, game theory is an extreme abstraction oversimplifying in many ways the actual state of affairs of a game or war situation. For it does not exhibit all the complexities of warfare and real games. But neither do all physical theories. For example, Newton's theory of gravitation gives short shrift to all the nuances of planetary shapes and sizes, bulldozing them all into mere dimensionless points where all their putative masses are condensed. Yet it is none the worse for its disregard of reality. It has been adequate for predicting the motions of planets ever since its inception. The worst discrepancy it has had to face is that of the orbit of Mercury, which unaccountably drifts from its predicted place by an amount so small that it is barely equivalent to an error of a foot at a distance of a mile per *century*. The upshot of this excursion into gravitational theory is that abstraction in a theory, provided it is of the right sort, lends it power. It is therefore no wonder that von Neumann and Morgenstern have had to resort to abstractions to secure a foothold for a first peep into the reality of conflict situations that arise in war or a game. For it is certainly as yet much too simple a theory to take into its stride all the aspects of interest in any military, economic, or social situation. Nevertheless, it is a tribute to von Neumann's genius that his theory, even in its infancy, is sufficiently general to illumine certain critical features of many interesting competitive situations.

What, then, is a game, according to von Neumann's general theory? A 'game', in his theory, is exactly what it means in ordinary parlance. That is, it is a contest between a number of players, played for fun or forfeit, according to some predetermined rules, and decided by skill, strength, or chance. Although a game may be played for mere fun or some non-monetary forfeit, for most econometric and social purposes it would do if it were assumed to be played for money or a 'utility' which we may suppose to be measurable. In most games played for monetary stakes, such as bridge, poker, and the like, the algebraic sum of the gains and losses of all the players is zero. Such a game is called a zero-sum game. In other words, most ordinary games are zero-sum games wherein the play does not add a single penny to the total wealth of all players. It merely results in a new distribution of their old possessions.

A game theory of economic behaviour can therefore deal only with a pure problem of distribution or imputation, that is, a problem wherein an economic group of Peters could be paid only by robbing a group of Pauls. In any actual economy, as also in many games, the real-life situation is different. For example, even poker may not be a zero-sum game if a certain percentage of the pot is cut for the 'house' before the final pay-off. Likewise, in real life most economically significant schemes cannot be treated as zero-sum games at all, for the sum of all the payments – the total social product – is in general not zero. It does not even remain a constant.

To take account of this important feature of social economy von

Neumann and Morgenstern broaden the concept of a game to include those in which the sum of the total proceeds of all players is not zero. But a non-zero-sum game may be transformed into a zero-sum game. This is done by including an additional fictitious player in the game. Thus a non-zero-sum poker game, where three players have to pay the 'house' a percentage cut, may be turned into a zero-sum game by adding an additional 'dummy' player, the 'house'. Then the sum of the gains of all four players including the 'house' is restored to zero. It is clear that in general any non-zero-sum game played by $(n-1)$ persons may be turned into a zero-sum $n$-person game by including an additional dummy player who receives (pays) the residual losses (gains) of all the original $(n-1)$ players. Consequently, the case of a zero-sum $n$-person game is sufficiently broad to cover the general problem of social economy, namely, the problem of imputation with or without the creation of 'utility' during the process of play. We shall therefore confine our description to the case of a zero-sum game.

## ZERO-SUM GAMES

The simplest such game is that of a single player playing solitaire or patience. As he faces no opponent his task is the extremely simple one of maximizing his own 'good', 'satisfaction', or 'utility'. At least it is so in theory. This case corresponds to a rigidly established dictatorship in which one unalterable scheme of distribution prevails and the interests of all the members of the society are assumed to be identical with those of the dictator. There is nothing further that the game theory can tell us in the solution of the imputation problem in this case.

Next in order of complexity is the case of a zero-sum two-person game. This case corresponds to a market wherein a single buyer 'bargains' with a single seller. The game becomes more complex when there are three or more players. The reason is that while in a two-person game there is always a total clash of interests, in a three-person game there occurs a partial mitigation of this total clash. The mere existence of a third player opens up possibilities of coalitions and alliances by any two of them against the third. This case corresponds to a duopolistic market wherein a buyer faces two producers of the same commodity and can play one against the other. The possibilities of such manoeuvres and coalitions increase enormously as the number (*n*) of players increases.

Nevertheless, it is often possible to reduce a general zero-sum *n*-person game to the simpler case of a zero-sum two-person game. For consider any particular player of the game. If he treats all the remaining players as one coalition the game becomes a two-person game, that is, one between himself and the rest of the group, at least to a degree of approximation. This is why the case of a zero-sum two-person game is quite fundamental in the whole theory. We shall therefore consider it in greater detail.

For the sake of simplicity we may visualize a zero-sum two-person game as a sequence of only two moves: a first move by player *A*, followed by a second move by player *B*. Let player *A* have a choice of 5 possible moves, designated by $A_1, A_2, A_3, A_4, A_5$, and let player *B* have a choice of 4, designated by $B_1, B_2, B_3, B_4$. Any actual play will give rise to some one of the 5 moves in *A*'s repertoire, followed by some one of the 4 in that of *B*. Clearly, there will in all be $5 \times 4$ different combinations of *A*- and *B*-moves, each one of which is an outcome of some particular play. The complete set of $5 \times 4$ pairs of *A*'s and *B*'s moves, covering the totality of all possible plays, defines the game *G*, as distinct from any particular play thereof. Now the rules of the game must also prescribe the pay-offs that each player has to make to the other as a result of each play. In other words, we must also prescribe the pay-off for each of the $5 \times 4$ possible combinations of *A*'s and *B*'s moves. As before, these $5 \times 4$ pay-offs can be arranged in matrix form, that is, as a 2-dimensional array of pay-off numbers in rows and columns. Let the pay-offs be as shown in the $5 \times 4$ matrix in Table 27.

The number shown in each box or square of Table 27 is the payment made by *B* to *A*, if *A* plays the move corresponding to the column of the matrix and *B* plays that corresponding to its row. Consider, for example, the pay-off number 4 in the box located in the first column and first row. This is the payment that the rules of the game require *B* to make to *A*, if *A* plays the move $A_1$ and *B*, the move $B_1$. Since the numbers shown in the pay-off matrix are payments received by *A* from *B*, the course of the play will be determined by the desire of *A* to maximize it and that of *B* to minimize it.

*Table 27.* Pay-off matrix of player *A* against player *B*.

| B's moves | A's moves | | | | |
|:---:|:---:|:---:|:---:|:---:|:---:|
| | $A_1$ | $A_2$ | $A_3$ | $A_4$ | $A_5$ |
| $B_1$ | 4 | 3 | 2 | −1 | −3 |
| $B_2$ | −2 | 1 | 3 | −3 | 2 |
| $B_3$ | −4 | −1 | −2 | −3 | −2 |
| $B_4$ | −1 | 2 | −2 | 1 | −3 |

Thus both concentrate on pay-off numbers shown in the matrix – one (*A*) with the intention of maximizing it and the other (*B*) with that of minimizing it. Suppose, now, *A* moves first. In doing so he will have to reckon with the fact that whatever move he may adopt, *B*, his opponent, will select that particular countermove which will minimize the pay-off. Thus, if *A* selects the move $A_1$, then *B* will reply by selecting $B_3$, as this corresponds to the *least* pay-off in the *first* column, corresponding to $A_1$. Any other choice of a move by *B* will only increase *B*'s loss. Similarly, if *A* plays the move $A_2$ he can only expect the minimum of the pay-off numbers in the second column, namely, −1, corresponding to *B*'s move $B_3$. In other words, whatever move *A* may adopt, he can expect only the minimum of the corresponding column pay-offs. These, corresponding to each *A*-move, are shown in Table 28.

*Table 28*

| *A*-move | Minimum of the column pay-offs |
|:---:|:---|
| $A_1$ | −4 (of first column) |
| $A_2$ | −1 (of second column) |
| $A_3$ | −2 (of third column) |
| $A_4$ | −3 (of fourth column) |
| $A_5$ | −3 (of fifth column) |

Naturally, *A*'s best move is the one that is the maximum of the column minima shown in Table 28, namely, −1, corresponding to his move $A_2$. Hence *A* will choose the move $A_2$, and *B* will then reply by choosing $B_3$ because any other move by the latter will only result in greater loss to him. The game will then consist of $A$ making the move $A_2$, followed by $B$ making the move $B_3$, and the resultant pay-off will be $-1$, that is, a loss of 1 to $A$.

In the foregoing $A$ was assumed to make the first move and declare it. Suppose $B$ were to make the first move and declare it. Will the game be played differently? If $B$ were to make the first move he would reason that whatever move he chose $A$ would make a move to maximize his pay-off. Thus, if $B$ played the move $B_1$ then $A$ would make the countermove $A_1$, as that corresponds to the *maximum* pay-off in the *first* row. In other words, $B$ will consider the *maxima* of the *rows* and choose the row corresponding to the *minimum* of the *row maxima*. A glance at the pay-off matrix will show that the row maxima are as shown in Table 29.

*Table 29*

| $B$-move | Maximum of the row pay-offs |
|:--------:|:---------------------------:|
| $B_1$ | 4 |
| $B_2$ | 3 |
| $B_3$ | $-1$ |
| $B_4$ | 2 |

The minimum of the row maxima is $-1$, corresponding to the move $B_3$ by $B$. In that case, $A$ would make the move $A_2$, as any other choice by $A$ would increase his loss. As it happens, the outcome of the game is the same in both cases, that is, $A$ plays $A_2$ and $B$ plays $B_3$, the resultant pay-off being $-1$ to $A$. The reason is that in this case the maximum of column minima is equal to the minimum of row maxima. In symbols,

Maximum of column minima = Minimum of row maxima

or,

Max. (column minima) = $-1$ = Min. (row maxima).

As a result, it is immaterial whether we first pick column *minima* and then choose their *maximum*, or pick row *maxima* and then choose their *minimum*. In such cases, when the maximum of column minima equals the minimum of row maxima, the pay-off matrix is said to have a *saddle point*. This is the point or rather the box of the pay-off matrix where the maximum of the column minima coincides with the minimum of the row maxima. Thus the saddle point of the pay-off matrix shown in Table 27 is the box with pay-off number −1 in the second column and the third row, where $A$'s move $A_2$, corresponding to the maximum of column minima, intersects $B$'s move $B_3$, corresponding to the minimum of the row maxima. The importance of the saddle point arises from the fact that, in general, the optimal play for each player consists in sticking to the moves which pass through it. To solve a game problem we need therefore merely look for the saddle point of the pay-off matrix. *If* it exists the problem is solved. Unfortunately, most pay-off matrices do not have any saddle point. Those which, like that of Table 27, have one do so because they are artificially constructed to yield the equality of the maximum of the column minima and the minimum of the row maxima. But as the two operations of picking the *maximum* of column *minima* and the *minimum* of row *maxima* are quite distinct, there is no reason in logic why they should lead to the same pay-off number except through special contrivance in initially rigging the pay-off matrix. If, for example, we substitute the pay-off matrix of Table 30 for the earlier one, the maximum of column minima will no longer be equal to the minimum of row maxima.

For the maximum of the five column minima corresponding to the five moves of $A$ is −2, the number marked [*] in the last row

*Table 30*

| $B$'s moves | $A$'s moves | | | | | Row maxima |
|---|---|---|---|---|---|---|
| | $A_1$ | $A_2$ | $A_3$ | $A_4$ | $A_5$ | |
| $B_1$ | 6 | −5 | 2 | −10 | 5 | 6 |
| $B_2$ | −1 | −3 | 4 | 5† | 3 | 5† |
| $B_3$ | 1 | 0 | −3 | 7 | 11 | 11 |
| $B_4$ | −2* | 4 | 8 | 3 | −5 | 8 |
| Column minima | −2* | −5 | −3 | −10 | −5 | |

entitled 'column minima', as a glance at Table 30 clearly shows. The same glance will also reveal that the minimum of the four row maxima corresponding to the four moves of $B$ is 5, the number marked [†] in the last column headed 'row maxima'. In this instance the *maximum* of *column minima*, $-2$, is no longer equal to the *minimum* of the *row maxima*, 5, so that the pay-off matrix has no saddle point. In such cases the minimax or maximin principle of solving a game problem breaks down.

MIXED MOVES

To meet such situations von Neumann and Morgenstern introduced a new concept, that of *mixed moves*. The novel feature worthy of note here is that, unlike the earlier case, in which plays were declared, whichever player now announced his move would be at a serious disadvantage. For his opponent would make full use of the intelligence received to increase his own gain. We could, however, make matters even between the two by requiring each of them to write his move on a secret ballot and determine the outcome by reading their choices simultaneously. How then should each player write the choice of his move on the secret ballot? It will no longer pay him to stick to any particular one move as in the earlier case – $A_2$ in case of $A$ and $B_3$ in case of $B$ – when the maximum of column minima happened to equal the minimum of row maxima. He will have to mix his moves, making sometimes one, sometimes another, in such a way that his average rake-off over a large number of plays of the game would be optimal, even though he may lose more in any individual play of the game.

To illustrate how the moves should be mixed in order to maximize the *average* pay-off over a large number of plays of the game, consider for the sake of simplicity the $2 \times 2$ pay-off matrix in Table 31.

The maximum of the column minima is 3, corresponding to $A$'s move $A_1$. Consequently, if $A$ adopts the move $A_1$ he will never receive a pay-off smaller than 3. Likewise, the minimum of the row maxima is 7, corresponding to move $B_1$ by $B$. So use of $B_1$ by $B$ ensures that $B$ will never lose more than 7. Since the two are not equal there is no clearly optimal move for either player. If $A$ stuck

132

*Table 31*

| B's moves | A's moves | | Row maxima |
| :---: | :---: | :---: | :---: |
| | $A_1$ | $A_2$ | |
| $B_1$ | 7† | 2 | 7* |
| $B_2$ | 3* | 11 | 11 |
| Column minima | 3* | 2 | |

always to $A_1$ he could make sure that he would gain at least 3. If
$B$ always played $B_1$, he could ensure that he never lost more than 7.
But if $A$ came to know that $B$ is *always* going to play $B_2$ in anticipation of his own move $A_1$, he might chose $A_2$ for a change and increase his pay-off to 11. On the other hand, if $B$ could rely on $A$'s
playing always $A_2$ he might forestall him by varying his move from
$B_2$ to $B_1$ and thus reduce $A$'s pay-off to only 2. This is indeed a
dilemma. Player $A$ as well as player $B$ must do something, and since
the steadfast election of either of the two moves open to each of
them will only permit his opponent to profit unduly, each must also
consider the remaining alternative to make both moves during the
course of various plays of the game. Now in any one play of the
game either player is constrained to make one or the other move,
because by definition each move is a complete course of action and
excludes the other. It follows therefore that $A$ must make the move
$A_1$ sometimes and $A_2$ at other times. In other words he needs a
grand strategy which can tell him when to make one move and
when to make the other. What holds for $A$ is equally true of $B$. He
too must mix his moves from play to play. The question is: how
must each player mix the two moves open to him in order to
optimize his own gain?

To do so he has to meet two requirements. First, since each of the
two players could profit unduly if he knew his opponent's intentions,
his main concern should be to avoid having his own intentions
divined rather than attempt to find out what his opponent is going
to do. This is why each player must vary in a wholly unpredictable
way his choice of the move he makes from one play to another. For

133

if he mixes the moves according to some regular pattern, such as (if he is $A$) choosing $A_1$ and $A_2$ alternatively, his opponent ($B$) will be able to guess his next move after observing his behaviour during the course of a number of plays. The only safeguard against such enemy anticipation is for each player to mix his moves in a random manner, by recourse to a chance mechanism such as the throw of dice or some equivalent process to be specified more precisely later. If he does so, he will give no clue to his opponent of what his next move is likely to be, for the simple reason that he himself will not know it, since he has delegated his discretion to decide to the chance mechanism he has contrived. Such delegation to a chance contrivance may seem at first glance quite a frivolous way of selecting a course of action, particularly if its outcome has important consequences. But actually, it is quite the reverse. Indeed, all the wisdom of the game theory is fed into making the chance mechanism. For it is not any odd chance device that the player uses but one that is specifically tailored to secure just that particular blend of moves which optimizes, as much as the rules of the game will allow, his over-all gain during the course of several plays. How then must each player tailor his chance apparatus to obtain his own optimal mixture of moves? This leads us to the second of the two requirements we mentioned earlier.

Obviously, the chance apparatus must have only two outcomes – such as '*heads*' or '*tails*' with the toss of a coin – since there are only two moves open to each player. But the probability of each alternative need not be identical, as is the case with the tossed unbiased coin. To decide the probabilities of the two outcomes consider first the chance apparatus of player $A$. Let us label its two outcomes $A_1$ and $A_2$, where the appearance of the former leads to the choice of *move $A_1$* and that of the latter to the *move $A_2$*. By definition, the probabilities with which the two outcomes $A_1$ and $A_2$ of the chance apparatus actually materialize are the same as those with which the two moves $A_1$ and $A_2$ must be selected in order to optimize $A$'s gain. If $A$'s optimal strategy is to mix his two moves, $A_1$ and $A_2$, with probabilities $p$ and $q$ respectively, where the sum of $p$ and $q$ is naturally unity, then clearly the final result of the game should be the same no matter what moves $B$ chooses to make. For if not, the mixed strategy $A$ adopts is not optimal. Suppose $A$

mixes his moves $A_1$ and $A_2$ with probabilities $p$ and $q$ against $B$'s strategy $B_1$. Recalling that the pay-offs corresponding to moves $A_1$ and $A_2$ against $B$'s move $B_1$ are

|       | $A_1$ | $A_2$ |
|-------|-------|-------|
| $B_1$ | 7     | 2     |

$A$'s net expected or average gain during the course of the play will obviously be $(7p+2q)$. Similarly, his net average gain against $B$'s strategy $B_2$ when the pay-offs are

|       | $A_1$ | $A_2$ |
|-------|-------|-------|
| $B_2$ | 3     | 11    |

will be $3p+11q$. Since $p$ and $q$ have been chosen to make $A$'s mixture of moves optimal against any of the two possible $B$-moves, the two gains must be equal. Hence

$$7p + 2q = 3p + 11q$$

where

$$p + q = 1.$$

Solving these two simultaneous equations in $p$ and $q$, we find that $p = 9/13$ and $q = 4/13$. In other words, $A$'s optimal play consists in mixing his two moves $A_1$ and $A_2$ in the proportion $9/13 : 4/13$, or $9 : 4$. A chance mechanism that will yield $A_1$ and $A_2$ moves at random but with probabilities $9/13$ and $4/13$, respectively, is to put in a hat 9 slips of paper marked $A_1$ and 4 slips marked $A_2$. To decide his move in any given play all that $A$ need do is to shake these slips thoroughly and pick one at random. He then plays the move written on the slip, naturally taking care that $B$ does not see it before making his own.

Similarly, $B$ too can make a chance mechanism designed to yield his optimal strategy by proceeding along analogous lines. Suppose he chooses his moves $B_1$, $B_2$ with probabilities $p'$ and $q'$, where $p'+q'=1$. Since the pay-offs to $A$ corresponding to $A$'s move $A_1$ are

|       | $A_1$ |
|-------|-------|
| $B_1$ | 7     |
| $B_2$ | 3     |

the expected average loss to $B$ against $A$'s move $A_1$ will be $7p'+3q'$. Likewise, the pay-offs to $A$ corresponding to $A$'s move $A_2$ being

the expected average loss to $B$ against $A$'s move $A_2$ will be $2p'+11q'$. Again, the two must be equal; otherwise $B$'s mixture of his two moves against any of the two possible $A$-moves will not be optimal. We thus again have two simultaneous equations

$$7p'+3q' = 2p'+11q';$$

where

$$p'+q' = 1$$

to determine $p'$ and $q'$. Solving, we find that

$$p' = 8/13 \text{ and } q' = 5/13.$$

Consequently, $B$'s chance mechanism that yields him *his* optimal play is *another* hat having 13 slips of paper, 8 of which are marked $B_1$ and 5 $B_2$ – all of them thoroughly mixed before $B$ draws a slip to decide his move.

While the calculation of probabilities with which each player must choose his own moves is simple, we can derive them by recourse to even a simpler short cut. For the proportion, $p:q$, in which $A$ must mix his moves for optimal play, is given by the equation

$$7p+2q = 3p+11q,$$

whence

$$(7-3)p = (11-2)q$$

or,

$$\frac{p}{q} = -\frac{2-11}{7-3} = \frac{9}{4}.$$

This suggests the following rule of thumb. We begin with $A$'s moves, $A_1$ and $A_2$,

| $A_1$ | $A_2$ |
|---|---|
| 7 | 2 |
| 3 | 11 |

and subtract the numbers in the second row from those in the first, obtaining

The proportion, $p:q$, in which $A_1$ and $A_2$ should be mixed, is simply the numbers so obtained, except that the number 9 to be associated with $A_1$ is to be found in the box under $A_2$, and vice versa, as indicated by the arrows. That is, the moves $A_1$ and $A_2$ should be mixed in the proportion 9* : 4 as we have already shown. Likewise, the proportion $p':q'$, in which $B$ must mix his moves, is given by the equation

$$7p'+3q' = 2p'+11q',$$

whence

$$(7-2)p' = (11-3)q',$$

or

$$\frac{p'}{q'} = -\frac{3-11}{7-2} = \frac{8}{5}.$$

This leads to the following analogous rule for $B$. We begin with the moves $B_1$ and $B_2$

| | $B_1$ | |
|---|---|---|
| $B_1$ | 7 | 2 |
| $B_2$ | 3 | 11 |

and subtract the numbers in the second *column* from those in the first, obtaining

---

*Negative signs are disregarded.

$$
\begin{array}{c|l}
B_1 & 7 - 2 = \boxed{5} \\
B_2 & 3 - 11 = -\boxed{8}
\end{array}
$$

The proportions in which $B_1$ and $B_2$ should be mixed are simply the numbers so obtained, except that the number to be associated with $B_1$ is to be found in the box opposite $B_2$, and vice versa. That is, the moves $B_1$ and $B_2$ should be mixed in the proportion 8 : 5, as we have already shown.

If both players mix their moves with the probabilities computed above, each will in the long run optimize his own pay-off within the constraints imposed by the rules of the game. Since the chance of selecting $A_1$ is 9/13 and that of $B_1$ is 8/13, the chance of simultaneous selection of moves $A_1$ *and* $B_1$, by the race-course principle, is obviously $9/13 \cdot 8/13 = 72/169$. In a similar way, the chance of each one of the four possible combinations can be calculated and is shown in Table 32.

*Table 32.* Chance of each of the 4 possible outcomes.

| | |
|---|---|
| $A_1 \cdot B_1 = \dfrac{9}{13} \cdot \dfrac{8}{13} = \dfrac{72}{169}$ | $A_2 \cdot B_1 = \dfrac{4}{13} \cdot \dfrac{8}{13} = \dfrac{32}{169}$ |
| $A_1 \cdot B_2 = \dfrac{9}{13} \cdot \dfrac{5}{13} = \dfrac{45}{169}$ | $A_2 \cdot B_2 = \dfrac{4}{13} \cdot \dfrac{5}{13} = \dfrac{20}{169}$ |

The probabilities of the aforementioned four outcomes obviously add up to 1, as they ought to, considering that some of them are certain to occur. The pay-offs and their corresponding probabilities in respect of each of the four possible outcomes will then be as shown in Table 33.

The numbers in parentheses in each box of Table 33 are the probabilities shown in Table 32 that the corresponding pay-off written

*Table 33*

| B's moves | A's moves | |
|---|---|---|
| | $A_1$ | $A_2$ |
| $B_1$ | $7$ $\left(\dfrac{72}{169}\right)$ | $2$ $\left(\dfrac{32}{169}\right)$ |
| $B_2$ | $3$ $\left(\dfrac{45}{169}\right)$ | $11$ $\left(\dfrac{20}{169}\right)$ |

in the box materializes. It follows therefore that the expected pay-off in a large series of plays is the sum of the products of each pay-off and the corresponding probability of its occurrence. In other words, it is the sum

$$7\left(\frac{72}{169}\right) + 2\left(\frac{32}{169}\right) + 3\left(\frac{45}{169}\right) + 11\left(\frac{20}{169}\right) = \frac{923}{169} = 5\cdot4.$$

Thus, the aforementioned grand strategy of mixed moves will make $A$'s net gain 5·4 in the long run. No other strategy can make his gain greater. *Per contra*, $B$'s net loss will be 5·4 in the long run, and no other strategy on his part will make it less. The optimal value of the game therefore is 5·4 in favour of $A$, and the optimal strategy of both players is the mixture of moves in the aforementioned pro-portions. If any player deviates from his own optimal proportion in which he ought to mix his moves he will only increase his opponent's gain.

What is true of the simple $2 \times 2$ pay-off matrix holds equally for any pay-off matrix no matter how complex. It can be shown that when the maximum of column minima is *not* equal to the minimum of row maxima (that is, when the pay-off matrix has no saddle point) both players can always find a way of mixing their moves in such a way as to optimize their respective gains. To be sure, the calculation of proportions according to which the available alter-natives should be mixed for optimal play is much more complicated when the pay-off matrix is no longer a simple $2 \times 2$ array. But the game theory guarantees that such proportions do exist, even though it is much more difficult actually to find them in any real-life case.

However, there are many game problems where simpler methods suffice to yield a solution. First, consider games having square pay-off matrices which have as many columns as rows, such as the $3 \times 3$ matrix shown in Table 34.

*Table 34*

|  | $A_1$ | $A_2$ | $A_3$ | Row maxima |
|:---:|:---:|:---:|:---:|:---:|
| $B_1$ | 3 | 0 | 4†† | 4†† |
| $B_2$ | 5 | 6 | 1 | 6 |
| $B_3$ | 2† | 8 | 3 | 8 |
| Column minima | 2† | 0 | 1 | |

A glance at the matrix shows that the minimum of row maxima (4) is *not* equal to the maximum of column minima (2). There is no saddle point and the minimax principle breaks down, so that no pure move is available to any player. Since pure moves do not exist, each must adopt a mixed strategy. If the probabilities of 3 $A$-moves which $A$ must mix for optimal play are $p, q, r$, then the 3 pay-offs to $A$ corresponding to each of the 3 countermoves of his opponent ($B$) must all be equal to the optimal value $G$ of the game. Since $A$'s pay-offs against the 3 $B$-moves, $B_1, B_2, B_3$, are respectively

$$3p+0q+4r,$$
$$5p+6q+1r,$$
$$2p+8q+3r,$$

we obtain 3 equations by equating each of these 3 $A$-weighted pay-offs to $G$. That is,

$$3p+0q+4r = 5p+6q+r = 2p+8q+3r = G,$$

or

$$-2p-6q+3r = 0,$$

and

$$3p-2q-2r = 0.$$

140

Hence,

$$\frac{p}{18} = \frac{q}{5} = \frac{r}{22}.$$

Consequently, $A$'s mixture of his 3 moves $A_1$, $A_2$, $A_3$ for optimal play must be in proportions $18:5:22$. Similarly denoting the probabilities used by $B$ for blending his 3 moves $B_1$, $B_2$, $B_3$ by the symbols $p'$, $q'$, $r'$, we find that $B$'s 3 average pay-offs against $A$'s moves $A_1$, $A_2$, $A_3$ are respectively,

$$3p'+5q'+2r',$$
$$0p'+6q'+8r',$$
$$4p'+1q'+3r'.$$

The equality of the 3 pay-offs to the optimal value of the game leads to the 3 equations

$$3p'+5q'+2r' = 0p'+6q'+8r' = 4p'+q'+3r' = G,$$

or

$$3p'-q'-6r' = 0,$$

and

$$4p'-5q'-5r' = 0.$$

Therefore,

$$\frac{p'}{25} = \frac{q'}{9} = \frac{r'}{11}.$$

Hence, for optimal play $B$ must blend his 3 moves $B_1$, $B_2$, $B_3$ in the proportions $25:9:11$.

## THE GRAPHIC METHOD

The procedure described above will generally work for any game whose pay-off matrix is a square with any number ($n$) of columns and rows, unless it has a saddle point, when the minimax principle naturally applies.* But it will not work when the pay-off matrix happens to be an $m \times n$ rectangle with $m$ rows and $n$ columns. In such cases a graphic short-cut is available if either $m$ or $n$ is two.

* There are no doubt some cases where it breaks down. But this is not because of the non-existence of an optimal way of mixing the players' moves. The game theory assures us that such ways do exist, even when our procedure for discovering them fails us.

For it enables us to substitute a much simpler $2 \times 2$ matrix for the original $m \times 2$ or $2 \times n$ matrix. To illustrate, consider the following $2 \times 6$ pay-off matrix:

*Table 35*

|  | $A_1$ | $A_2$ | $A_3$ | $A_4$ | $A_5$ | $A_6$ | Row maxima |
|---|---|---|---|---|---|---|---|
| $B_1$ | 1 | 3† | −1 | 4† | 2 | −5 | 4† |
| $B_2$ | −3 | 5 | 6 | 1 | 2 | 0 | 6 |
| Column minima | −3 | 3† | −1 | 1 | 2 | 0 | |

Since there is no saddle point we proceed to apply the graphic short-cut by plotting on 2 different vertical axes the 2 pay-offs corresponding to each of the 6 columns. The pay-off numbers in the first row are plotted on axis 1 and those in the second row on axis 2 some distance away but parallel to it, as shown in Figure 30. Thus the 2 pay-off numbers 1 and −3 in the first column are denoted respectively by point $P$ on axis 1 and point $Q$ on axis 2. Line $PQ$ then denotes $A$'s move $A_1$. By plotting the pay-off numbers of

*Figure 30*

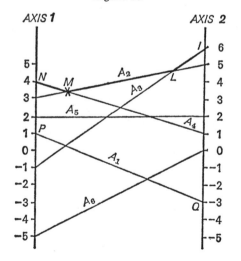

each of the remaining 5 columns on the 2 axes we obtain in all 6 lines like the line $PQ$ which correspond to the 6 $A$ moves (see Figure 30). If, using a thick line, we draw the segments which bound the figure from the top, namely, the segments $NM$, $ML$, and $LI$ shown in Figure 30, and mark the *lowest* point ($M$) on this boundary, the two lines passing through it identify the two critical moves of $A$ which, combined with two of $B$, yield the $2 \times 2$ matrix which can be used to determine the optimal strategies of the two players of the original game. Thus, in the case under review, the critical moves of $A$ are $A_2$ and $A_4$, as $M$ is the intersection of lines $A_2$ and $A_4$ in Figure 30. Although $A$ is allowed 6 moves he need use only these 2 critical ones, $A_2$ and $A_4$, ignoring the remaining 4 altogether for his optimal play. The game thus becomes one with the following $2 \times 2$ pay-off matrix:

$$\begin{array}{c|c|c} & A_2 & A_4 \\ \hline B_1 & 3 & 4 \\ \hline B_2 & 5 & 1 \end{array}$$

Proceeding on familiar lines, $A$ must mix his 2 moves $A_2$ and $A_4$ in the proportion $3 : 2$

and $B$ his 2 moves $B_1$ and $B_2$ in the proportion $4 : 1$

$$\begin{array}{c|c} B_1 & 3 - 4 = -① \\ \hline B_2 & 5 - 1 = ④ \end{array}$$

for optimal play. Since $A$ need never use his other 4 moves ($A_1$, $A_3$,

$A_5$, $A_6$), the proportions in which he must mix the 6 moves allowed him are

$$0 : 3 : 0 : 2 : 0 : 0,$$

while $B$ will mix his 2 moves in the ratio 4 : 1. The case of pay-off matrices having only 2 columns but more than 2 rows is entirely analogous, except that in the diagram we draw we thicken the line segments which bound the figure from the *bottom* and take the *highest* point on this boundary. For example, consider the pay-off matrix:

|        | $A_1$ | $A_2$ |
|--------|-------|-------|
| $B_1$  | $-2$  | 5     |
| $B_2$  | $-5$  | 3     |
| $B_3$  | 0     | $-2$  |
| $B_4$  | $-3$  | 0     |
| $B_5$  | 1     | $-4$  |
| $B_6$  | 5     | $-1$  |

Figure 31 shows the pay-off numbers from each row represented as points on 2 vertical axes 1 and 2. Thus line $B_1$ joins the first pay-off

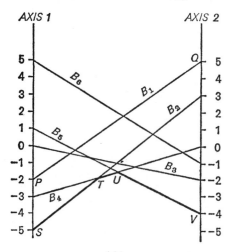

Figure 31

144

number $-2$ in the first row, represented by $P$ on axis 1, and the second pay-off number 5 in the first row, represented by $Q$ on axis 2. Similarly, lines $B_2$, $B_3$, $B_4$, $B_5$, and $B_6$ join the corresponding representations of pay-off numbers in the second, third, fourth, fifth, and sixth rows. The segments $ST$, $TU$, and $UV$, drawn in thick lines, bound the figure from the bottom, and their highest intersection $U$, through which lines $B_4$ and $B_5$ pass, defines the 2 relevant moves $B_4$ and $B_5$ that alone $B$ need use. The solution of the original game therefore boils down to that of the simpler game with the following $2 \times 2$ pay-off matrix:

|       | $A_1$ | $A_2$ |
|-------|-------|-------|
| $B_4$ | $-3$  | $0$   |
| $B_5$ | $1$   | $-4$  |

The graphic short-cut described above is a convenient device for isolating the 2 dominant moves that are so obviously superior *vis-à-vis* others that a player may with impunity choose never to use the latter. The segregation of dominant moves from these recessive ones that need never be considered is an important step in simplifying complex game problems. There is no simple way of identifying such moves when the matrix is no longer restricted to having only either 2 columns or 2 rows. When the number of both columns and rows exceeds 2 our graphic procedure is not applicable. Nevertheless, a close inspection of a matrix may now and then reveal that there are some moves so patently inferior *vis-à-vis* another that they should never be played. Consider, for instance, the pay-off matrix

|       | $A_1$ | $A_2$ | $A_3$ | $A_4$ |
|-------|-------|-------|-------|-------|
| $B_1$ | 3     | 4     | 2     | 1     |
| $B_2$ | 0     | 5     | 3     | 4     |
| $B_3$ | 2     | 1     | $-1$  | 0     |

If we compare the pay-offs that $A$ is due to receive if he plays $A_2$

with those due him under either move $A_3$ or $A_4$, it is obvious that $A_2$ is so superior to both $A_3$ and $A_4$ that the latter have no chance before the former. Thus, if $B$ plays $B_1$, move $A_2$ will fetch $A$ a gain of 4 against only 2 by $A_3$ and 1 by $A_4$. If $B$ plays $B_2$, move $A_2$ gains him 5 against 3 under $A_3$ and 4 under $A_4$. Finally if $B$ plays $B_3$, move $A_2$ will yield him 1 whereas $A_3$ will cost him 1 and $A_4$ will fetch him nothing at all. In all cases, no matter what move $B$ chooses to make, $A$ gains more by playing $A_2$ rather than $A_3$ or $A_4$. In other words, move $A_2$ is so dominant over both $A_3$ and $A_4$ that he may as well reject both $A_3$ and $A_4$ out of hand. Likewise, if we compare $B$'s move $B_1$ against $B_3$, we find that no matter what move $A$ makes, $B$'s losses are less under $B_3$ than under $B_1$. Move $B_1$ is therefore so uniformly inferior to $B_3$ that player $B$ may as well discard it out of hand. If $B$ rejects $B_1$, and $A$ rejects both $A_3$ and $A_4$ altogether, the pay-off matrix becomes the simpler $2 \times 2$ matrix

|       | $A_1$ | $A_2$ |
|-------|-------|-------|
| $B_2$ | 0     | 5     |
| $B_3$ | 2     | 1     |

which may be solved in the usual way.

The solution of a matrix game with $m$ columns and $n$ rows of pay-off numbers having neither a saddle point nor redundant or obviously rejectable moves is somewhat more difficult. What we require is $A$'s $m$-probabilities with which he must mix $m$ moves available to him and $B$'s $n$-probabilities with which he must blend his own $n$ moves and the expected optimal value $G$ of the game that may be computed by weighting each pay-off number in the matrix by the probability of its occurrence during the course of several plays. There are therefore in all $(m+n+1)$ unknowns to be evaluated, namely, $m$-probabilities of $m$ $A$-moves, $n$-probabilities of $n$ $B$-moves, and the expected optimal value $G$ of the game. To find them we have on the one hand $n$ inequalities, which express the fact that the average of the set of $m$ pay-off numbers in *any* row, duly weighted by $m$ $A$-probabilities, must be either equal to or greater than the optimal value $G$. There being $n$ rows in all, this consideration yields us $n$ inequalities. A similar consideration in respect of columns leads to *m* inequalities. For the average of the set of *n* pay-off numbers in any of the *m* columns, duly weighted by *n* *B*-probabilities, must likewise be less than or at most equal to *G*. We thus obtain $(m+n)$ inequalities. In addition, the sum of the set of *A*-probabilities as well as that of *B*-probabilities must equal unity, while each of the $(m+n)$ probabilities is a positive fraction which can never fall below 0. It can be shown, as L. S. Shapley and R. N. Snow have done, that a basic solution of such a system of linear inequalities is, in turn, the unique solution of a suitably chosen subsystem of linear *equations*. As a result, the solution (if unique) or the full set of solutions (if more than one exists) can be derived by solving a set of linear simultaneous equations. Unfortunately, solution of linear simultaneous equations, even though very simple in theory, is exceedingly cumbersome in practice when the numbers, *m* and *n*, of rows and columns increase inordinately. This is why the solution of a large-scale matrix game by the method outlined above is indeed a formidable if not impracticable task.

## REAL GAMES

However, having to deal with large-scale $m \times n$ pay-off matrices much larger than the simple $2 \times 2$ arrays is not the only complication of real games. There are many more which game theory is as yet quite helpless to resolve. Here we need mention only two. First our assumption that a game is decided in a single pair of moves – an *A*-move and its associated response by *B* – is a gross oversimplification of the actual state of affairs. In most cases the game consists of a large succession of such pairs of *A*- and *B*-moves. We have therefore to apply the aforementioned minimaxing procedure that yields us our 'pure' or 'mixed' optimal moves, as the case may be, for each pair of the complete series of *A-B* twin moves that makes up the game. Unfortunately, the series often goes on the rampage, rapidly proliferating itself beyond all control. In the case of chess, for example, a game may easily involve examination of such an enormous number of pairs of moves as cannot be completed during the entire putative age of the universe, even if we had a computer to examine 1,000,000,000 move-pairs per *second*. The avalanche of permutations that other games let loose is scarcely less overwhelming, with no way of getting round it yet in sight, although some interesting existence theorems have been proved. A case in point is E. Zermelo's theorem on extensive two-person games in which each player is informed of the complete previous history of the play. The theorem asserts that such games can always be solved by pure strategies without randomized mixing. In other words, there is always a saddle point in the pay-off matrix of such games. Thus Zermelo's theorem guarantees that, in the case of chess, one and only one of the following three alternatives is valid:

(i) White has a pure strategy that wins no matter what Black does
(ii) Both players have pure strategies that ensure at least a draw no matter what the other does
(iii) Black has a pure strategy that wins no matter what White does.

But the theory gives no clue for deciding which assertion is true.

The second complication on our list arises because the mathematical definition of 'rationality' that the theory adopts to enable the players to choose their optimal moves is likely to overreach itself in certain cases. Thus, if one or more players resort to bluffing or other 'deviations' from 'textbook' strategies, the situation may well be like that of Nanda in the following apocryphal dialogue:

NANDA: Where are you going?
CHANDA: To Baroda.
NANDA: Shame on you, Chanda! You say so to make me believe you are going to Maroda. But I know you are going to Baroda.

This sort of Baroda-to-Maroda out-think in game theory is the counterpart in logic of the Cretan Epimenides' paradox: 'All Cretans are liars.' Did the Cretan speak the truth? Whether we answer *yes* or *no* there is logical embarrassment in either case.

Nevertheless, while a host of difficulties (of which we have cited only two) remain to be overcome, von Neumann and Morgenstern's classic, *Theory of Games and Economic Behavior*, is by common consent the one single book which 'posterity may regard as one of the major scientific achievements of the first half of the twentieth century'.* We may therefore confidently expect to hear more of it as this lusty infant grows to adult vigour and maturity. Meanwhile, we may simply remark that even in its present state its relevance to our present theme of operations research is obviously great. For conflict is the basic ingredient of most situations that an operations-research worker usually encounters. Remember, he has to struggle against other human competitors and/or impersonal nature. Such being the case, we can often transcribe an operations-research situation in the game-theory idiom by making use of the identity of its structure with that of a game. Thus the model of the situation an operations-research worker faces has the following general skeleton. There is a set of mutually exclusive actions or moves $A_1, A_2, \ldots, A_i, \ldots, A_n$, of which one and only one must be taken. One examines each possible action, $A_i$, and determines its consequence, $C_i$, taking into account the reactions and counter-moves of his competitors, if any, as well as other possible states of nature that are likely to arise. The consequences ($C_i$) of these various actions are described in one common unit such as dollar profit, cost, or some other efficacy index to make them mutually comparable like the pay-off numbers of the game theory. Indeed, the efficacy measure $C_1, C_2, \ldots, C_i, \ldots, C_n$ of the consequences of available actions or moves $A_1, A_2, A_3, \ldots, A_i, \ldots, A_n$ are the exact counterparts of pay-off numbers. Having thus described the consequences of each action the problem is simply to make a clear and quantitative comparison of their merits in order to pick the optimal alternative. In other words, the aim is to establish a clear basis for rational decision exactly as in a game situation. Indeed, it is strange but true that the mathematical theory of zero-sum two-person games is precisely the same as that of linear programming as well as of statistical decisions. For it can be proved that to every zero-sum two-person game there corresponds a linear-programming problem and vice versa. It therefore results that numerical methods of solving the former can be applied to the latter and vice versa. In particular, all manner of diverse problems amenable to linear-programming treatment can be handled as well by the theory of games.

* A. H. Copeland in *Bulletin of the American Mathematical Society*, Vol. 51 (1945), pp. 498–501.

Similarly Wald's theory of decision functions, which includes the Neyman–Pearson theory of critical regions described in Chapter 4, can be interpreted as a zero-sum two-person game. All that need be done is to set up the following correspondence:

*Table 36*

| Decision problem | Two-person game |
|---|---|
| Nature | Player $A$ |
| Experimenter | Player $B$ |
| Loss function | Pay-off matrix |

Wald shows that the analogy between the decision problem and a zero-sum game is complete except for one feature, namely the absence of a sharp clash of interests between the two players in a game. While it is true that the experimenter wishes to minimize the loss function, we could hardly say that nature opposes him by endeavouring to maximize it. However, Wald counters this objection with the suggestion that it is not unreasonable for the experimenter to act as if nature wanted to maximize the loss function. This is, no doubt, playing it safe, but the trouble is that it is apt to be too safe in many cases.

For instance, we saw earlier how the minimax solution of the decision problem facing a manufacturer wishing either to sell his product with a double-your-money-back guarantee in case of a defective article, or to dump the lot, was irrationally overcautious.* This is because, interpreted as a game, the problem views nature as a hostile opponent endeavouring to make the player lose as much as possible. But actually, in many situations, far from actively opposing the experimenter, nature may even help him. Some post-Waldian work on compound decision functions seems to show that there exist situations in which one would profit by discarding the Wald view of expecting either definite hostility or even belligerent neutrality from nature and actually planning an experiment on the basis of anticipations of positive help.

The remarkable versatility of the game-theory approach to so many diverse fields gives some measure of its latent power in tack-

*See page 76.

ling hyper-complex problems of business, administration, and industry. In brief, its main contribution to organization man is a framework of ideas in which he can work on the difficult decision problems facing him, even though they are in many cases strictly not solvable by the procedures it prescribes. The concept of strings of moves called the players' strategies, of the head-on clash of their interests, of pay-off matrices as modes of quantifying the relative worth of each strategy to each player, of minimaxing as a way of devising optimal strategies whether 'pure' or 'mixed' provide beacon lights to all men of affairs groping for a way out of their dilemmas and multilemmas in the heat and fog of conflict.

# CHAPTER 8

# Queueing Theory:
## How to Handle Bottleneck Problems

A QUEUEING or bottleneck problem arises when the service rate of a facility such as a booking office or telephone exchange falls short of the flow rate of its clients or calls. An obvious remedy is duplication of the facility. But equally obviously, it is one to be adopted only as a last resort when a more judicious deployment of existing units cannot meet the demand. A simple but classic case in point is the suggestion made by an operations-research worker who happened to visit an army canteen. He found that after meals there were large queues at the wash basins for washing and rinsing the plates. There were 4 basins, of which 2 were allotted for washing and 2 for rinsing, on the basis of equal division of available facilities between the 2 operations. The operations-research worker, however, observed that while the washing operation at the basin took only 1 minute, that of rinsing the plates took 3. This led him to earmark 3 basins for rinsing and only 1 for washing. He thus secured a 50-per-cent increase in service that eliminated the queues.

A more profitable example is that of the Moghalsarai yard cited in Chapter 1. Some years ago the Indian railways encountered a serious bottleneck at the Moghalsarai yard because of the growth of traffic. As a result there arose long queues of trains all along the main line waiting admission to the yard. The actual humping capacity of the yard was about 30 trains per day. However, the service time, that is, the time taken from the commencement of a humping operation to its finish, was 24 minutes, or 24/60 hour. Hence, if it were possible to continue the humping operations without any interruption, the ideal capacity would be

$$\frac{24}{24/60} = \frac{24 \times 60}{24} = 60.$$

But as the actual output was only 30 trains per day, that is, barely

50 per cent of the theoretical capacity, obviously there were impediments preventing a better yield. One of them was the loss of about 10 minutes per humping operation necessitated by the need to send the switch engine to the receiving yard before it could begin the next humping. In other words, inadequate switching power led to a good deal of this loss of capacity. When a second switch engine was provided the interval between two successive humping operations – the sum of the actual humping operation (24 minutes) and the time taken to reverse the switch engine on the next train (10 minutes) – was reduced from 34 to 24 minutes. As a result, the capacity of the yard increased by about 50 per cent, and the increase sufficed to ensure free reception of all the trains that were offered at the time as well as for a long while after.

Simple though the removal of the bottleneck proved to be, this account has oversimplified the actual situation. For it would be a mistake to imagine that the increase in the humping capacity of the yard was brought about by merely providing a second switch engine in the yard. It also required collateral action to accelerate the flow of the humped cars from the classification yard. For in a dynamic system removal of one bottleneck often shows up another elsewhere.

Another instance of the same kind is the case of the Andal yard, where coal cars drawn from collieries had also to be weighed while being marshalled into trains for various destinations. Since a single weighbridge clerk observed the weight of a car as well as recorded it the marshalling-*cum*-weighing operation was interrupted every time he missed an observation. As a result the operation became an awkward alternation of stops and starts. By providing a second clerk to read the scale and leaving the first free only to record what the second observed the former 'stop–go' style of working was turned into a quick, continuous, smooth flow of cars into the classification yard. The mere provision of a single clerk thus eliminated almost instantaneously the long queues of trains that used to wait for hours on the main line for lack of room in the yard.

Such radical improvement in working by simple clerical assistance at a crucial stage of the service operation is not peculiar to railway working alone; it is equally rewarding in many other spheres of industrial activity. An illustration is that of a steel mill rolling billets which was repeatedly obliged to cease rolling when the subsequent process of handling, inspecting, repairing, and dispatching the billets became overloaded. It developed in the course of a study that all the individual finishing processes were quite adequate for dealing with fluctuations in the rate with which the billets arrived from rolling, but the production plan was faulty in that it allowed too much time for each process, causing the billets awaiting dispatch to pile up. The pile-up of billets in turn congested the finishing area, slowing down the finishing processes. By altering the planning allowance for individual processes and by imposing a simple clerical control system which ensured adherence to the plan, it was found possible to reduce the delivery time. Even though the reduction was very slight, it sufficed to relieve the bottleneck in the finishing area. In both these cases queues were eliminated by a relatively minor improvement in servicing time of the incoming 'clients': by the provision of an additional engine in one case and a clerk in the other.

As both the aforementioned illustrations clearly show, the nub of any queueing problem is the proper matching of the service rate of its 'clients' to that of their arrival. This is why queueing theory is really an exploration of ways of making the former faster than the latter in the *most economical manner*. Since the object is to service as many customers with as few facilities as possible it might seem prudent to create a situation in which the service rate exactly equals the average rate of arrival. A deeper examination, however, shows that this is often an unsatisfactory solution. Consider, for example, a facility whose average service rate, say, 5 minutes per customer, exactly equals the average gap of 5 minutes between 2 consecutive arrivals. If the customers arrive regularly, that is, 1 every 5 minutes, each customer will be served just before the arrival of the next so that no congestion can possibly arise. But such a regular flow of customers is seldom the case in any real queueing situation. As a rule, customers arrive irregularly, at random. A typical instance of random arrivals is represented graphically in Figure 32, where the arrival of 10 customers during the first 48 minutes is denoted by crosses. The numbers shown between any 2 consecutive crosses are the gaps measured in minutes between the

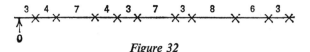

*Figure 32*

arrivals of corresponding customers. Thus the first customer arrives 3 minutes after the commencement of the service; the second 4 minutes after the first arrival; the third 7 minutes after the second, and so on. Since initially there is no customer, there will naturally be no service. It begins 3 minutes later, with the arrival of the first comer. Service time being 5 minutes, the second, arriving 4 minutes later, will have to wait for 1 minute before being attended to. Since the third arrives 7 minutes later, the second will be completed 1 minute before the arrival of the third and the service counter will be idle again for 1 minute. Since such idling intervals when no customer is present are lost irretrievably, the actual number served during any sufficiently long period can never equal the number of arrivals if the average gap between successive arrivals equals the service rate. As a result, queues must arise and grow indefinitely with passage of time. Indeed, in all queueing systems where the customer input rate exactly balances their outgo infinitely long queues and infinite waiting times are inevitable. Such queueing situations are particularly sensitive to even marginal improvements or deteriorations in service procedures. They tend to produce, for better or worse, disproportionately large changes in mean waiting time as well as mean queue length. Thus if the service time of customers in the case under review is reduced by even a single minute, from 5 minutes per customer to 4, the probability of a customer's having to wait will be only 4 chances out of 5 instead of a dead certainty. The corresponding mean waiting time will be only 16 minutes against the earlier infinite value. This is typical of all queueing situations. As soon as the service rate begins to approach the mean arrival rate, both waiting time and queue length change disastrously for the worse. It is in this delicate area that queueing problems most frequently arise. The variety of contexts in which they occur, their susceptibility to some form of analysis, mathematical or otherwise, and above all the very real possibility of

155

making large gains by mere marginal changes suggested by studying the queue in relation to the entire operation make them particularly amenable to operations-research treatment.

Take first the variety of contexts in which we are likely to encounter queueing problems. They may be divided into three main categories:

(i) Telephone switching problems

(ii) Traffic problems such as the bunching of trains at railway stations, of ships in sea ports, of automobiles at traffic lights, or of aeroplanes wanting to land at airports

(iii) Machine breakdown and feed problems.

In all such cases, whether that of a pile of broken-down machines waiting for attention by the repairman or a fleet of ships waiting for a berth in the harbour, the five features common to any queueing situation are:

(i) 'Customers' or 'clients', which may be persons, trains, machines, ships, or aeroplanes

(ii) One or more gates or service counters, such as a booking office, classification yard, repairman, berth in a habour, or airstrip in an airport

(iii) An input process governing the arrival of 'clients'

(iv) Some queue discipline, such as the 'first-come-first-served' rule or any other system of priority of service

(v) A service mechanism, such as the issue of tickets at a booking office, humping of a train in a marshalling yard, or discharge of the cargo of a ship in a port.

An abstract description of the queueing problem in general then is that there are 'customers' arriving for service either randomly or in a regular stream as on a conveyor. As each customer moves to the service 'counter' time is taken in serving him, after which he leaves and is usually no longer a part of the problem. Any customers who arrive while another is being served must wait their turns, that is, form a queue. The queue need not be a physical line of clients. It may be a dispersed list of persons 'wait-listed' for a berth on a train, for a meal in a restaurant, or for a trunk telephone call. Even though the persons affected may not feel the tedium of being in an actual queue, to a servicing agency like the railway or telephone company these lists are as real as physical queues.

No matter whether queues are physical lines or mere lists of clients, the elements of interest in an analysis of the situation are mainly two. First is the average number of customers in the queue at any time, that is, the mean queue length when the situation reaches a stationary state if it ever does. Second is the average waiting time of the customer in the queue.

Such a twofold study of queues is particularly rewarding when the queueing 'clients' are large and expensive physical items like ships, trains, aircraft waiting to land, or broken-down machines awaiting repair. For in such queues time lost in waiting is often expensive in terms of money, equipment, and perhaps even lives. A case in point is the state of saturation that may come to pass at an air base in wartime after an all-out raid. Returning planes would all tend to arrive at the home airport at the same time, each with little spare fuel and anxious to land. The situation can rapidly approach over-saturation, with planes being brought in for landing at the rate of one a minute or faster, as was the case in wartime Britain. This landing pace, however, can be stretched only so long as there are no accidents. Unfortunately, aircraft operation at over-saturation levels is hazardous, having all the elements of self-aggravation. For even if a single aircraft running out of fuel radios for immediate clearance to land, the hasty rearrangement of schedules required to accommodate the emergency might consume so much time as to make two other planes run dangerously low on fuel. If planes are obliged to make 'dead-stick' landings there is always the possibility that they will ground-loop or otherwise obstruct the landing strip, thereby causing other emergency landings. In such situations the waiting time is a vital point for consideration.

Luckily, many self-aggravating queueing situations can also be turned into self-improving ones by small technological or organizational changes that produce even minor improvements in servicing rate. Thus at the Dongargarh yard the mere provision of a water column at the switching neck to free the reception lines turned a self-aggravating traffic situation on the main line into a self-ameliorating one. On such small things does the destiny of a trunk route often turn!

The object of queueing theory is to show whether a transition from self-aggravation to self-amelioration is at all possible and, if so, how to bring it about in the most economical manner. This may be done by making a mathematical model of the queueing problem under consideration. Consider, for the sake of simplicity, the case of queues at a single service 'counter'. To begin with we may label the customers 1, 2, 3, . . ., in order of their arrival after a given instant of time. Next, we need to make certain assumptions about the input and output processes according to which the clients arrive and obtain the service they require. Thus they may arrive at random or in a regular continuous stream. Again, the service time may be a fixed constant or a variable, depending on the particular needs of the client. Finally, we have to take note of the queueing discipline, which may or may not require service to be given in order of arrival without provision for any preferential treatment for any client. The problems for investigation are whether or not there exists a stationary state of equilibrium at which the queue approaches neither infinity nor zero, and whether any remedy can be applied to mitigate the waiting 'agony' of the clients.

A mathematical solution of such a queueing problem naturally requires a more explicit specification of the particular type among the many kinds of arrival patterns, service mechanisms, and queue disciplines that are possible in theory. Consider first the arrival patterns. Among the several ways in which customers can arrive at a service counter two are noteworthy in that one is physically and the other mathematically the simplest. In the former, which is by no means the easiest to handle mathematically, customers arrive singly at equally spaced intervals like discrete objects delivered by a uniformly moving conveyor belt. In the latter, which is mathematically the simplest as well as most commonly useful in practical applications, the arrivals are completely random, as for example is the case with customers coming according to the pattern in Figure 32. The chief attribute of the random pattern is that customers arrive one at a time, as before, but irregularly, so that gaps between successive arrivals are random numbers like those shown in Figure 32. Although these random numbers measuring the intervals between successive arrivals seem to vary irregularly there is nevertheless a method in their apparently mad variation. For in spite of their random fluctuations, their long-term average does tend to stabilize itself at a steady level. We may actually see it happen in the case of the arrival pattern of Figure 32 if we compute the cumulative averages of the successive gaps between consecutive arrivals as done in Table 37.

*Table 37*

| Customer number | Gap between two consecutive arrivals | Cumulative sum | Number of gaps | Cumulative average gap |
|---|---|---|---|---|
| 1  | 3 | 3            | 1  | $3/1 = 3 \cdot 0$   |
| 2  | 4 | $3+4 = 7$    | 2  | $7/2 = 3 \cdot 5$   |
| 3  | 7 | $7+7 = 14$   | 3  | $14/3 = 4 \cdot 7$  |
| 4  | 4 | $14+4 = 18$  | 4  | $18/4 = 4 \cdot 5$  |
| 5  | 3 | $18+3 = 21$  | 5  | $21/5 = 4 \cdot 2$  |
| 6  | 7 | $21+7 = 28$  | 6  | $28/6 = 4 \cdot 7$  |
| 7  | 3 | $28+3 = 31$  | 7  | $31/7 = 4 \cdot 4$  |
| 8  | 8 | $31+8 = 39$  | 8  | $39/8 = 4 \cdot 9$  |
| 9  | 6 | $39+6 = 45$  | 9  | $45/9 = 5 \cdot 0$  |
| 10 | 3 | $45+3 = 48$  | 10 | $48/10 = 4 \cdot 8$ |
| 11 | 6 | $48+6 = 54$  | 11 | $54/11 = 4 \cdot 9$ |
| 12 | 9 | $54+9 = 63$  | 12 | $63/12 = 5 \cdot 2$ |
| 13 | 6 | $63+6 = 69$  | 13 | $69/13 = 5 \cdot 3$ |
| 14 | 4 | $69+4 = 73$  | 14 | $73/14 = 5 \cdot 2$ |
| 15 | 7 | $73+7 = 80$  | 15 | $80/15 = 5 \cdot 3$ |
| 16 | 3 | $80+3 = 83$  | 16 | $83/16 = 5 \cdot 2$ |
| 17 | 6 | $83+6 = 89$  | 17 | $89/17 = 5 \cdot 2$ |
| 18 | 6 | $89+6 = 95$  | 18 | $95/18 = 5 \cdot 3$ |
| 19 | 1 | $95+1 = 96$  | 19 | $96/19 = 5 \cdot 0$ |
| 20 | 4 | $96+4 = 100$ | 20 | $100/20 = 5 \cdot 0$ |
| 21 | 6 | $100+6 = 106$ | 21 | $106/21 = 5 \cdot 0$ |
| 22 | 5 | $106+5 = 111$ | 22 | $111/22 = 5 \cdot 0$ |

A glance at the right-hand column of Table 37 will show that after some initial irregular changes in the value of the cumulative average gap between successive individual customers it settles down to a constant value – five minutes in the case under review. This constancy of the long-term average of random gaps between two successive customer arrivals is an important attribute of the pattern under consideration. Indeed, it is the sole parameter of arrivals that we need to know to completely predict customer behaviour provided only we make the additional assumption that the chance of a customer's arriving at any particular instant is the same as at any other. Thus, suppose we have a mode of arrivals, wherein the average gap between successive customers is some number $\alpha$ units of time. Since a customer arrives, on the average, after $\alpha$ units of time, in any fairly long interval $T$ a total of $T/\alpha = m$ customers will arrive. If we now divide the interval $T$ into a very large number of $n$ sub-intervals each of small duration $\delta t$, we have $T = n\delta t$. Since customers appear completely at random any one of the $m$ customers who arrive during time $T$ may do so during any one of the $n$ sub-intervals of duration $\delta t$ into which we have divided $T$. In other words, any one of the $m$ customer arrivals during total time $T$ can occur with *equal* chance in any one of the $n$ sub-intervals into which we have divided $T$. Hence, the probability of any single customer's arriving during any one of the $n$ sub-intervals of small duration $\delta t$ is

$$\frac{m}{n} = \frac{T}{\alpha} \div \frac{T}{\delta t} = \frac{\delta t}{\alpha}.$$

*Per contra*, the probability of a customer's *not* arriving during the same small sub-interval $\delta t$ is $(1 - \delta t/\alpha)$.

Consider now any period of time $t$ reckoned from any arbitrary origin coinciding with an arrival instant. Let $f(t)$ be the probability that the *next* customer does *not* arrive during the interval $t$. Then $f(t + \delta t)$ is the probability that neither does the customer appear during the extended interval $t + \delta t$. Now the latter event – the non-appearance of a customer during the extended time $t + \delta t$ – is the result of the conjunction or simultaneous occurrence of two events. First, that the customer does not appear during the interval $t$. The probability of this event is by definition $f(t)$. Second, that he does not appear during the small extension of $t$ by $\delta t$. The probability of this second event is, as shown above, $\left(1 - \dfrac{\delta t}{\alpha}\right)$. Consequently, by the race-course principle described in Chapter 3, the probability

$f(t+\delta t)$ that the customer does not appear during the extended interval $t+\delta t$ is simply the product

$$f(t) \left( 1 - \frac{\delta t}{a} \right).$$

It therefore follows that

$$f(t+\delta t) = f(t) \left( 1 - \frac{\delta t}{a} \right)$$

or

$$f(t+\delta t) - f(t) = -f(t) \frac{\delta t}{a}$$

or

$$\frac{f(t+\delta t) - f(t)}{\delta t} = \frac{-f(t)}{a}.$$

Proceeding to the limit when $\delta t$ tends to zero, we have

$$\frac{df}{dt} = -\frac{f(t)}{a}.$$

It therefore follows that

$$f(t) = ce^{-t/a} \qquad \text{(i)}$$

where $c$ is a constant whose value may be determined by recalling that the origin of time has been chosen to be an arrival instant. That is to say, that the probability of the *next* customer's arriving at the same time, $t = 0$, is nil, and therefore of its non-arrival at $t = 0$ is 1.* In other words, $f(0) = 1$. Substituting $t = 0$ in (i), we therefore find that $c = 1$. We conclude then that the probability of the *next* customer's *not* arriving till $t$ units of time after the arrival of the last one is $e^{-t/a}$.

It is indeed remarkable that only two very broad features of the arrival pattern – the constancy of the long-term average of gaps between successive customer-arrivals and the complete statistical independence of arrivals in any period of those in any other – should enable us to compute the probabilities of the arrival of the next customer at all possible times after the arrival of its pre-

---

* It is recalled that the customers arrive singly and therefore no two do so at the same instant.

decessor. A number of consequences flow from the computation of these probabilities. First, the probability that the gap between two consecutive customers is exactly $t$ can be easily deduced. For the event, the arrival of the next customer exactly at the instant $t$, is the conjunction of two events, namely, (*a*) that the next customer does *not* arrive before the instant $t$ and (*b*) that he does arrive within an infinitesimal interval $\delta t$ immediately following the instant $t$. The probability of (*a*) has already been shown to be $e^{-t/a}$ while that of (*b*) is $\delta t/\alpha$. It therefore follows, again by the race-course principle, that the probability that the gap between two successive arrivals lies between $t$ and $(t+\delta t)$ is $e^{-t/a}\,\delta t/\alpha$. In other words, the probability that the gap between two consecutive arrivals will be exactly $t$ is $(1/\alpha)e^{-t/a}\,\delta t$.

Secondly since the probability of a gap of duration $t$ is $(1/\alpha)e^{-t/a}\,\delta t$ its mean value is obviously the 'weighted' sum of all possible values of $t$ from zero to infinity – each particular value in this range being 'weighted' by its probability of occurrence. In other words, it is the sum

$$\sum_{t=0}^{t=\infty} \frac{t}{a}e^{-t/a}\,\delta t,$$

which for sufficiently small $\delta t$ becomes the integral

$$\int_0^\infty \frac{t}{a}e^{-t/a}\,dt = \alpha.$$

This is indeed exactly as it ought to be, since we assumed at the outset that the long-term average of the gaps between successive arrivals is $\alpha$. The same probability distribution enables us to prove that the standard deviation of the gap interval is also $\alpha$. For it is simply the integral

$$\int_0^\infty (t-\alpha)^2 \frac{e^{-t/a}}{\alpha}\,dt,$$

which is easily shown to be $\alpha$.

Thirdly, since the value of $e^{-t/a}$ is maximum at $t=0$ and decreases as the length of the interval, $t$, increases, the shorter the interval, the greater the likelihood of its occurrence. Thus, short intervals or gaps between customer arrivals are relatively more frequent than long ones. This is why a completely random series shows a considerable tendency to cluster, as illustrated in Figure 33.

A completely random mode of arrival whose characteristic features we have outlined above is thus a special form of arrival and not any haphazard way of customer irruption. And yet for all its speciality it is no mere artificial construct devised for the sake of mathematical simplicity or convenience. It is a pattern that often arises, at least to a close degree of approximation, in actual practice in a wide diversity of fields. Broadly speaking, arrivals conform to

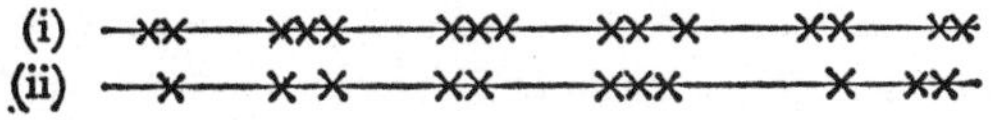

(i) —xx——xxx——xxx——xx-x——xx——xx
(ii) —x——x-x——xx——xxx——x—xx-

*Figure 33*

such a pattern when the customers are drawn from a very large pool of individuals all behaving independently of one another, as in the case of incoming calls at a telephone exchange over a fairly short period, the landing of aircraft at busy airports, arrival of trains in large marshalling yards, stoppages of machines produced by mechanical breakdowns or, in textile processing, by end-breakages, and the like.

Having deduced a simple mathematical formalism fully adequate to describe the arrival pattern it is time to consider the service mechanism. But this sets no new problem, for the sole feature relevant to our present context is the time taken to serve a customer. These service durations may, for greater generality, be also assumed to behave like the gaps between successive arrivals. That is, we assume (*a*) that the service time of a customer is not uniform but varies randomly, and (*b*) that its long-run average tends to a constant value, $\beta$, exactly as that of the gap between successive arrivals did to another constant, $\alpha$. Under these two assumptions the probability that service time will be *t mutatis mutandis* is easily seen to be $e^{-t/\beta} \delta t/\beta$. As a result, both its average and standard deviation can be shown to be $\beta$, just as $\alpha$ was shown to be the corresponding value of the self-same parameters of the arrival pattern.

Given $\alpha$ and $\beta$, the respective rates of client input and service, and assuming that a single-service counter functions according to the 'first-come-first-served' rule, we can predict completely the behaviour of the queueing system. Briefly, what it will do depends neither on $\alpha$ nor on $\beta$ singly but jointly on their ratio $\rho$, called the utilization factor:

$$\rho = \frac{\beta}{\alpha} = \frac{\text{Average service time of a single customer}}{\text{Average gap between two consecutive arrivals}}.$$

It can be shown that a knowledge of $\rho$ alone suffices to yield us the average size of the queue as well as the probability of its exceeding any prescribed length $n$. While the former is $\rho/(1-\rho)$, the latter is $\rho^{n+1}$. Two interesting corollaries follow immediately. First, the average waiting time of a customer is obviously the time taken to serve the average number $\rho/(1-\rho)$ of customers waiting in the queue. It is therefore $\beta\rho/(1-\rho)$. Secondly, since the probability of queue size exceeding zero is $\rho$, that of its *not* exceeding zero is $(1-\rho)$. Hence the probability of a customer finding the service counter free (queue size not exceeding zero) is $(1-\rho)$. Table 38 shows for values of $\rho$ ranging from 0·1 to 1·0 the values of the aforementioned 3 expressions for each of the following:

(i) The probability of a customer finding the service
counter free $= 1-\rho$

(ii) The average queue size $= \dfrac{\rho}{1-\rho}$

(iii) The probability of the queue size exceeding any
prescribed length $n$ $= \rho^{n+1}$

It will be observed that as $\rho$ tends to unity, that is, when the average service time just begins to equal the average gap between successive arrivals, queue size tends to infinity, and so also the average waiting period of a customer. In fact, queues begin to appear even when $\rho$, the utilization factor, is as low as 0·5 or even lower. The fact need cause no surprise because the congestion that occurs in any queueing system depends in an essential way on the irregularities in the system and not just on its average properties. However, while queues will no doubt sometimes arise even with $\rho$ no more than 0·5 the situation remains fairly comfortable as the average queue size does not exceed one, so that the average waiting time remains less than the average service time. But by the time $\rho$ reaches 0·8 the queueing situation already becomes quite distressful, the average

*Table 38*

| Utilization factor ($\rho$) | Probability that service counter is free or idle $(1-\rho)$ Item (i) | Average queue size $\dfrac{\rho}{1-\rho}$ Item (ii) | Average waiting time $\beta\,\dfrac{\rho}{1-\rho}$ Item (iii) | Probability of queue size exceeding 4 and 9 Item (iv) | |
|---|---|---|---|---|---|
| | | | | 4 ($\rho^5$) | 9 ($\rho^{10}$) |
| 0·1 | 0·9 | 0·111 | 0·111$\beta$ | 0·000 | 0·000 |
| 0·2 | 0·8 | 0·250 | 0·250$\beta$ | 0·000 | 0·000 |
| 0·3 | 0·7 | 0·429 | 0·429$\beta$ | 0·002 | 0·000 |
| 0·4 | 0·6 | 0·667 | 0·667$\beta$ | 0·010 | 0·000 |
| 0·5 | 0·5 | 1·000 | 1·000$\beta$ | 0·031 | 0·001 |
| 0·6 | 0·4 | 1·500 | 1·500$\beta$ | 0·077 | 0·006 |
| 0·7 | 0·3 | 2·333 | 2·333$\beta$ | 0·168 | 0·028 |
| 0·8 | 0·2 | 4·000 | 4·000$\beta$ | 0·327 | 0·107 |
| 0·9 | 0·1 | 9·000 | 9·000$\beta$ | 0·590 | 0·348 |
| 1·0 | 0·0 | Infinity | Infinity | 1·000 | 1·000 |

waiting time being four times the service time. How distressful this rise becomes may be seen by a glance at Figure 34, showing the relationship between the mean number in the queue *vis-à-vis* the utilization factor $\rho$. For values of $\rho$ exceeding 0·8 even a slight further rise in traffic intensity begins to entail a disproportionately sharp rise in waiting time as well as queue length. This is why service counters with utilization factors exceeding 0·8 are very sensitive to mere marginal increases in input rate and are apt to run into very serious congestions at the mildest provocation. In such situations one has to balance the cost of likely congestions against that of accelerated service. Table 38 provides useful clues as to how much service acceleration we need provide to secure a prescribed reduction in mean queue length and waiting time. We may use it to compare the cost of service acceleration versus the loss of clientèle. However, in many cases the loss of 'clients' due to increasing queue length and waiting time when the utilization ratio $\rho$ even slightly exceeds 0·75 is so great compared with any additional cost required to accelerate the service that it is superfluous to make any detailed calculation to balance the two. Such, for example, is the case with traffic congestion in railway marshalling yards when the input rate increases sufficiently to make $\rho$ exceed 0·75. For in such cases the loss of earnings due to the bottleneck curtailing even a single train per day is many times (about 100 to 1,000 times) greater than the cost of providing additional staff, switch engine, and the like, to accelerate the service rate in order to make a marginal reduction in $\rho$.

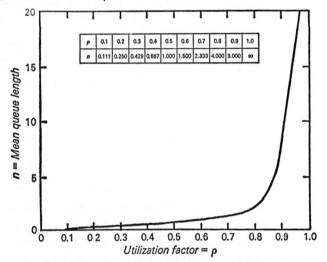

| $\rho$ | 0.1 | 0.2 | 0.3 | 0.4 | 0.5 | 0.6 | 0.7 | 0.8 | 0.9 | 1.0 |
|---|---|---|---|---|---|---|---|---|---|---|
| $n$ | 0.111 | 0.250 | 0.429 | 0.667 | 1.000 | 1.500 | 2.333 | 4.000 | 9.000 | ∞ |

*Figure 34.* Relationship of queue length to the utilization factor $\rho$.

To illustrate, consider the case of the Moghalsarai yard already cited. Just before the onset of congestion that a slight increase in its input rate sparked, the average gap $\alpha$ between the arrivals of any 2 successive customers (i.e. trains) was 48 minutes, for the yard received about 30 trains per 24 hours. The average service time $\beta$, including the time taken to reverse the switch engine to begin switching service on the next train, was 36 minutes. The utilization factor, $\rho = 36/48 = 0·75$, was thus already high enough to cause queues of 3 trains, on the average, as the substitution of $\rho = 0·75$ in the expression $\rho/(1-\rho)$ for average queue size clearly shows. Nevertheless, the situation remained reasonably comfortable. For with 10 receiving lines in the yard it could accommodate train queues up to 9.* This covered 95 per cent of all the possible con-

* Excluding one required to be kept free all the time to reverse the switch engine from the crest of the hump to the rear of the next train for humping

tingencies, as the probability of the remaining ones when the queue size exceeds 9 is only $\rho^{10} = (0.75)^{10} = 0.05$. That is, the really distressful contingencies when the yard had to hold 10 or more trains – the stage at which congestion began to overflow on to the main line and seriously to impair traffic mobility – arose only 5 per cent of the time. This is a rare enough chance – rarer than a run of four 'heads' in four successive throws of a coin. All the same, the stage had been reached at which the yard situation was sufficiently sensitive to resent even a modest increase in input rate by 10 per cent. For with an input of 33 trains per day $\alpha$ was reduced to about 43 minutes so that $\rho$ rose to $36/43 = 0.84$. As a result mean queue length became about 6 and the chance of queues of 10 or more trains arising rose to $(0.84)^{10} = 0.2$, or one chance out of five. This is quite an intolerable situation in a yard which lets congestion overflow on to the main line with such alarming frequency.

As we mentioned earlier, the congestions that began to arise because of increased input were eliminated by providing a duplicate switch engine and several other collateral accelerations in various aspects of yard working. With these modifications of the service mechanism, $\beta$, the average service time, dropped from its former value of 36 minutes to 24. In consequence, utilization factor $\rho$ became only $24/43 = 0.56$. As a reference to Table 38 will show, at this level of utilization factor the average queue size is about 1 train, and the chance of queues of 10 or more trains arising only $(0.56)^{10} = 0.003$, or three chances out of one thousand.* In fact, the modified service mechanism was adequate for even a much larger increase in input rate – up to 50 per cent. For with an input of 45 trains per day the average gap ($\alpha$) per train is $(24 \times 60)/45 = 32$ minutes, so that utilization factor $\rho$ is $24/32 = 0.75$, the same as before the onset of the original 10 per cent increase. It is obvious that even with an input of 45 trains per day the new situation is no more (but also no less) critical than previously. Consequently, any further increase in utilization factor is likely to be as disastrous as previously, unless steps are taken to reduce once again the service time $\beta$. The required reduction may be secured by various means such as by substituting diesel switch engines in lieu of steam and/or

* This is rarer than a run of eight 'heads' in a series of eight throws of a coin.

automation. Or, alternatively, if the cost of further acceleration is likely to be prohibitive, we may seek to reduce the chance of the yard's getting into distress by the provision of additional holding lines in the receiving yard. Which of these alternatives would be optimal can again be inferred from Table 38. As a reference to Table 38 will show, $(\rho = \beta/\alpha)$ should not exceed 0·7 or 0·75 if congestions and unduly long queues are to be avoided. Hence $\beta$, the average service time, should lie between $0·7\alpha$ and $0·75\alpha$. For any specified value of $\alpha$, the input rate, we can select the cheapest service mechanism whose average service time $\beta$ approximates most closely to $0·7\alpha$ or $0·75\alpha$. A review of available switching facilities in marshalling yards, including the holding capacity of the receiving yard on these lines, is likely to be very rewarding.

•There are, however, other situations where the gains expected from additional clients by service improvements are *not* so overwhelmingly great as to make the balancing of additional gains against additional costs superfluous. Such, for example, is the case when we have to consider whether or not to open a second service counter for repairing a group of broken-down machines. In such cases we need to balance the cost of the idle time of the service counter against loss of revenue when broken-down machines have to queue up for service. When we have to make such precise balancing calculations we need to know the proportion of the time the facility idles or is free and the mean waiting time of a client. To illustrate, suppose we have a repair counter with one attendant to repair a waiting line of broken-down machines. Let the average time $(\alpha)$ between consecutive arrivals of clients (broken-down machines) be 60 minutes and the average service time $(\beta)$ be 50 minutes. The utilization ratio $\rho$ then is $\beta/\alpha = 50/60 = 5/6 = 0·833$. A reference to Table 38 will show that while the average waiting time per machine, excluding repair time, is $\beta[\rho/(1-\rho)] = 50(0·833/0·167) = 250$ minutes $= 4·17$ hours per machine, the attendant at the service counter is free or idle for a proportion $1-\rho = 1-0·833 = 0·167$ (or 16·7 per cent) of his time. Consequently, if the cost of idle time of a machine is, say, a dollar an hour, the total cost of idle time of 24 machines arriving during the day is $24(1)(4·17) = 100$ dollars. On the other hand, if the cost of idle time of the service, including wages of the attendant, is 5 dollars an hour, the cost of its idle time is $24(0\cdot167)(5) = 20$ dollars a day. Obviously, with one service counter we are incurring a very large machine-waiting time (100 hours) in relation to the counter-idle time (4 hours). *Prima facie* therefore there is a case for duplicating the service facility, even at the cost of increasing its idle time, in order to reduce the machine-waiting time. Under the new conditions of a second service counter the average service time $\beta$ now becomes $\frac{1}{2}$, or 25 minutes, so that the utilization ratio $\rho$ is $\frac{1}{2}(0\cdot833) = 0\cdot417$. A reference to Table 38 again yields the corresponding values of the proportion of the time the service counter idles, namely, $(1-\rho) = (1-0\cdot417) = 0\cdot583$, and mean waiting time of the machines, or $\beta[\rho/(1-\rho)] = 25[0\cdot417/(1-04\cdot17)] = 25(0\cdot417/0\cdot583) = 0\cdot3$ hours. The cost of the idle time of the service facility now is $24(0\cdot583)(5) = 70$ dollars a day against the cost of waiting time of the machines $24(1)(0\cdot3) = 7\cdot20$ dollars. The total cost of the two idle times now is $(70+7\cdot20) = 77\cdot20$ dollars against the earlier total of $(20+100) = 120$ dollars. Thus by increasing the idle cost of the service facility even by a factor exceeding three we have secured a significant over-all decrease in total unproductive costs because of the great reduction in the waiting time of the machines by duplicating the service facility.

In making the above balancing calculation we have assumed that the patterns of client arrival as well as of service are completely random, that is, that their distribution conforms to the negative exponential law and the queue discipline is the first-come-first-served rule. With other patterns and other disciplines the system will naturally behave differently. Unfortunately, the mathematics of queueing situations, when modes of arrival and service are no longer of the exponential type we have hitherto considered and when other priority schedules of service are in force, becomes exceedingly complicated and very often even intractable. Fortunately, we can in many cases resolve the difficulty by resort to Monte Carlo simulation, as we shall show in the next chapter.

# CHAPTER 9

# Monte Carlo Simulation

'MONTE CARLO' is the code name given by von Neumann and S. M. Ulam to the mathematical technique of solving problems too expensive for experimental solution and too complicated for analytical treatment. Originally, the concept referred to a situation in which a difficult but determinate problem is solved by resort to a chance process. A simple illustration of the idea is the problem of finding the surface area of an irregularly shaped lake enclosed in a rectangle $R$, as shown in Figure 35. Instead of computing the area by geometrical methods we apply the following chance process. A

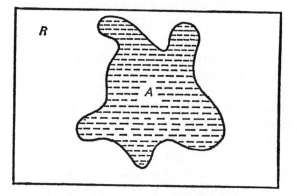

*Figure 35.* Lake of area $A$ enclosed in rectangle of area $R$.

large number of pebbles are projected by means of a catapult whose elastic is stretched to randomly varying lengths at angles which too vary equally randomly. The area $A$ of the lake then is simply

$$A = R\left(\frac{\text{Number of pebbles falling in water}}{\text{Total number of pebbles projected}}\right).$$

The underlying rationale of the process is that the probability that a pebble will fall in water, that is, the frequency ratio of throws falling in the water to the total number of throws, is equal to the ratio of the areas of the lake and its enclosing rectangle. We have here a probabilistic process that yields us the solution of a determinate problem, namely, the area of the irregular lake. Another instance of the same kind is the problem of evaluating numerically $\pi$, the ratio of the circumference of a circle to its diameter. There are a number of analytical procedures of varying degrees of complexity for making the calculation directly. But we can also use J. Buffon's theorem to invent a chance process for evaluating it. Buffon calculated the probability of a very thin needle of specified length $l$ intersecting one of the lines of a ruled board on which it is thrown at random (see Figure 36).

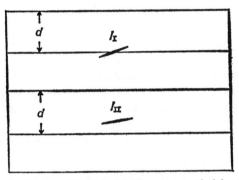

*Figure 36.* Needle of length $l$ falling on a ruled board with parallel lines distance $d$ apart. Needle $l$ in position I intersects a line of the board but does not in position II.

He showed that if the parallel lines on the board are ruled at a distance $d$ apart ($d$ being greater than $l$) the probability $p$ in question will be

$$p = \frac{2l}{\pi d}.$$

It therefore follows that

$$\pi = \frac{2l}{dp};$$

or

$$\pi = \frac{2l}{d} \frac{\text{Total number of times the needle is thrown}}{\substack{\text{Number of times the needle intersects} \\ \text{a line of the board}}}.$$

171

The astronomer R. Wolf actually threw a needle 36 mm. long 5,000 times on a board ruled with parallel lines 45 mm. apart. He observed that the needle intersected one of the parallel lines 2,532 times. He thus found that

$$\pi = \frac{2(36)\,(5000)}{45(2532)} = 3\cdot159.$$

This differs from the standard value by less than 0·02.

The difficulty in applying Wolf's procedure is that a very large number of trials is necessary to obtain a reasonably accurate estimate, as a few trials are likely to yield a grossly misleading result. Thus 10 trials may lead to a value as wide of the mark as 2·5, and even 100 trials may not improve it materially. Indeed, it can be shown that the accuracy of a Monte Carlo approximation improves only as the *square* of the number of trials. To double the accuracy of the estimate the number of trials has to be quadrupled; to treble it they must increase ninefold, and so on. This is why even the 5,000 trials of Wolf gave him an estimate barely correct to 6 per cent. But a large number of trials can be very fatiguing. If you tried

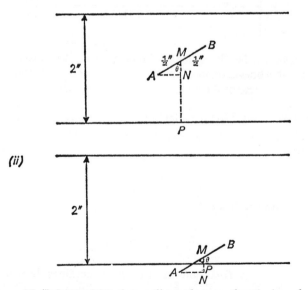

*Figure 37.* (i) $MN<MP$: the needle not intersecting the board line. (ii) $MN>MP$: the needle intersecting the board line.

172

Wolf's experiment, it is more than likely that your arm would be tired long before you reached the one thousandth trial, so that even the 5,000 repetitions that Wolf completed would have to be secured in several instalments.

One way of avoiding the tedium and fatigue of an enormous number of trials is to resort to computer simulation, that is, make a little calculating machine that will do the work. It is not difficult to programme a computer to carry out operations which will reproduce the results of dropping a needle on a ruled board. All we need do is to devise a way of describing the situation of the needle relative to the nearest line in a manner intelligible to the machine. Consider, for the sake of definiteness, the case of a needle 1 inch long which is dropped on a board with parallel lines 2 inches apart. A glance at Figure 37 will show that two numbers suffice to specify the position of the needle, namely, the distance $MP(r)$ of its midpoint $M$ from the nearest line, and the angle $A\,MP(\theta)$ made by the needle with the perpendicular ($MP$) to the line. Given these two quantities, $r$ and $\theta$, the machine can easily decide whether the needle intersects a line. For it can calculate the distance $MN$ (it is simply $\frac{1}{2}\cos\theta$) and compare it with $MP = r$. The needle obviously intersects the line if and only if $MN$ exceeds or equals $MP$. Hence if the machine computes the difference ($MN-MP$), or ($\frac{1}{2}\cos\theta-r$), the sign of the difference determines what the needle will do. It will intersect a line if the difference is positive or zero, but otherwise not.

Now to find out by experiment in what proportion of trials a needle dropped at random would touch the line we would like to test all possible positions in which the needle might fall. That is, we would have to consider all possible combinations of the values of distance $r$ and angle $\theta$. But as we cannot possibly complete such an unending task we have to make do with a random sample of their values. The selection of such a random sample is the heart of Monte Carlo method.

If we are content to measure the angle (which can vary only from 0 to 90 degrees) correct to the nearest degree, we may select its value at random by a spin of a roulette wheel having 91 compartments (see Figure 38). A spin of such a wheel would select the angle for us in a random manner, and over many trials each of the 91 values of the angle would be selected with about equal frequency. To select the distance *r* at random we may employ another wheel with an appropriate number of compartments. Thus, if we decide to measure *r* correct to 0·01 inches, we may divide the full range of *r*'s

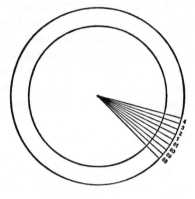

*Figure 38*

variation, namely, from 0 to 1 inch,* into 100 equal parts, so that *r* is assumed to have one of the 101 possible values:

0·00, 0·01, 0·02, 0·03, 0·04, 0·05, 0·06, . . ., 1·00.

A spin of a roulette wheel with 101 compartments representing 101 different distances of the midpoint *M* from the nearest line will choose for us a value of *r* at random (see Figure 39). A series of spins of the two wheels would give us a random set of positions just as if we had actually dropped a needle at random on a ruled board.

If you object that wheel-spinning will be even more cumbersome and tiring than dropping the needle, you will be right. But there are simpler ways of going about the same thing with a computer provided with a random number table. These random numbers are groups of 10 numbers (0 to 9), or 100 numbers (from 00 to 99), or 1,000 numbers (from 000 to 999), or any other larger similar group.

---

*The parallel lines being 2 inches apart, the midpoint of the needle from the nearest line will naturally vary between 0 and 1. For the moment *MP* exceeds 1, it will be closer to the parallel line on the other side and we could reckon its distance from the latter.

174

In each case, the order in which the numbers are placed is absolutely fortuitous or random, so that they have no beginning and no end. They can be read in any way – vertically, horizontally, or diagonally. However we may read them, so long as they are picked up in some regular fashion from the table they will appear absolutely at random, no number in the group enjoying any preference over any other. Table 39, for example, is a miniature facsimile

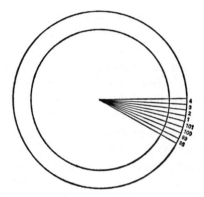

*Figure 39*

of 80 random numbers lying between 00 and 99 taken from R. A. Fisher and F. Yates's table of random numbers.

*Table 39*

| | | | | | | | | | |
|---|---|---|---|---|---|---|---|---|---|
| 44 | 16 | 16 | 58 | 09 | 79 | 83 | 86 | 19 | 62 |
| 84 | 16 | 07 | 44 | 99 | 83 | 11 | 46 | 32 | 24 |
| 82 | 97 | 77 | 77 | 81 | 07 | 45 | 32 | 14 | 08 |
| 50 | 92 | 26 | 11 | 97 | 00 | 65 | 76 | 31 | 38 |
| 83 | 39 | 50 | 08 | 30 | 42 | 34 | 07 | 96 | 88 |
| 40 | 33 | 20 | 38 | 36 | 13 | 89 | 51 | 03 | 74 |
| 96 | 83 | 50 | 87 | 75 | 97 | 12 | 25 | 93 | 47 |
| 88 | 42 | 95 | 45 | 72 | 16 | 64 | 36 | 16 | 00 |

We could take a random-number table of the aforementioned type and score out all numbers exceeding 91. A computer having access to such a table in its storage would be able to select one of these numbers at random. Since each of the numbers lying between 0 and 91 has the same chance of selection as any other, it is completely equivalent to choosing $\theta$ by a spin of the roulette wheel having 91 compartments. Likewise, provision of another appropriately devised table of random numbers would enable the computer to select $r$ at random. Having selected $\theta$ and $r$ it would easily compute the difference $(\frac{1}{2}\cos\theta - r)$ and decide from its sign, without actually dropping the needle at all, whether or not the needle intersected the nearest parallel line. A moderately fast computer could simulate within one minute 100 trials, and a really high-speed one as many as 5,000 trials.

We have outlined above Monte Carlo simulation of a determinate problem, namely, the determination of the numerical value of $\pi$. But the merit of the idea for our present purpose is that if chance processes can be invented to solve difficult determinate problems, they can be devised to handle probabilistic ones too. Consider, for example, the problem of evaluating the probability $P$ that a tank will be knocked out by either a first or second shot from an anti-tank gun assumed to possess a constant kill probability of $\frac{1}{2}$. It can be shown that $P = \frac{1}{2} + \frac{1}{2}(1-\frac{1}{2}) = \frac{3}{4}$. But we could also invent a Monte Carlo procedure by simulating each round of the anti-tank gun by the flip of a coin. Since the probability of a 'head' is the same as that of a kill, we may call it a hit when the coin turns up a 'head', and otherwise a miss. If we now flip the coin a large number of times the value of $P$ may be calculated by merely counting the number of times a 'head' turns up *at least* once in two successive throws. The frequency ratio of such occasions to the total pairs of throws is the required probability. Clearly, the use of Monte Carlo procedure is a poor substitute for the theoretical calculation in this simple case. But many real-life systems are so complicated that it is all but impossible to transcribe them in mathematical equations or to solve the equations even if they could be so transcribed. It happens that while mathematical equations cannot transcribe them, a step-by-step verbal description of the sequence of actions is often possible. It is such situations that Monte Carlo simulation has been designed to handle. In particular, it provides the simplest possible solutions for queueing problems which would otherwise be completely intractable. For in queueing theory, where customer arrival is entirely random and service time may also be a random variable, Monte Carlo simulation often neatly cuts the queueing tangle in a truly Gordian fashion.

As the name suggests, simulation is a way of representing one system such as a field operation or a physical phenomenon by a model to facilitate its study. Cases in point are model aeroplanes imitating flight conditions in a wind tunnel or fatigue-test models attempting to duplicate the normal wear-and-tear of years in a few days or weeks. Such kinds of simulation models, based on the principle of similitude, have been in use for a long time. But Monte Carlo simulation is a recent operations-research innovation. The novelty lies in making use of pure chance to construct a simulated version of the process under analysis, in exactly the same way as pure chance operates the original system under working conditions. Thus, the use of flips of coin enabled us to simulate tank kill by anti-tank fire. We could do so because the probability of a kill as well as of a 'head' was the same, that is, $\frac{1}{2}$. But if it had been different, we would have had to use a biased coin with the same probability of turning up a 'head' as the anti-tank gun has of a kill. Instead of making biased coins to simulate chance situations we can also use a table of random numbers to simulate throws of a biased coin with any pre-assigned probability of a 'head' or 'tail', exactly as we simulated earlier throws of Buffon's needle. As we saw, the essence of Monte Carlo simulation is to use random-number tables to reproduce on paper the operation of any given system under its own working conditions. To illustrate this, consider any concrete operation subject to chance, such as the arrival of trucks at a loading bay. Suppose we observe their actual arrivals on a number of days, the larger the better. We can summarize the observations made in two complementary ways. First, we may group the number of trucks arriving every hour: 7–8, 8–9, 9–10 a.m. and so on till 4–5 p.m., assuming that no trucks arrive before 7 a.m. nor any after 5 p.m. Thus if 2, 4, 6, 5, 3 trucks arrive between 7 and 8 on 5 days of the period under observation, the mean number of trucks arriving during the hour 7–8 will be

$$\frac{2+4+6+5+3}{5} = \frac{20}{5} = 4.$$

Since there are 10 hours in which truck arrivals have been classified there will be 10 such mean values. Table 40 is a specimen of 10 means of truck arrivals for every hour we may possibly obtain.

*Table 40.* Mean truck arrivals per hour.

| Hourly period | Mean arrivals |
|---|---|
| 7–8 A.M. | 4·0 |
| 8–9 | 5·4 |
| 9–10 | 1·4 |
| 10–11 | 2·4 |
| 11–12 | 1·4 |
| 12–1 P.M. | 1·6 |
| 1–2 | 1·4 |
| 2–3 | 4·6 |
| 3–4 | 3·0 |
| 4–5 | 2·0 |

This is the first summary. We supplement it by making a second which takes into account the deviations of actual arrivals from the corresponding mean hourly arrival. Thus for the hour 7–8 the mean hourly arrival for the whole period of 5 days is 4. But the deviations from the mean value 4 on the 5 days in question are

$$(2-4), \ (4-4), \ (6-4), \ (5-4), \ (3-4).$$
$$-2, \quad 0, \quad 2, \quad 1, \quad -1$$

Likewise, there will be another set of 5 deviations from the mean hourly arrival during the next hour, 8–9 a.m., and so on to the tenth hour, 4–5 p.m. There will thus be 10 sets of 5 deviations from each of the 10 mean hourly arrivals during the hours beginning with 7–8 a.m. and ending with 4–5 p.m. Table 41 shows the frequency of the deviations from their respective means according to their magnitude.

The penultimate column in Table 41 shows the frequency of each value of deviation as a percentage. In the last column is shown the allotment of 100 random numbers from 00 to 99, both inclusive, according to the percentage frequency of the deviation. Thus, deviation to the extent of $+4$ from the mean, having 0 frequency percentage, has no random number allotted to it. The next deviation to the extent of 3·5, occurring only once out of a total of 50 and therefore having a frequency percentage of 2, has 2 random numbers, 00 to 01, allotted to it. The next deviation of $+3$, with a percentage frequency of 8, has the next 8 random numbers, 02 to 09, allotted to it. Proceeding thus we find that the last deviation,

*Table 41.* Deviation of truck arrivals per hour from mean.

| Deviation from mean | Frequency | Percentage frequency | Random numbers allotted |
|---|---|---|---|
| +4·0 | 0 | 0 | — |
| +3·5 | 1 | 2 | 00–01 |
| +3·0 | 4 | 8 | 02–09 |
| +2·5 | 4 | 8 | 10–17 |
| +2·0 | 5 | 10 | 18–27 |
| +1·5 | 6 | 12 | 28–39 |
| +1·0 | 4 | 8 | 40–47 |
| +0·5 | 3 | 6 | 48–53 |
| −0·5 | 5 | 10 | 54–63 |
| −1·0 | 3 | 6 | 64–69 |
| −1·5 | 4 | 8 | 70–77 |
| −2·0 | 3 | 6 | 78–83 |
| −2·5 | 2 | 4 | 84–87 |
| −3·0 | 2 | 4 | 88–91 |
| −3·5 | 1 | 2 | 92–93 |
| −4·0 | 3 | 6 | 94–99 |
| Total | 50 | 100 | |

−4, shown in the table, with percentage frequency 6, is allotted the last 6 random numbers, from 94 to 99. The object of these allotments is to derive by simulation the actual number of trucks that may be expected to arrive during any given hour. Thus, suppose we need to know how many trucks may be expected to turn up on a particular day during the hour 10–11 a.m. Table 40 shows that the mean arrival during this hour is 2·4. If we could ascertain the deviation of the actual arrivals from the mean we could easily compute the former. To do so, we refer to Table 39 of random numbers and select any two-digit numbers at random. Suppose it is the first, viz. 44. Since 44 lies between 40 and 47, the 8 random numbers allotted to the deviation of magnitude +1, the deviation of actual arrivals from the mean will be (+1) on that day. In other words, the actual arrivals for 10–11 will be 2·4+1 = 3·4, so that we may assume that 3 trucks will arrive between 10 and 11 a.m. on the day in question.* The underlying rationale of the simulation

*The fraction, being less than half, has been dropped in rounding.

procedure described above is that every deviation from its corresponding mean has the same chance of occurring by random number selection as in the actual case, because each deviation has as many random numbers allotted to it as its frequency percentage in the general pool of all deviations derived from earlier observations of the process at work. Its actual incidence in the paper version simulated by random number selection will therefore equal the probability of its occurrence in the actual process.

A simple variant of the same random number technique will even tell us the actual arrival instant of the trucks arriving during any stipulated hour. For after ascertaining the number of trucks likely to arrive during any hour, say, 10–11 a.m., all we need know is the minutes past the hour (10 o'clock in this case) when each of the 3 trucks does turn up at the loading bay. If we are content to reckon the arrival instant correct to within 5 minutes the required number of minutes past the hour can take a value only in one of the 12 intervals (0–5 minutes, 6–10 minutes, 11–15 minutes, . . . 56–60 minutes) into which any hour may be divided. Now, given the actual arrivals during the hours 7–8, 8–9 a.m., . . ., and 4–5 p.m. for all the days under observation, we can easily make a frequency table showing how many trucks arrive within 5 minutes, how many within 6–10 minutes past the hour, and so on for the remaining 10 5-minute intervals into which we have chosen to split the hour. Table 42 shows the frequency with which the arrivals may occur within the stipulated number of minutes past the hour.

It also shows the same frequency expressed as a percentage of the total according to which random numbers from 00 to 99 are allotted to each 5-minute interval. Thus the first interval, 0–5 minutes, with a frequency percentage of 23, has the first 23 random numbers, 00 to 22, assigned to it; the next interval, 6–10 minutes, with a frequency percentage of 12, the next lot of 12 random number, 23 to 34, and so on for the other intervals. If we now pick a random number from Table 39 we may find it to be, say, 17. A reference to Table 42 shows that it occurs in the range 00 to 22 allotted to the interval 0–5 minutes. It therefore follows that the first of the 3 trucks arriving between 10 and 11 a.m. arrives at 5 minutes past 10. Picking two new random numbers, namely, 36 and 58, we find from Table 42 that they are assigned respectively to

*Table 42.* Frequency of truck arrivals within the number of minutes past the hour.

| Number of minutes past the hour | Frequency of truck arrivals | Percentage frequency Col. (ii) × 100 / 136 | Random numbers allotted |
|---|---|---|---|
| (i) | (ii) | (iii) | (iv) |
| 0–5  min. | 30 | 23 | 00–22 |
| 6–10 min. | 16 | 12 | 23–34 |
| 11–15 min. | 8 | 6 | 35–40 |
| 16–20 min. | 19 | 14 | 41–54 |
| 21–25 min. | 4 | 3 | 55–57 |
| 26–30 min. | 8 | 6 | 58–63 |
| 31–35 min | 18 | 13 | 64–76 |
| 36–40 min. | 7 | 5 | 77–81 |
| 41–45 min. | 6 | 4 | 82–85 |
| 46–50 min. | 7 | 5 | 86–90 |
| 51–55 min. | 10 | 7 | 91–97 |
| 56–60 min. | 3 | 2 | 98–99 |
| Total | 136 | 100 | |

Note: In our illustration 136 trucks are assumed to arrive during five days, that is, 27·2 trucks per day. The frequency of arrivals during these five days within the stipulated number of minutes past the hour is shown against each.

the intervals 11–15 and 26–30 minutes. Thus the second and third trucks arrive at 15 and 30 minutes past 10, respectively. Proceeding in an analogous way we can make a frequency table showing the number of trucks loaded within intervals of varying magnitudes, say, 10 minutes, 10–20 minutes, and so on. Each of these loading intervals or service durations can then be allotted a set of 100 random numbers, 00 to 99, according to the *percentage* frequency of its occurrence, to provide a basis for simulating the pattern of available service. In other words, by repeated use of random-number tables we can simulate both the arrival pattern of trucks as well as that of the loading service given them.

This is one illustration of how the arrival as well as service patterns in a queueing system may be derived by Monte Carlo simulation. It is obvious that both are far too refractory to be trapped in a neat mathematical expression like the exponential function we could devise earlier, on the assumption that the chance of arrival of a customer at any instant is the same as at any other. For a glance at Table 40 will show that while the chance of any truck arriving during the period after 5 p.m. or before 7 a.m. is nil, that of its arrival even during the period 7 a.m. to 5 p.m. is not uniform and varies according to the hour. For instance, it is four times greater between 8 and 9 than between 11 and 12. With such pronounced preference for arrivals during certain hours of the day it is all but impossible to deduce mathematically the salient features of the arrival pattern. In situations like this, simulation method stands us in very good stead indeed. For it is often an adequate substitute for the purely mathematical formalism and enables us to predict not only the number of customers likely to arrive during any stipulated period but also the very instants at which they do. As we have seen, similar application of Monte Carlo technique can simulate the pattern of customer service and indeed the whole operation. Such simulation of an actual operation or process on the basis of its own past working is, however, only the first step. It paves the way for the next, which is to predict the changes in its behaviour likely to result from innovations that we may wish to introduce. These innovations can be introduced (on paper) at no expense, and the application of a fresh series of random numbers at the appropriate stages would cause the model to operate just as if the same alterations had actually been made. We can thus assess at practically no cost at all the likely effect of contemplated changes in the system of working.

Consider, for the sake of illustration, a factory loading bottled chemicals in trucks at two loading bays. Because of the irregularities of truck arrivals as well as of loading service there will be times when trucks have to wait for service while at others the loading gangs will have no trucks to load. Suppose actual observation of the operation shows that the daily waiting times of trucks averages 96 truck-hours and that of loading gangs 50 man-hours. It then becomes necessary to determine whether the reduction in waiting time of trucks by improved service, e.g. operating one or more additional loading bays, will balance the increased waiting time of the servicing facilities. By observing the actual operation – truck arrivals and loadings on a sufficient number of days – we can simulate on paper the modified operation that would result by working 3 or 4 bays instead of the actual 2. Thus we could easily predict by the random number technique already explained the

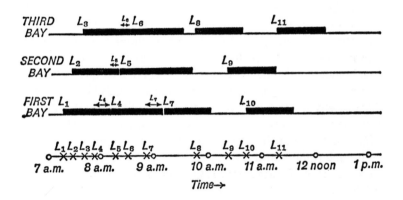

*Figure 40.* The crosses $L_1$, $L_2$, $L_3$, . . ., on the bottom line denote the arrival instants of the first, second, third, . . ., trucks. The 3 lines at the top indicate the state of the 3 loading bays at various times, the thick line showing occupation and the thin line idling. The waiting time of a truck, if it happens to arrive when all 3 bays are busy (as is the case with $L_4$, $L_5$, $L_6$, and $L_7$), is shown by a double arrow connecting the instant at which it arrives and that at which service can begin, thus: $\xleftarrow{\quad L_4 \quad}$. As can be seen, trucks $L_4$, $L_5$, $L_6$, and $L_7$ have to wait because all 3 bays happen to be engaged at the time of their arrival.

times at which the trucks arrive during the day. Similar simulation of service pattern will enable us to determine time taken to service each truck. We thus have both the elements – the arrival and service pattern – to determine how long each truck has to wait even when 3 bays are at work instead of the actual 2, or *per contra* how long each loading bay remains idle (see Figure 40). As a result, we can determine the total waiting time of trucks and idling time of loading gangs under the modified setup. We may find, for example, that with 3 loading bays the waiting time of trucks is 25 truck-hours and that of the gangs 126 man-hours. The introduction of the third bay will thus reduce the waiting time of trucks by 71 truck-hours, but at the cost of increasing the idling time of loading gangs by 76 man-hours. Since a truck-hour obviously costs a good deal more than a man-hour it will certainly pay the factory to provide the additional facility of a third loading bay. In coming to this conclusion we have merely reproduced on paper the likely outcome of setting up an additional loading bay without actually doing so. Monte Carlo simulation therefore provides a means of discovering in advance at practically no cost at all whether or not the expense incurred in making the changes envisaged would be worthwhile. This is why it has been applied to a wide diversity of problems, ranging from the arrival of trucks at loading bays to the behaviour of markets, by an ingenious adaptation of linear-programming technique (input–output analysis) recently developed by Wassily Leontief, L. V. Kantorovich, T. C. Koopmans, G. B. Dantzig, and others.

*Part III*

# IMPROVISATIONS

CHAPTER 10

# The Confrontation Theorem

IN operations research a micron of theory sometimes yields a mega-buck of cash. This was recently illustrated in India by the experience of the Northeast Frontier Railway, which had to face a new situation as a result of the outbreak of hostilities between India and Pakistan in September 1965. One consequence of this conflict was the sudden suspension of the two independent Indo–Pakistan lines of supply for West Bengal, Assam, North East Frontier Agency, Tripura, and Nagaland – the River Steam Navigation Company's river route through Pakistan waters and the Indo–Pakistan rail routes via East Pakistan Railways. Although the Northeast Frontier Railway had no spare capacity to carry the traffic previously moving by these routes by an all-India route, it managed to create it overnight by resorting to a remarkably ingenious artifice based on what may be called the confrontation theorem.

The main idea underlying the confrontation theorem is the quantification of the commonplace observation that on a single-line railway trains from opposite directions have to confront and cross at crossing stations. When they do, at least one, if not both, must necessarily halt for a while. One may expect such crossings to increase directly with the number of trains run. But a more precise calculation shows that they increase, not directly as the number ($n$) of trains run, but even more rapidly than its square. It is therefore worthwhile studying how fast these confrontations or crossings grow with increasing train service.

Consider, for example, any given section whereon run a number of trains all moving at the same speed and all enjoying equal priority. The total running time $T$ of each train will be the same in all cases. Assume further that the total number of trains run in each direction during $T$ hours, the lifetime of a train, is $x$. Then our master chart will have $x$ paths for *up* trains and an equal number of *down* trains, all equally spaced in the interval of time $T$ as shown

187

in Figure 41. If the departure instant of the first *up* train is the zero

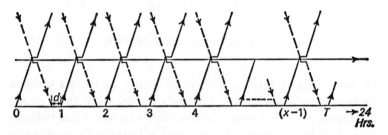

*Figure 41.* Simplified model of train crossings.

hour from which we reckon time, the departure instants of **the** second, third, fourth, . . ., *x*th *up* trains will respectively be

$$\frac{1}{x} T, \frac{2}{x} T, \frac{3}{x} T, \ldots, \frac{x-1}{x} T.$$

Likewise, let the arrival instants of the first, second, third, . . ., *x*th *down* trains be each *d* hours *prior* to the departure of the second, third, fourth, . . ., *up* trains as shown in Figure 41. Consequently, the departure instants of the *x up* trains and the arrival instants of the corresponding *down* trains will be as shown in Table 43.

*Table 43.* Departure and arrival instants of *x* trains.

| Trains | First train | Second train | Third train | Fourth train | . . . | *x*th train |
|---|---|---|---|---|---|---|
| Departure instants of *up* trains | 0 | $\frac{1}{x} T$ | $\frac{2}{x} T$ | $\frac{3}{x} T$ | . . . | $\frac{x-1}{x} T$ |
| Arrival instants of *down* trains | $\frac{1}{x} T - d$ | $\frac{2}{x} T - d$ | $\frac{3}{x} T - d$ | $\frac{4}{x} T - d$ | . . . | $\frac{x}{x} T - d$ |

It will be observed that according to the symmetrical model of service assumed there is a sequence of one *up* train departing followed by a *down* train arriving. With such a symmetrical pattern of arrivals and departures the cycle of $x$ trains repeats itself periodically every $T$ hours. In each cycle the first train will encounter all the $(x)$ *down* trains during the interval $T$, the period of the cycle, which is also the life span of every individual train. The second *up* train of the cycle will encounter $(x-1)$ *down* trains, the third *up* train $(x-2)$ *down* trains, and so on. The last or $x$th *up* train will encounter only one *down* train during the period $T$ of the cycle. The total number of crossings during the time $T$ will therefore be

$$x+(x-1)+(x-2)\ldots3+2+1 = x\frac{(x+1)}{2}.$$

Now the life span $T$ of a train is made up of two parts: the actual running time $r$ and the stationary time spent in crossings. Since each train has $x$ crossings in the course of its career, the stationary time is $px$, where $p$ is the crossing delay in hours per crossing. Hence

$$T = px+r. \tag{i}$$

Now if the daily number of trains running on the section is $n$, then

$$n = \frac{x(24)}{T}$$

or

$$x = \frac{nT}{24}. \tag{ii}$$

Consequently, the total number of crossings during time $T$, the life span of a train or the period of the cycle, is

$$\frac{x(x+1)}{2} = \frac{1}{2}\left(\frac{nT}{24}\right)\left\{\frac{nT}{24}+1\right\}.$$

Therefore, the number $(N)$ of crossings per day is

$$N = \frac{1}{2}\left(\frac{nT}{24}\right)\left\{\frac{nT}{24}+1\right\}\frac{24}{T}$$

$$= \tfrac{1}{2}n\left(\frac{nT}{24}+1\right). \tag{iii}$$

189

But

$$T = px + r$$

$$= p\left(\frac{nT}{24}\right) + r.$$

Or

$$T = \frac{24r}{24 - pn}.$$

Substituting for $T$ in (iii), we have

$$N = \tfrac{1}{2}n\left(\frac{nr}{24 - pn} + 1\right)$$

$$= kn^2 + \tfrac{1}{2}n, \qquad \text{(iv)}$$

where

$$k = \frac{1}{2}\left(\frac{r}{24 - pn}\right).$$

It thus results that the number $N$ of crossings per day is the sum of two parts: one part directly proportional to the number ($n$) of trains per day, and the other, the more dominant part, varying directly as $n^2$. It is to be noted that $k$, the constant of proportionality for the dominant part, is not a true constant. It too increases slightly with increasing $n$. This is why diminution of even one train reduces the number of crossings so significantly when the number of trains ($n$) is very high.

It is true that in deriving expression (iv) we have assumed a highly oversimplified situation. But any departure from the simple symmetrical situation envisaged in the model will only worsen the crossing delays. It is a general principle that a symmetrical situation leads to an extremum. Consider, for instance, a point $P$ inside a triangle $ABC$. The sum of three distances $PA, PB, PC$ is *minimal* when $P$ is situated *symmetrically* with regard to the three vertices. That is, when all the three angles $APB, BPC$, and $CPA$ are equal, each being 120°. One may assume as a heuristic principle that a symmetrical model of an operating situation will lead to minimal delays. However, if anyone is dissatisfied with the foregoing analysis merely because of its extreme simplicity he is welcome to prove the heuristic principle cited above. But even he will concede, without demanding a formal proof, that the gains in eliminating crossing delays in any actual non-symmetrical situation will be more than even those given by equation (iv). Consequently, we can take it that crossing delays derived from equation (iv) are a lower limit of actual delays likely to occur when the service pattern departs from the symmetrical model assumed.

To illustrate, let the average speed of trains be 20 miles per hour and the length of the section be 100 miles. Then $r = 100/20 = 5$ hours. Let $p = 2/3$ hours, the crossing delay per crossing. Then for values of $n = 15$, 14, and 13 the number of crossings per day, from (iv), will approximately be

for $n = 15$,

$$N = \frac{1}{2}\left(\frac{5}{24-\frac{2}{3}(15)}\right)(15 \times 15) + \frac{15}{2} = \frac{15}{84}(225) + \frac{15}{2} = 48$$

for $n = 14$,

$$N = \frac{1}{2}\left(\frac{5}{24-\frac{2}{3}(14)}\right)(14 \times 14) + \frac{14}{2} = \frac{15}{88}(196) + \frac{14}{2} = 41$$

for $n = 13$,

$$N = \frac{1}{2}\left(\frac{5}{24-\frac{2}{3}(13)}\right)(13 \times 13) + \frac{13}{2} = \frac{15}{92}(169) + \frac{13}{2} = 34.$$

By reducing the number of trains by one, from 15 to 14, the number of crossings decreases by nearly 17 per cent at least. Likewise, by reducing the number of trains by two, from 15 to 13, the number of crossings decreases by nearly 41 per cent at least. If therefore we arrange to combine one pair of passenger trains by running them coupled, that is, two trains on a single path, we save one path without really sacrificing the passenger train. We thus reduce the crossing delays by at least 17 per cent. By coupling two pairs of passenger trains we have a minimal reduction of 41 per cent. This is why the Northeast Frontier Railway was able to catapult its diesel-engine-kilometers per engine-day in use by 39 kilometers – a rise of over 20 per cent – in a single *coup*, by combining one pair of passenger trains between New Gauhati and Katihar, thereby saving one path. The quantum of passenger service remained the same. But the change in the mode of service itself yielded a rich dividend in the increase in the diesel-engine-utilization index.

The gains secured by coupling one pair of passenger trains proved lucrative enough to call for an extension of the scheme. This was done by coupling an additional pair of express trains running between Gauhati and Barauni, effective 1 December 1965. As a result the mobility of the fleet of diesel engines as well as cars improved still further. From August 1965 to February 1966 the diesel-engine- kilometers per engine-day in use increased from 207 to 280, an increase of 35 per cent.

It is interesting to watch the persistent climb of diesel-engine usage, month by month, since the onset of the operations-research exercise in September 1965.

*Table 44*

|  | 1965 | | | | | 1966 | | |
|---|---|---|---|---|---|---|---|---|
|  | Aug. | Sept. | Oct. | Nov. | Dec. | Jan. | Feb. | Mar. |
| Diesel-engine kilometers per engine-day in use (all services) | 207 | 229 | 241 | 246 | 265 | 272 | 280 | 278 |

The reason the diesel-engine usage improved in stages after each of the two amalgamations of a pair of passenger trains instead of in a single stroke is this. In railway transportation one bottleneck removed is very often another revealed. When after combining a pair of passenger trains in September 1965 the diesel-locomotive power availability improved, it unmasked many other bottlenecks – in yards, sheds, sick lines, and control offices. It took time and detailed field studies to discover ways of overcoming these bottle- necks. Cases in point are the New Gauhati and Lumding yards, where input of traffic increased greatly beyond the limits to which they were used. Thus, during November 1965 nearly 11,000 loaded cars were received at New Gauhati, against 6,150 during the corresponding month of 1964. Likewise, the number of cars moved out of Lumding into the difficult Lumding–Badarpur Hill Section increased considerably, from 1900 in November 1964 to 3,000 in the corresponding month of 1965. To handle the increased traffic, steps were taken to keep New Gauhati fluid to enable it to form long-distance trains for South Bank destinations Lumding and beyond. This was done (*a*) by rigidly enforcing line nomination, because previously free mixing of sorting lines was the rule, and (*b*) by suitably regulating input into New Gauhati, keeping the 'overflow' at Pandu yard, a relic of the old days of ferry crossings before the construction of the Brahmaputra Bridge in 1962. This yard, which had been kept as a standby in case the ferry had to be used again, was now brought into use as a satellite of New Gauhati to enable the latter to form long-distance trains (see Figure 42).

Similarly, the pit-line bottlenecks at the Lumding and Badarpur yards were overcome by another ingenious device in addition to that of enforcing line nomination. It may be pointed out that the Lumding–Badarpur Hill Section traverses a very difficult terrain, and gradients as steep as 1 in 37, sharp curves of 10 degrees or more, and long tunnels are frequent. Accordingly, all stock has to be intensively examined over a pit line at Lumding as well as Badarpur before dispatch. Since heavy incidence of damage would inevitably occur after pit-line examination the re-sorting of the examined load naturally took a heavy toll of the limited sorting capacity of the yards. The remedy was found by repairing the stock on the pit line itself after the necessary reorganization of the yard working.

It is to be noted that every significant increase to input produced one or more fresh bottlenecks. Thus, when in December 1965 diesel availability further improved after a second pair of passenger trains was amalgamated, a new bottleneck arose at Lumding itself. It was now found that the yard did not have a sufficient number of holding lines for the further increase of input that occurred in January 1966. By this time the Hill Section clearances out of Lumding had increased from 3,000 in November 1965 to 3,720 in January 1966 – almost double the corresponding month of 1965. The solution was found by giving the yard two fresh steam engines coupled tender to tender. This pair of coupled engines was used to shuttle every train formed in the yard to one or another of the crossing loops at two of the adjacent stations on both the *up* and *down* sides of the yard. The coupled engines enabled the trains to

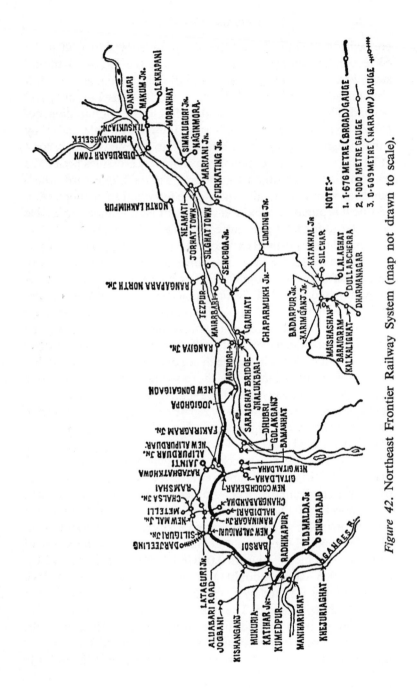

*Figure 42.* Northeast Frontier Railway System (map not drawn to scale).

be shuttled both ways as required without having to turn the engine. The unit worked as a departure switch engine, with the loop lines of these stations as a sort of substitute departure yard, albeit dispersed in space.

In brief, the first bottleneck – lack of adequate locomotive power to move the increased traffic – was overcome by coupling first one pair of passenger trains in September 1965 and another pair in December 1965, and running each pair on a single path instead of two. As the increased input into the various yards made possible by better diesel usage showed specific bottlenecks, special field studies were made to overcome them. In this way Northeast Frontier Railway was able to increase steadily its mobility sufficiently to meet freely for the first time all demands of freight traffic. All quotas and limitations imposed on receipt of traffic by the railway could thus be removed. The various dividends of the operations-research exercise, as shown by the greatly improved indices of mobility as well as productivity during the seven months from September 1965 to March 1966, are recorded in Table 45, below.

Spectacular as the operational gains were, the financial gains were even more remarkable. Since the freight earnings are ultimately due to the larger volume of freight traffic carried as a result of increased capacity generated thereby, it is necessary to evaluate the increase in traffic carried as a result of the operations-research exercise. The simplest unit of traffic carried is, of course, the tonne-kilometer. Table 46 gives the tonne-kilometers carried on the meter-gauge (M.G.) portion of the Northeast Frontier Railway.

It will be observed that of the total increase of 222 millions in tonne-kilometers in the year 1965–6 over 1964–5, 203 million accrued during the seven months from September 1965 to March 1966 after the initiation of the operations-research exercise, as against only 19 millions during the first five months, April to August 1965, prior to its initiation. Thus, over 91 per cent of the year's increased tonne-kilometers accrued in the latter seven months of the year, as against only about 9 per cent during the first five months.

The phenomenal increase in meter-gauge tonne-kilometers was also crucial in sparking a corresponding increase on the broad-gauge (B.G.) portion of the Northeast Frontier Railway. It may be

*Table 45*

| | 1965 | | | | | 1966 | | |
|---|---|---|---|---|---|---|---|---|
| | Aug. | Sept. | Oct. | Nov. | Dec. | Jan. | Feb. | Mar. |

### Indices of Mobility

| | | | | | | | | |
|---|---|---|---|---|---|---|---|---|
| Diesel-kilometers per engine-day in use (all services) | 207 | 229 | 241 | 246 | 265 | 272 | 280 | 278 |
| Car-kilometers per car-day on line | 40·3 | 42·5 | 43·5 | 42·9 | 43·5 | 45·5 | 48·4 | 48·1 |
| Speeds of through freight trains | 13·0 | 13·8 | 14·8 | 14·7 | 15·1 | 15·0 | 15·9 | 15·8 |
| Speeds of all freight trains | 10·7 | 11·4 | 11·7 | 11·7 | 12·0 | 11·9 | 12·3 | 12·4 |

### Indices of Productivity

| | | | | | | | | |
|---|---|---|---|---|---|---|---|---|
| Net tonne-kilometers per engine-hour | 2151 | 2224 | 2323 | 2408 | 2439 | 2237 | 2482 | 2414 |
| Net tonne-kilometers per car-day effective | 355 | 388 | 396 | 430 | 416 | 398 | 440 | 430 |
| Percentage of loaded car-kilometers to total | 72 | 75 | 84 | 80 | 78 | 71 | 72 | 71 |
| Total input into Assam east of Siliguri plus transhipment at New Bongaigaon (in cars) | 460 | 537 | 500 | 605 | 594 | 532* | 559 | 605 |

*The drop in the January input was due to reduced input by the neighbouring North Eastern Railway into Northeast Frontier Railway by 100 meter-gauge cars a day because the former had to run a large number of additional special passenger trains on the occasion of Kumbh Mela, a large religious festival that occurs once in twelve years and attracts millions of pilgrims from all over the country. This feature had an effect during part of February as well.

*Table 46.* Meter-gauge tonne-kilometers (in millions).

| Month | 1964–5 | 1965–6 | Increase/Decrease |
|---|---|---|---|
| April | 233 | 227 | −6 |
| May | 240 | 241 | +1 |
| June | 227 | 218 | −9 |
| July | 202 | 224 | +22 |
| August | 220 | 231 | +11 |
| | | | Total    +19 |
| September | 212 | 244 | +32 |
| October | 222 | 247 | +25 |
| November | 212 | 254 | +42 |
| December | 229 | 254 | +25 |
| January | 211 | 244 | +33 |
| February | 206 | 233 | +27 |
| March | 242 | 261 | +19 |
| | | | +203 |
| | | | Grand total   +222 |

mentioned that the broad-gauge system is of recent origin and still has plenty of spare capacity. But as almost all the increased traffic moving over it in 1965–6 was intended to meter-gauge destinations after transhipment at New Bongaigaon and New Jalpaiguri, the potential capacity available on the broad gauge could hardly have been actualized without developing the additional capacity on the meter-gauge system of the railway. Consequently, the operations-research exercise, though confined only to the meter-gauge system, was crucial in actualizing the broad-gauge potential as well. All in all, the total increase in the tonne-kilometers on the railway as a whole was as shown in Table 47.

*Table 47.* Total tonne-kilometers (in millions).

| | 1964–5 | 1965–6 | Increase | Per Cent Increase |
|---|---|---|---|---|
| Apr.–Aug. | 1278 | 1358 | 80 | 6·28 |
| Sept.–Mar. | 1785 | 2352 | 567 | 31·8 |
| Total | 3063 | 3710 | 647 | 21·1 |

It will be observed that the rate of increase in terms of *additional* tonne-kilometers rose from 6·28 per cent to 31·8 per cent, an increase by a factor of five, as a result of the operations-research exercise.

One consequence was a very welcome increase in freight earnings from 20 million dollars to 27 million dollars, that is, by about 33 per cent. If the total increase of 7 million dollars in freight earnings is distributed in the ratio of additional tonne-kilometers accruing in these two periods, namely 80 : 567 or 1 : 7, we find that increase in freight earnings directly attributable to the operations-research exercise is of the order of $(7 \times 7)/8 = 6$ million dollars during the seven-month period of its operation from September 1965 to March 1966. Given full scope for the year 1966–7 as a whole the operations-research exercise should enable the Northeast Frontier Railway to increase its freight earnings by about 10 million dollars per annum.

In short, even for the brief space of seven months the operations-research exercise had been in operation, it enabled the Northeast Frontier Railway to increase its freight earnings sufficiently to reduce its operating ratio (expenditure per 100 dollars earned) from 118 in the year 1964–5 to 105 in 1965–6. During the year 1966–7, with a full year's operation, it should enable Northeast Frontier Railway to break even if not to show a small profit.

# CHAPTER 11

# Operations Research and the Language Question

IT may at first sight seem odd to couple two such apparently un-related entities as language and operations research as has been done in the title of this chapter. This coupling becomes meaningful, however, when we recall that the sole repository of language or human speech is the living brain of man. In fact, the two are so intimately related that some neurophysiologists now believe that human speech may well be a window through which they can observe cerebral life. Now, as it happens, both the over-all cerebral capacity of the living brain, regarded as a neurophysiological machine, as well as the fraction absorbed in learning a language, may be calculated by resort to algebra. Since operations research mistrusts verbal arguments and substitutes algebraic reasoning for verbal wranglings, it follows that a computation of this sort, even of the crudest kind, should provide some scientific basis for deciding the language question.

Consider, to begin with, the capacity of the human brain. To compute it we must first devise a unit for measuring cerebral power analogous to the unit (horse-power) for measuring the muscle power of machines, whether these be biological like the mule or mechanical like the motor car. Fortunately we do not have to look far to find one, thanks to the efforts of communications engineers and cyberneticians. It is simply the *binary digit* or 'bit' for short, invented by them to measure the 'information' content of any given text, message, or instruction. If the text is transmitted by telegraph via the morse code the number of dashes and dots in the code translation is the number of bits of information contained therein. It is in terms of bits of information that can be stored in the memory of the computer or the human brain that their capacity is usually measured. Thus, while the storage capacity of some of the largest computers of today is of the order of a few million bits ($10^6$ or $10^7$), that of the human brain has been estimated to be a billion times greater, that is ($10^{15}$) bits.

Unfortunately, we cannot use all this colossal cerebral power of ours in *any* way we like. For only a tiny fraction thereof is free in the sense that it is not tied to performing some specific biological function such as maintaining blood sugar, temperature, or pressure at a particular level or regulating breathing rate or heart beat and the like. The fact is that there is a fundamental difference between living or natural automata such as animals and artificial automata such as computers. For while no computer is ever made merely to maintain itself – its primary function being to duplicate some special human skills like counting, computing, or sorting – the sole purpose of the animal machine (that is, life) is, apart from reproduction, simply to keep on living, notwithstanding what some people may have to say about the 'higher' aims of human life. It is therefore no wonder that almost the whole of our cerebral power is 'bound' to the performance of myriad physiological functions of the body, leaving only an infinitesimal residue for cultural purposes, of which speaking a language is only one. Indeed, this is obvious from even a superficial comparison of the cerebral cortex of *homo sapiens* with that of other animals, say, the chimpanzee. Although the cerebral power of the latter is of the order of $10^{14}$ bits – 100,000,000 times that of the largest computer – the chimpanzee has no *free* cerebral power to enable it to learn a language. All of its cerebral power is used up in merely keeping the animal on the go.

The question relevant to our present theme, then, is: what fraction of the total cerebral power of the human brain is available for the pursuit of cultural aims of human life such as speaking languages, practising medicine, playing politics, advancing technology, defending the nation, or learning science? We do not yet know the answer, but some informed guesses have been made by various authorities. The most plausible one seems to be that of A. M. Turing, the celebrated English logician. Delving deeply into the mystery of the 'thinking' process and its machine simulation he estimated that of the total storage capacity of $10^{15}$ bits available in the human brain barely one millionth, that is, $10^9$ bits, might be *free* and could be utilized for the practice of culture. The basis of Turing's surmise was the hope that it should be possible to make by the end of the century a computer or thinking machine with the storage capacity of $10^9$ bits. When made, such a machine could be expected to hold its own if pitted against any human genius. That is, it could confront a human prodigy and deceive him into thinking that he was facing another human prodigy. For the total information content of all the volumes of the *Encyclopaedia Britannica* is about a billion bits, so that a machine with ready access to that much information could reasonably be expected to outmatch any human prodigy in a face-to-face confrontation. Such a confrontation could, for example, begin with the human interlocutor asking the machine to write a sonnet. The machine would write one. Having written it, the interlocutor could put the machine to a *viva voce* test to discover whether it really understood what it was doing or just wrote it parrot-wise without any real 'comprehension'. Turing suggested that it could in fact sustain impromptu a dialogue of the kind quoted below:

INTERROGATOR: In the first line of your sonnet which reads 'Shall I compare thee to a summer's day', would not a 'spring day' do as well or better?

WITNESS: It wouldn't scan.

INTERROGATOR: How about a 'winter's day'? That would scan all right.

WITNESS: Yes, but nobody wants to be compared to a winter's day.

INTERROGATOR: Would you say Mr Pickwick reminded you of Christmas?

WITNESS: In a way.

INTERROGATOR: Yet Christmas is a winter's day and I do not think Mr Pickwick would mind the comparison.

WITNESS: I don't think you are serious. By winter's day one means a typical winter's day, rather than a special one like Christmas.

And so on.

It is true that a Turing machine capable of playing the sort of imitation game outlined above has not yet been made. But this is because modern computer-technology has still not come of age to implement Turing's design. The design itself makes it reasonably certain that the upper limit of 'free' cerebral power in a human prodigy may well be about $10^9$ bits.

However, fixing the upper limit of free cerebral power of the human brain, while necessary, is not sufficient. We must also discover its lower limit, or rather the full range of its variation from one individual to another. For in this respect, as in most others, it takes all kinds to make a world and our language policy cannot afford to consider only prodigies. To overcome this new difficulty we may recall that although individual human beings differ a good deal in every respect the pattern of variation of almost all anthropometric attributes – from height, foot length, or pull strength of the arm to cerebral power of the brain – is the same. It conforms to the so-called 'normal' or gaussian law. If so, and if further the average cerebral power is assumed to be a proportion ($p$) of the prodigy, a simple reference to the published tables of normal distribution enables us to deduce the lower limit ($x$) of cerebral power so as to include any given frequency or percentage of population. Table 48 shows for a few specimen values of $p = 1/2, 2/5, 1/4$, and $1/5$ the frequency of persons having bit power exceeding $x$ millions, under the assumption that an average person has a proportion ($p$) of the cerebral capacity of the prodigy.

*Table 48*

| Frequency of persons having free cerebral power exceeding $x$ million bits | Number ($x$) of bits in millions for various values of $p$ | | | |
|---|---|---|---|---|
| | $p = 1/2$ | $p = 2/5$ | $p = 1/4$ | $p = 1/5$ |
| 50 per cent | 500 | 400 | 250 | 200 |
| 60 per cent | 458 | 350 | 187 | 133 |
| 69 per cent | 417 | 300 | 125 | 65 |

Having computed the lower limits of free cerebral power available to 50, 60, 69 (or any other pre-assigned) percentage of population it is time to compute the bit power absorbed in learning a language. This requires the evaluation of the information content per letter of its alphabet, in case of a written language, or per phoneme, the basic unit of the phonetic alphabet, in case of its spoken version. For the sake of definiteness as well as simplicity, I will confine myself here to the written version of the English language. It has 26 letters in its alphabet. But if we include the punctuation marks, capital and lower cases, 10 numerical digits, as well as various ways adopted in printing and handwriting, the number of basic elements or symbols in its repertoire would easily exceed 64. Considering that a 2-letter alphabet such as the dash and dot of morse code gives one bit of information per symbol, one would expect over 6 bits of information per letter in the case of a language with more than 64 basic symbols. The reason is this: because $2^6 = 64$ we will require permutations of 6 such binary symbols to code all the 64 letters of our alphabet. Accordingly each letter has 6 times the information content of the binary symbols.

I am aware that the actual information-content per letter of the English alphabet is much less because of its built-in redundancy (redundancy is simply spare or surplus information already absorbed by the human mind before any text is presented to it). For our present purpose we need the information-content per letter without making any allowance for redundancy. The reason is that what we require is the total cerebral power absorbed in someone's learning a language if he knows nothing about its rules and regularities of structure, prior knowledge of which reduces the information-content per letter. Consequently, the information that a man is able to provide by himself *after* he has learned the language – which is what redundancy really is – must *not* be taken into account.

Taking the average content of information per letter as 6 the information content of a page of printed text of 400 words each on the average of 4 letters will be $6 \times 4 \times 400 = 9,600$ bits. A book of 250 pages will thus have an information content of about 2·4 million bits. I have no idea how many books of information about its vocabulary, grammar, orthography, and the like, will suffice to give one a working knowledge of English. But even if it is as low as four books, the requirement per mode of learning comes to about 10 million bits. But there are four modes of learning: reading, writing, speaking, and hearing. Each one of them will absorb its own bit equivalent of cerebral power. For many people some modes of learning are more difficult than others. Consequently, the requirement of bit power for one or more of these modes will have to be weighted by a factor exceeding one. But even if we neglect the weighting and treat them all on a par, the requirement for all four modes of learning comes to 40 million bits. Working knowledge of one or two additional languages would consume, not twice or thrice as much, but much more. For in neurophysiology as in other walks of life, the rule is first-come-first-served. The latecomers have a much harder time of it. That is why the first language one learns – one's own mother tongue – consumes the least cerebral power. It requires, as we have seen, some 40 million bits. But the languages learned later will need much greater bit power. It therefore follows that a three-language formula would absorb something like 120 to 150 million bits of cerebral power, perhaps considerably more.

Now it is not likely that an average person would rank in respect of cerebral power much higher than one-quarter of a prodigy. If so, assuming $p = \frac{1}{4}$, three languages will consume all the available cerebral power even if we tried to cover only 69 per cent of the population. We could do somewhat better if we applied the three-language formula to only 50 to 60 per cent of the population. For then we would consume between 60 to 80 per cent of the available cerebral power. In whatever way we may choose to restrict the scope of the three-language formula the tax on cerebral power would appear to be quite severe even if we rate a prodigy as no more than four times as clever as the average man.

I am fully aware of the weak links in the chain of argument leading to the above conclusion. To mention only one, values have been assigned to the various parameters either by guessing or on a factual basis that is admittedly flimsy. But I am not one to be deterred from beginning an investigation until all the unknowns are determined. If one were to wait for a rigorous evaluation of all the parameters one needs one would wait forever. This is where algebra stands us in such good stead. It is not merely that algebra mistrusts verbal arguments and therefore substitutes a chain of logical-*cum*-quantitative reasoning that cannot be twisted, as verbal arguments often can be, to serve any interest. But more importantly, the upshot of algebraic reasoning is often insensitive to the inevitable uncertainty in the estimates of parameters it has to employ. It is able to do so because, while the possible range of variations of parameters is theoretically infinite, the admissible range of actions open to one is often very restricted. As a result, a given parameter within any plausible range of variation leads in most cases to the same conclusion. A case in point is the value of $p$.

As a reference to Table 48 will show, for all values of $p$ not exceeding 2/5, the cerebral tax entailed by a three-language formula confined only to the upper 50 per cent of the population will not be less than 38 per cent of the total cerebral capacity.

In sum, an algebraic analysis of the language problem has several merits. Being algebraic, it imposes an exactness lacking in the verbal postulates made in the usual discussions of the question. For the same reason it is obliged to base itself on ideas which clarify the issues, rather than on interests which only befog them. Such imperviousness to the interest of any particular language – English, Hindi, Punjabi or any other – saves the discussion from generating emotional heat otherwise inevitable in such discussions. But alas, there is one fatal drawback. The algebraic analysis shows no simple way out of the stern dilemmas facing us. At best, it may merely help us make a bad compromise in place of a much worse one that would otherwise result. At worst, it may be dismissed as telling us no more than what we already know and only trying to prove in a roundabout way what is in any case obvious. Nevertheless, trying to prove the obvious is a favourite pastime of mathematicians. But it is a pastime not wholly useless. For in pursuing it one discovers sometimes that the 'obvious' is not even true, as actually happened when mathematicians failed to prove the parallel postulate till then regarded as self-evident. Alternatively, one may actually succeed in proving it, as in Zermelo's beautiful proof of the 'obvious' proposition that in any chess game White will either win, lose, or draw with Black. In either case, a new insight is gained.

If the above exposé of the 'obvious' limitations of the human brain as a neurophysiological machine proves to be also an exposure of the inexorable incompatibilities in the various goals we wish to pursue, it may enable us to make a choice balanced in the light of cold reason rather than one made in the heat of passion. Thus, in pursuit of three distinct goals, namely,

(i) having Hindi as our national language

(ii) retaining English as our national 'window' on world science and technology

(iii) requiring the Hindi-speaking people to learn one regional language to secure parity between the Hindi and non-Hindi speaking candidates in competitive examinations

if the people of India adopt a three-language formula they must appreciate all the consequences thereof. To cite one, enforcement of a three-language formula in place of the virtual two-language formula hitherto in effect for the *élite* would mean that in trying to handicap equally both the Hindi and non-Hindi-speaking people the people of India cannot escape handicapping themselves against the world. A recent study of the Irish experience of bilingualism by John Macnamara, an educational psychologist, should be an object lesson. He claims that bilingualism in Ireland is at least in part responsible for the fact that a child leaving an Irish primary school is $37\frac{1}{2}$ months behind an English child of the same age in ability to use and understand the English language – the native tongue of both. With a three-language formula retardation of an Indian child would be much worse. And yet, so great is the appeal of a national language for a newly independent nation that independence without one's own language is not considered real in India or Ireland alike. This is one instance of a hidden incompatibility in the complex of our national goals that today's leaders must squarely face.

# *Epilogue*

FROM the account given in this book it will be obvious that operations research is no routine application of prefabricated techniques such as linear programming and queueing theory. It is rather a free creation of the manager as he attempts to solve his own complex of problems. In pursuit of this goal he is guided by the following six heuristic principles:

(i) Operations research is eclectic. That is, it is an omnibus interdisciplinary activity that does not hesitate to make any branch of science carry grist to its own mill.

(ii) Operations research believes that while ideas illumine, interests only befog, thereby implementing Mills's maxim, 'One man with ideas counts as much as a hundred who have merely interests.'

(iii) Operations research mistrusts verbal arguments and therefore substitutes algebraic reasoning for verbal wrangling.

(iv) Operations research makes the structure of its algebraic reasoning robust in the face of an inevitable uncertainty in the values of the unknown parameters it has to employ. It is able to do so for the reason that, while the possible range of variation of parameters is theoretically infinite, the possible range of actions available is almost always very restricted. As a result, given parameters within any plausible range of variation often lead to the same result.

(v) Operations research often yields rather bad answers but improves on existing worse ones.

(vi) Operations research unmasks hidden incompatibilities in the complex of organizational goals in order to enable management to decide which of the incompatible goals should be chosen.

Since a mere enumeration of operations-research principles in the abstract might seem like preaching Christianity without showing a single living Christian, it is appropriate to illustrate these principles by concrete examples. Thus one may cite the case of an

207

operations-research worker mentioned by R. Ackoff who solved an escalator problem by recourse to his knowledge of human psychology. The director of a large office was plagued with complaints of inadequate escalator service. After examining various alternatives the operations-research expert suggested installing large mirrors in the lobby; while people were waiting they could overcome their boredom by looking at themselves in the glass. To take another instance, one might consider the bridging problem dealt with in the Appendix. Here, the question of selecting the site of a major railway bridge over the Ganges was settled by recourse to algebra, even though the issue had originally excited a good deal of emotion. The example shows not only the power of algebra to solve a rather emotional issue but also the strength of its underlying (algebraic) reasoning in spite of the uncertainty of some of the parameters of traffic pattern likely to emerge in the future. But the single case that illustrates all the six principles listed above is that of operations research on the language question discussed in Chapter 11. Here, operations research is eclectic, leaning as it does on a wide gamut of disciplines from information theory to neurophysiology. It is indifferent to the interests of any particular language – English, Hindi, Punjabi or any other. It is algebraic. Its reasoning is strong as the result is not materially affected by various assumptions made to give algebra a foothold. It gives no facile solution to the severe dilemmas facing the manager – other than to help supply a bad compromise in place of a much worse one that would otherwise result. Finally, it unmasks the incompatibilities in various goals, forcing the administration to face such incompatibilities squarely. Any successful use of operations research in solving management problems requires the application of some or all of these principles.

# The Bridging Problem

ONE of the problems facing the Indian Railways soon after independence was the location of a major rail-*cum*-road bridge on the river Ganges in Bengal or Bihar. Four alternative sites – Patna and Mokameh in Bihar and Sakrigali Ghat and Farakka in Bengal – were suggested. As usual each alternative had its partisans with a vested interest of their own, befogging all debate on the relative merits of the different sites. The problem was solved by substituting algebraic reasoning for verbal wrangling. It is true that statistical data to sustain the algebraization was lacking. Nevertheless, as will be apparent later, the conclusions of the algebraic reasoning devised were not materially affected by the inevitable uncertainty in the values of the unknown parameters that had to be employed. This is often possible. For while the range of variation of parameters is theoretically infinite, the possible range of actions or decisions available is almost always very restricted. As a consequence a given parameter within any plausible range of variation often leads to the same result. In the case under review, for example, corresponding to an infinite number of possible realignments of the flow of current traffic, there were available only four choices or decisions, namely, the four alternative sites already enumerated. Accordingly it became possible to assess quantitatively the relative merits of the four sites despite all the uncertainties in the pattern of traffic flow likely to materialize as a result of various factors at play. But to make this analysis of relative merits intelligible it is necessary to recall a few features of the river Ganges and the region through which it flows.

The river Ganges with a total drainage area of 392,000 square miles rises in the Gangotri Glacier in the Himalayan Range at lat. 30°50'N. long. 79°7'E., and after flowing south and subsequently east falls in the Bay of Bengal after a journey of about 1,600 miles along its winding length. While no fewer than six broad-gauge railway bridges span the river Ganges during the first half of its length up to Banaras, there is no bridge along its 800-mile-long course from Banaras to the Bay of Bengal. To be precise, there is just one, namely, the Hardinge Bridge at Sara some 300 miles north of Calcutta, but since Partition of the country this bridge is no longer in the territory of the Indian Union, having gone under the jurisdiction of Pakistan. For want of a rail bridge over the Ganges below Banaras, communications between the two parts of the country into which it is divided by the Ganges have been gravely hampered. Even prior to Partition, the only means of interchange of traffic between the broad-gauge railway system south of the river Ganges and the meter-gauge railway system north thereof was by means of ferries at Patna, Mokameh Ghat, Monghyr, Bhagalpur and Sakrigali Ghat. Of these the most important was Mokameh Ghat (about 250 miles downstream from Banaras) as it was the only point between Banaras and Sara where freight traffic could be crossed over in railway cars from one bank to the other bank of the Ganges. Since Partition its importance has grown all the more since it is now the only point between Banaras and Calcutta in the Indian Union where rail traffic can be crossed in full cars from one bank to the other. It is thus now, more than ever before, the main link between the two parts of the extensive stretch of the country between Banaras and Calcutta of which the river Ganges is the dividing line.

Mokameh Ghat on the south bank of the Ganges is served by the East Indian (EI) Railway and Semaria Ghat on the opposite bank is served by the Oudh Tirhut (OT) Railway. Meter-gauge cars are loaded on barges at Semaria Ghat and the barges are ferried by steamers to the opposite bank. Transhipment of meter-gauge cars to broad-gauge cars and vice versa is performed at Mokameh Ghat.

On account of the location of the car ferry at Mokameh Ghat almost the entire bulk of freight traffic interchanged between the two parts of the country into which the river Ganges below Banaras divides this territory has been concentrated at Mokameh Ghat. It is true that since Partition traffic at other ferry stations such as Bhagalpur, Sakrigali Ghat (which, prior to Partition, were of minor importance) has increased considerably.

This is due to the fact that traffic between Assam and North Bengal towards the north of Ganges on the one hand and the Calcutta area and South Bihar towards the south of the Ganges on the other has now to pass through either of these points in order to follow a route which remains within the limits of the Indian Union all the way. Nevertheless, in spite of the great increase in traffic passing through these two points (Bhagalpur and Sakrigali Ghat), Mokameh Ghat still carries by far the great bulk of freight traffic interchanged between the two regions on account of the fact that Mokameh Ghat alone of the three points has a car ferry.

If the bridge were built at any of the four proposed sites it would be reasonable to assume that almost the entire bulk of traffic at present passing through Mokameh Ghat plus the overflow passing through Bhagalpur and Sakrigali Ghat would pass over the bridge. We shall compare the relative merits of the proposed sites on the basis of this assumption.

Since four alternative sites – Patna, Mokameh, Sakrigali Ghat, and Farraka – have been proposed, it would mean six comparisons, as two sites out of four can be selected and compared two at a time in six different ways. But as Farraka is almost next door to Sakrigali Ghat, the relative merits of Farraka versus Patna and Farraka versus Mokameh from the traffic point of view can be judged from a similar comparison between Patna and Sakrigali Ghat, and Mokameh Ghat and Sakrigali Ghat, respectively. We shall, therefore, compare the relative merits of the first three of the proposed sites and judge that of the fourth by treating it as of the same merit as Sakrigali Ghat on account of the close geographical proximity of the two sites.

We shall thus make the following three comparisons:

(*a*) Mokameh versus Patna
(*b*) Mokameh versus Sakrigali Ghat
(*c*) Patna versus Sakrigali Ghat

### (*a*) COMPARISON BETWEEN MOKAMEH GHAT AND PATNA ROUTES

Which of the two alternative sites under consideration, namely, Mokameh Ghat and Patna, is better from the traffic point of view? The answer, of course, depends largely on the comparison of the average leads by the two routes of traffic likely to cross the river Ganges after the construction of the bridge. The route which gives the shorter lead will naturally be preferable. It is, therefore, necessary to compute what increase or decrease in average lead is likely to occur if all traffic at present crossing the Ganges by car ferry at Mokameh Ghat as well as that transhipped at other less important transhipment points, namely, Bhagalpur and Sakrigali Ghat, is diverted via Patna. It is easy to see in a general qualitative way the effect on average lead of diverting goods traffic from via Mokameh Ghat route to via Patna route. There are only four directions on the O T Railway from and to which traffic flows (see map on page 216). They are:

(i) from Sonepore to Chupra and stations north and west of Chupra

(ii) from Muzaffarpur to Bagaha and stations on Narkatiaganj Loop

(iii) from Bachhwara to Darbhanga and beyond

(iv) from Barauni to Khagaria and stations north and east of Khagaria.

Now the distance of any station in the first group to any station between Howrah and Kiul (including Sahibganj Loop and branches) on the Main Line of the East Indian Railway is the same by either route. But the corresponding distances of all stations in the other groups via Patna exceed those via Mokameh Ghat. Hence, in the case of traffic moving either from stations between Howrah and Kiul to the O T Railway or in the reverse direction the average lead must increase by diverting the traffic to the via Patna route. Now the bulk of loco coal – over 90 per cent of the total – originates from the Raniganj Coalfields, that is, stations between Howrah and Kiul, and the bulk of freight traffic from the O T Railway – again over 90 per cent – moves to stations between Howrah and Kiul. It therefore follows that the average lead per ton for loco coal from the East Indian to the O T Railway and freight traffic from the O T to the EI Railway must increase by diverting this traffic to the via Patna route. To compute the exact lead difference we must proceed on rather different lines.

Strictly speaking, in order to calculate the lead difference between the via Patna and via Mokameh Ghat routes we should consider the volume of traffic moving between every possible pair of stations on the EI and OT Railway systems, calculate the difference in distance between them by the two routes under consideration, and then multiply this lead difference (with its appropriate sign) by the tonnage moving between the two stations. We thus obtain the increase (or decrease) in ton-miles by diverting traffic between these two stations to the via Patna route. If all the increases (or decreases) thus obtained in respect of every possible pair of stations are added up we obtain the total increase (or decrease) in ton-miles by diverting the entire traffic via Patna. Dividing this aggregate by the total tonnage of traffic we obtain the average increase (or decrease) in lead per ton.

It is, however, quite impossible to follow this method, as the number of possible pairs of stations to be considered would run to several hundred thousand. It is far easier to group all stations for which the lead difference by the two routes is identical into one zone and then assess the volume of traffic moving in and out of that zone. Thus, for instance, the lead difference via Patna and via Mokameh Ghat for all stations between Howrah and Kiul on the East Indian Railway is the same, viz. +57 miles, and they can all be grouped in one zone. In fact, all the stations on the East Indian Railway can be grouped in seven zones of identical lead difference as shown in Table 49.*

*Table 49.* Zones of constant lead difference on the East Indian Railway.

| | Lead difference + when via Patna route is longer |
|---|---|
| *Zone 1* | |
| (i) From Howrah to Kiul via Main Line and via Barharwa–Bandel Branch and via Sahibganj Loop including branches | |
| (ii) Luckeesarai to Dumra on Main Line | +57 miles |
| (iii) Kulti to Barakar on Grand Chord | |
| (iv) Sirari to Warisaliganj on South Bihar Branch | |

*These zones include nearly all the stations of the EI Railway system except a few which do not fall in any of the zones, but traffic to and from these stations is insignificant and may be safely ignored.

### Zone 2
(i)  Dhanbad–Pathardihi
(ii) Dhanbad–Kusunda–Katrasgarh  } +6 miles

### Zone 3
Gomoh to Khalari on Central Indian Coalfield
Section                                      −30 miles

### Zone 4
Mohuamilan to Ankorha                        −41 miles

### Zone 5
Nimiaghat to Manpur                          −34 miles

### Zone 6
Gaya to Durgauti                             −42 miles

### Zone 7
(i)   All stations above Moghal Sarai (inclusive)
(ii)  Stations between Moghal Sarai and Dinapore
      and Moghal Sarai to Karmnasa            } −58 miles
(iii) Stations between Simra and Bela on Patna–Gaya
      Branch

Similarly, all stations on the OT Railway can be divided into four zones of constant lead difference as noted in Table 50.*

*Table 50.* Zones of constant lead difference on the OT Railway.

|  | Lead difference + when via Patna route is longer |
|---|---|
| **Zone 1**<br>From Sonepore to Chupra and all stations North and West of Chupra including stations between Captainganj and Bagaha (exclusive) | −57 miles |

*A few stations which do not fall into any of the four zones have been ignored as traffic from and to these stations is insignificant.

## Appendix: The Bridging Problem

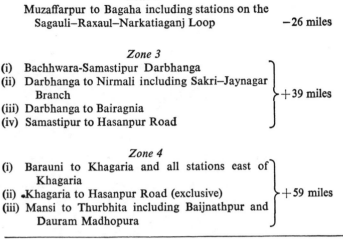

### Zone 2
Muzaffarpur to Bagaha including stations on the
Sagauli–Raxaul–Narkatiaganj Loop      −26 miles

### Zone 3
(i) Bachhwara-Samastipur Darbhanga
(ii) Darbhanga to Nirmali including Sakri–Jaynagar
    Branch
(iii) Darbhanga to Bairagnia
(iv) Samastipur to Hasanpur Road
              +39 miles

### Zone 4
(i) Barauni to Khagaria and all stations east of
    Khagaria
(ii) .Khagaria to Hasanpur Road (exclusive)
(iii) Mansi to Thurbhita including Baijnathpur and
     Dauram Madhopura
              +59 miles

Having divided the stations on the East Indian and the Oudh Tirhut Railway systems into appropriate zones of constant lead difference, it now remains to estimate the volume of traffic moving in and out of each zone.

For the purpose of estimating the volume of traffic moving in and out of each zone it would be best to divide the traffic into three categories:

(i) Public coal, that is to say, coal booked on public account for public uses.

(ii) Loco coal, that is, coal booked on account of railways for use on locomotives, workshops, pumping stations, and so on.

(iii) All other freight traffic.

### Coal Traffic

PUBLIC COAL. Coal traffic originates only from coalfield stations of the East Indian Railway which are in Zones 1, 2, and 3 of that railway. From an examination of the statistics of dispatches of public coal from coalfield stations to via Mokameh Ghat, Bhagalpur, and Sakrigali Ghat during the two financial years 1949–50 and 1950–51 it is ascertained that the following per-

215

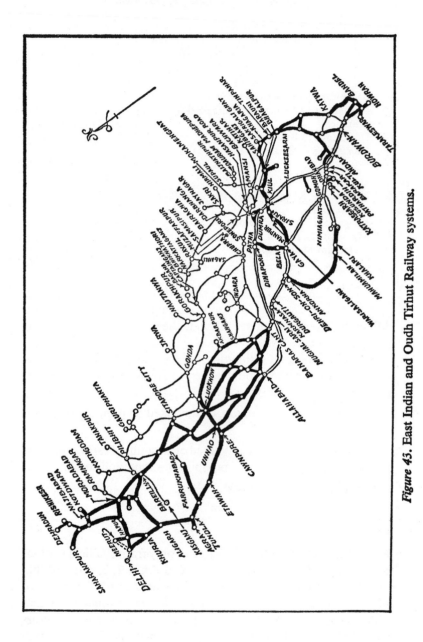

*Figure 43.* East Indian and Oudh Tirhut Railway systems.

centages of the total public coal traffic originated from coalfield stations in Zones 1, 2, and 3.

| Zone 1 | Zone 2 | Zone 3 |
|--------|--------|--------|
| 87·3%  | 12·2%  | 0·5%   |

If the total tonnage of public coal dispatched from the coalfield stations be taken as $T$ tons, its distribution from the three zones will be

| | |
|---|---|
| From stations in Zone 1 | 0·873 $T$ tons |
| From stations in Zone 2 | 0·122 $T$ tons |
| From stations in Zone 3 | 0·005 $T$ tons |

Now by diverting coal from stations in Zone 1 to the via Patna route an additional haulage of 57 miles is incurred. Similarly, by diverting the tonnage from stations in Zone 2 an additional haulage of 6 miles is involved, and by diverting the tonnage from stations in Zone 3 there is a reduction in haulage by 30 miles. Thus the total additional haulage in ton-miles involved on the East Indian Railway by diverting public coal traffic from the via Mokameh Ghat to the via Patna route will be

$$0·873\ T\,(57) + 0·122\ T\,(6) + (0·005)\ T\,(-30)\ \text{ton-miles}$$
$$= 50·343\ T\ \text{ton-miles.}$$

In other words, the proposed diversion would involve the East Indian Railway in an additional haulage of 50·3 miles for every ton of public coal. It would be observed that this increase in average lead of traffic is independent of the quantum of traffic as long as its zonal distribution remains unchanged. With the present location of the coalfields it is unlikely that these proportions would change appreciably for a long time to come.

We have now to calculate the average lead difference on the Oudh Tirhut Railway. For this purpose we require the proportions of traffic moving into the four zones of constant lead difference into which Oudh Tirhut Railway has been divided. The proportions of traffic moving into the four zones of Oudh Tirhut Railway were fairly steady during the pre-war and pre-Partition years. Thus, based on statistics of traffic during the ten years ending 1943–4, these proportions were

| Zone 1 | Zone 2 | Zone 3 | Zone 4 |
|--------|--------|--------|--------|
| 57·4%  | 18·6%  | 21·6%  | 2·4%   |

But later, as a result of the Japanese entry in the Second World War in 1942, these proportions began to change. After the war the Partition of the country had a still greater disturbing effect on these proportions. Thus the actual proportions of public coal traffic moving into the four zones during the year 1948–9, the latest year for which figures are available, are

| Zone 1 | Zone 2 | Zone 3 | Zone 4 |
|--------|--------|--------|--------|
| 66%    | 7%     | 13%    | 14%    |

The most significant change in the proportions is in the proportion of traffic moving into Zone 4, from 2·4 per cent to 14 per cent. This proportion would be greater still if we had worked it out on the basis of later-year figures, as the traffic moving into Zone 4 (which includes North Bengal and Assam stations) is increasing and is likely to increase still further, especially immediately after the bridge is constructed. When, therefore, the traffic stream is known to be in a state of avulsion, it would be hazardous to base our calculation of lead differences on the proportions calculated from 1948–9 figures or for that matter even any later figures. We shall adopt here a method which would reduce to a minimum the effect of this likely change in the existing distribution of traffic.

In order to avoid making arbitrary assumptions let us assume that the volume of public coal traffic moving into the O T Railway is $T$ tons and that which has to move into North Bengal and Assam via Katihar because of the effect of Partition is $t$ tons. If formerly the proportions of traffic moving into the four zones were $p, q, r, s$, respectively, then the volume of O T Railway traffic moving into the four zones would be

| Zone 1 | Zone 2 | Zone 3 | Zone 4 |
|--------|--------|--------|--------|
| $pT$   | $qT$   | $rT$   | $sT$   |

If now $t$ tons of Assam and North Bengal traffic also move in

Zone 4, the total quantity $T+t$ tons will be distributed into the four zones:

| *Zone 1* | *Zone 2* | *Zone 3* | *Zone 4* |
|----------|----------|----------|----------|
| $pT$ | $qT$ | $rT$ | $sT+t$ |

Hence the new proportions moving into the four zones will be

$$\frac{T}{T+t}p, \frac{T}{T+t}q, \frac{T}{T+t}r, \frac{T}{T+t}s + \frac{t}{T+t}.$$

We can thus derive the actual proportions likely to arise by applying the correction factor $T/(T+t)$ to the proportions worked out on the basis of the ten years' statistics referred to above. This procedure will be better than calculating the lead differences on the basis of proportions derived from even the latest figures, for the reason that the traffic has not yet found its steady level or the level it is likely to attain with the construction of the bridge. The safest course, therefore, would be to calculate the new proportions by applying the aforementioned corrections to the values of proportions as calculated from the statistics of traffic during a period when it was in a steady state. Hence, adopting the method of lead differences described above, the additional lead via the Patna route on the O T Railway would be on the average:

$$\frac{pT}{T+t}(-57) + \frac{qT}{T+t}(-26) + \frac{rT}{T+t}(39) + \frac{sT+t}{T+t}(59) \text{ miles}$$

$$= \frac{T}{T+t}\{-57p - 26q + 39r + 59s\} + \frac{t}{T+t}(59) \text{ miles}.$$

The expression within the brackets $\{\quad\}$ may be worked out by substituting the aforementioned values of $p, q, r, s$, viz. $p = 0.574$, $q = 0.186$, $r = 0.216$, $s = 0.024$ and is found to be $-27.7$. Hence the additional lead on the O T Railway per ton is

$$-\frac{27.7T}{T+t} + \frac{59t}{T+t} \text{ miles}$$

or,

$$-\frac{27.7}{1+(t/T)} + 59\frac{t/T}{[1+(t/T)]} \text{ miles}.$$

Now if we can estimate the ratio $t/T$ correctly we should be able to calculate the lead difference even though we may not be able to estimate the individual tonnages $t$ and $T$. As far as $t$ is concerned the volume of traffic actually moving via the two routes, viz. Sakrigali Ghat and Bhagalpur after the opening of the Assam Link, was as shown in Table 51.

As the traffic is still increasing it is not advisable to take $t$ as the average of these two years. On the other hand the coal Commissioner of Assam is of the opinion that the demand for public coal is far in excess of what is being met. His forecast of this traffic is 300,000 tons. However, we shall derive our lead difference without any speculative estimate of $t$. We shall assume it to be 53,995$n$ tons, where the factor $n$ may be left undetermined for the time being. As

*Table 51*. Public coal in tons to O T and Assam Railways.

| Year | Via Sakrigali Ghat | Via Bhagalpur | Total |
|---|---|---|---|
| 1949–50 | 13,140 | 262 | 13,402 |
| 1950–51 | 35,453 | 18,542 | 53,995 |

far as $T$ is concerned we may take it as the pre-war average, 253,666 tons. It is true that the wartime average was only 91,142 tons and even during the post-war period it is only 98,474 tons. But this is certainly due to our inability to carry the traffic. There is no reason why we should not reach the pre-war level once the ferry bottleneck is broken as a result of the construction of the bridge. Taking then $t = 53,995n$ tons and $T = 253,666$ tons the lead difference on the O T Railway per ton would be

$$\frac{-27\cdot7}{1+0\cdot2n}+\frac{59(0\cdot2n)}{1+0\cdot2n} = \frac{-27\cdot7+11\cdot8n}{1+0\cdot2n} \tag{i}$$

For $n = 1$, the value of (i) is $-13\cdot2$

$n = 2$, the value of (i) is $-3$

$n = 3$, the value of (i) is $+5$

$n = 4$, the value of (i) is $+11$.

Hence the average net increase in lead per ton on both the railways would be

$$
\begin{aligned}
\text{For } n &= 1, 50{\cdot}34 - 13{\cdot}2 = 37{\cdot}14 = 37 \text{ miles} \\
n &= 2, 50{\cdot}34 - \ 3 \quad = 47{\cdot}3 \ = 47 \text{ miles} \\
n &= 3, 50{\cdot}34 + \ 5 \quad = 55{\cdot}34 = 55 \text{ miles} \\
n &= 4, 50{\cdot}34 + 11 \quad = 61{\cdot}34 = 61 \text{ miles.}
\end{aligned}
$$

We observe that at the very least, so long as Assam traffic remains at as small a level as it reached in 1950–51, Patna site would mean an additional haul of 37 miles on the average to every ton of coal carried over that route. If this traffic doubles or trebles itself, as it will certainly do, it would mean an additional average haul of 47 and 55 miles, respectively, to every ton. Even if we consider the forecast of the Coal Commissioner, viz. $t = 300{,}000$ tons, as inflated, it is not likely to be less than 100,000 to 150,000 tons. This would mean that Patna site would mean an additional haul of at least 47 and possibly 55 miles to every ton of public coal carried over the bridge. We may therefore confidently state that the Patna site would involve an additional haul of 50 miles to every ton of public coal.

LOCO COAL. The calculation can be made on exactly the same lines as in the case of public coal. During the financial years 1949–50 and 1950–51 the following percentage of the total loco coal dispatched via Mokameh Ghat, Sakrigali Ghat, and Bhagalpur originated from stations in Zones 1, 2, and 3 of the East Indian Railway:

| Zone 1 | Zone 2 | Zone 3 |
|--------|--------|--------|
| 98·44% | 0·72%  | 0·84%  |

Proceeding as before, the additional ton-miles involved in hauling this tonnage via Patna would be

$$
0{\cdot}9844 \, T \, (57) + 0{\cdot}0072 \, T \, (6) - 0{\cdot}0084 \, T \, (30) \text{ ton-miles}
$$
$$
= 55{\cdot}9 \, T \text{ ton-miles.}
$$

Thus every ton of loco coal would have to be hauled 55·9 miles longer on the East Indian Railway if this traffic were diverted via Patna.

the demand for loco coal has been met to a much greater extent than that of public because of a higher priority being accorded to movements of loco coal. But a rise in its volume should not be ruled out altogether. Nevertheless any such rise would be comparatively small. We may, however, assume $t$ to be 104,396$n$ tons where $n$ is an undetermined factor. As regards $T$, we may take it to be the post-war average during the two years 1949–50 and 1950–51, when restrictions were comparatively less severe and movement relatively free. (The pre-war average was lower.) $T$ is then 324,520 tons. Our value for the lead difference on the O T Railway is thus:

$$\frac{-24\cdot3}{1+0\cdot32n}+\frac{59(0\cdot32n)}{1+0\cdot32n} = \frac{-24\cdot3+18\cdot88n}{1+0\cdot32n} \qquad \text{(i)}$$

For $n = 1$     value of (i) is $-4$   miles
$n = 1\cdot1$   value of (i) is $-2\cdot6$ miles
$n = 1\cdot25$ value of (i) is $-0\cdot5$ miles
$n = 1\cdot33$ value of (i) is $+0\cdot6$ miles
and $n = 1\cdot5$   value of (i) is $+2\cdot7$ miles.

Hence the net average increase in lead per ton on both the railways would be

For $n = 1$,     $55\cdot9-4$   $= 51\cdot9 = 52$ miles
$n = 1\cdot1$,   $55\cdot9-2\cdot6 = 53\cdot3 = 53$ miles
$n = 1\cdot25$, $55\cdot9-0\cdot5 = 55\cdot4 = 55$ miles
$n = 1\cdot33$, $55\cdot9+0\cdot6 = 56\cdot5 = 56$ miles
$n = 1\cdot5$,   $55\cdot9+2\cdot7 = 58\cdot6 = 59$ miles.

Thus, at the very least every ton of loco coal would have to be hauled 52 miles extra via the Patna route, and if the loco coal for the Assam shows a 25 to 33 per cent rise, as might happen, the extra haulage would be 55 miles.

We may, therefore, conclude that whatever the future quantum of public and loco coal for the Assam Railway the average *increase* in lead on both the railways would most probably be within the following limits:

Public coal     47 and 55 miles
Loco coal      52 and 55 miles.

## Appendix: The Bridging Problem

### Table 54

|  | Lead difference + when via Sakrigali route is longer |
|---|---|
| *Zone 1* Giridih Coalfields Area | +93 miles |
| *Zone 2* Gomoh to Sitarampur on the Grand Chord Tori to Gomoh on Central Indian Coalfield | +32 miles |
| *Zone 3* Ondal area | −10 miles |
| *Zone 4* Asansol area | +22 miles |

Having divided the stations on the East Indian and Oudh Tirhut Railways systems into appropriate zones of constant lead difference it now remains to estimate the volume of traffic moving in and out of each zone.

Since the lead differences for Zone 1 and Zone 2 of Oudh Tirhut Railway are +71 and +84 miles, we shall get a lower limit for the lead difference if we treat both zones as one with a common lead difference of 71 miles. Similarly, an upper limit can be obtained by treating both zones as one with a common lead difference of 84 miles. This would obviate the necessity of ascertaining the proportions of traffic moving in and out of the Zones 1 and 2 of Oudh Tirhut Railway. We may thus treat the meter-gauge railway system north of the Ganges as divided into two zones only, one consisting of all stations west of Katihar and the other stations east thereof. The latter are all Assam Railway stations. If $T$ is the traffic moving to the O T Railway west of Katihar and $t$ to the Assam Railway east of Katihar the additional haulage in ton-miles incurred on the Oudh Tirhut Railway by diverting all traffic via Sakrigali Ghat would lie between

Upper limit $84T - 139t$, and lower limit $71T - 139t$.

225

The limits for the average lead difference per ton would thus be

$$\text{Upper limit } \frac{84T-139t}{T+t} = \frac{84-139(t/T)}{1+(t/T)} \text{ miles}$$

$$\text{Lower limit } \frac{71T-139t}{T+t} = \frac{71-139(t/T)}{1+(t/T)} \text{ miles.}$$

We may now calculate these limits for public and loco coal.

PUBLIC COAL. As before, we take $t = 53{,}995n$ tons and $T = 253{,}666$ tons. Hence $t/T = 0 \cdot 2n$.

The limits for the lead difference on the OT Railway are therefore

$$\text{Upper limit } \frac{84-(139)\,(0 \cdot 2n)}{1+0 \cdot 2n} \text{ miles}$$

$$\text{Lower limit } \frac{71-(139)\,(0 \cdot 2n)}{1+0 \cdot 2n} \text{ miles.}$$

For $n = 1, 2, 3$, these values are

| $n$ | Upper limit | Lower limit |
|---|---|---|
| 1 | 47 | 36 |
| 2 | 20 | 11 |
| 3 | 0 | −8 |

To calculate the average lead difference on the East Indian Railway we observe from dispatches of public coal to via Mokameh, Sakrigali Ghat, and Bhagalpur during the two years 1949–50 and 1950–51 that the following percentages originated from the four zones of the East Indian Railway:

| Zone 1 | Zone 2 | Zone 3 | Zone 4 |
|---|---|---|---|
| 3·2% | 59·3% | 26·7% | 10·8% |

The lead difference would thus be

$$0 \cdot 032(93)+0 \cdot 593(32)-(0 \cdot 267)\,(10)+(0 \cdot 108)\,(22) \text{ miles}$$
$$= 21 \cdot 70 \text{ miles.}$$

The net increase in lead over both the railways by diverting public coal via Sakrigali Ghat would thus be for various values of $n$ as below:

| $n$ | Upper limit | Lower limit |
|---|---|---|
| 1 | $47 + 21 \cdot 7 = 68 \cdot 7 = 69$ | $36 + 21 \cdot 7 = 57 \cdot 7 = 58$ |
| 2 | $20 + 21 \cdot 7 = 41 \cdot 7 = 42$ | $11 + 21 \cdot 7 = 32 \cdot 7 = 33$ |
| 3 | $0 + 21 \cdot 7 = 21 \cdot 7 = 22$ | $-8 + 21 \cdot 7 = 13 \cdot 7 = 14$ |

Thus at the present level of public coal traffic to Assam every ton of coal would have to be hauled between 58 to 69 miles extra via the Sakrigali Ghat route compared to the Mokameh route. This advantage in favour of the Mokameh site would be reduced should the public coal for Assam increase beyond its present level. This increase is, of course, inevitable, and assuming that it would double itself the via Mokameh Ghat route would still be more economical as it would save an extra haul of between 33 to 42 miles to every ton of coal. Even if the Assam traffic increases threefold, the Mokameh site would still be preferable, being on the average 14 to 22 miles shorter.

LOCO COAL. Here $t = 104,396n$ tons and $T = 324,250$ tons. Hence $t/T = 0.32n$. Our limits for lead difference on the O T Railway are therefore

$$\text{Upper limit} \quad \frac{84 - (139)\,(0 \cdot 32)n}{1 + 0 \cdot 32n} \text{ miles}$$

$$\text{Lower limit} \quad \frac{71 - (139)\,(0 \cdot 32)n}{1 + 0 \cdot 32n} \text{ miles.}$$

For $n = 1, 1 \cdot 1, 1 \cdot 25, 1 \cdot 33$, and $1 \cdot 5$, we have the following values of the limits:

| $n$ | Upper limit | Lower limit |
|---|---|---|
| 1 | 30 | 20 |
| 1·1 | 26 | 16 |
| 1·25 | 20 | 11 |
| 1·33 | 17 | 8 |
| 1·50 | 12 | 3 |

To calculate the lead difference on the East Indian Railway we observe from dispatches of loco coal during the two years 1949–50 and 1950–51 that the following percentages originated from the four zones of the East Indian Railway:

| Zone 1 | Zone 2 | Zone 3 | Zone 4 |
|--------|--------|--------|--------|
| 6·7% | 32·3% | 54·4% | 6·6% |

The lead difference on the East Indian Railway would thus be

$$0·067(93)+0·323(32)-(0·544)(10)+(0·066)(22)$$
$$= 12·57 \text{ miles} = 13 \text{ miles.}$$

The net increase in lead over both the railways by diverting loco coal via Sakrigali Ghat would thus lie between

$$30+13 = 43 \quad \text{and} \quad 20+13 = 33 \text{ miles,}$$

if loco coal for Assam Railway remains at its existing level ($n = 1$).

Even if the loco coal for Assam Railway increases by about 25 per cent of its present level these limits would still be

$$20+13 = 33 \quad \text{and} \quad 11+13 = 24.$$

It follows, therefore, that for loco coal as well the Mokameh route is more economical. By diverting traffic to the Sakrigali site we should have to haul every ton of loco coal on the average at least about 24 to 33 miles extra and possibly more.

We may, therefore, state that whatever the future quantum of public and loco coal for the Assam Railway the average increase in lead on both the railways as a whole would most probably be within the following limits:

| | |
|--------|--------|
| Public coal | 33 and 42 miles |
| Loco coal | 24 and 33 miles. |

### (c) COMPARISON BETWEEN PATNA AND SAKRIGALI SITES

We have thus found that the Mokameh route is more economical than Patna as well as the Sakrigali route as far as coal traffic is concerned. Our comparison also shows that via Mokameh Ghat is the best route and that the next best from the traffic point of view is the Sakrigali Ghat route and the least economical route the Patna route. However, if the Mokameh site is ruled out for any reason and our choice is limited to only two sites, viz. the Patna and Sakrigali sites, we can deduce the average difference for these two routes from the calculations already made. This comparison, however, is only of an academic interest and is being given here for the sake of completeness.

Suppose $T$ tons is the total traffic passing over the proposed bridge. Let $P$ be the ton-miles involved if it is sited at Patna and $M$ the ton-miles if it is sited at Mokameh. If $d$ miles is the average lead difference per ton, then

$$P - M = dT \qquad \text{(i)}$$

Similarly if $S$ is the ton-miles if the bridge is sited at Sakrigali Ghat and $d'$ is the average lead difference per ton compared with Mokameh site,

$$S - M = d'T \qquad \text{(ii)}$$

Hence subtracting (ii) from (i), $P - S = (d - d')T$. It follows, therefore, that the average lead difference per ton is simply the difference between the two average lead differences pertaining to the Mokameh versus Patna and Mokameh versus Sakrigali sites. We have therefore the following results.

PUBLIC COAL. $d$ was estimated to lie between 47 and 55 miles, the most likely value being 50 miles. Likewise, $d'$ was found to lie between 33 and 42 miles, the most likely value being 36 miles. The Patna route would, therefore, be on the average longer by about 14 miles for every ton compared to the Sakrigali site. The comparatively small value of the lead difference should not, however, blind us to the fact that it is essentially a comparison between two relatively uneconomic routes.

LOCO COAL. In this case $d$ was found to lie between 52 and 55 miles, the most likely value being 55. Likewise $d'$ was found to lie between 24 and 33 miles, the most likely value being 27 miles. The Patna route, therefore, would on the average be longer than the Sakrigali route by about 28 miles for every ton of loco coal carried over the bridge. Here again this is only a measure of the relative demerit of the Patna site compared to the Sakrigali site, which itself is an uneconomical route compared to the Mokameh route.

We may, therefore, put the three sites in descending order of merit as far as haulage of coal traffic is concerned: *Mokameh, Sakrigali Ghat, Patna.*

## FREIGHT TRAFFIC

We have now to assess the relative merits of the three sites in so far as the movement of freight traffic other than coal is concerned. We shall take up the three comparisons:

(*a*) Mokameh Ghat versus Patna,

(*b*) Mokameh Ghat versus Sakrigali Ghat,

(*c*) Patna versus Sakrigali Ghat,

*seriatim.*

### (*a*) Comparison of Mokameh Ghat and Patna sites

We shall first consider the movement of freight traffic from the EI to OT Railway. To calculate the average lead difference over the EI Railway we require the proportions of traffic moving out of the seven zones of constant lead difference. Now no station-to-station statistics of freight traffic are maintained on the EI Railway. It is, therefore, not possible to estimate accurately the proportions of total traffic moving in or out of each of the seven zones of constant lead difference. Nevertheless, it is known that by far the greater bulk of freight traffic – over 90 per cent – flows in and out of Zone 1 (in which Calcutta is situated), for the reason that Calcutta is the nearest port serving this area. Hence even if the exact distribution of the remaining 10 per cent among the remaining six zones is known only approximately, it will not make appreciable difference in the estimate of average lead difference. To obtain an approximate estimate of proportions of traffic moving out of the remaining six zones, station-to-station statistics for the six months January, April, June, August, October, and December, 1951, were specially compiled. It was found that via Mokameh Ghat traffic originates from the seven zones in the following proportions:

| Zone 1 | 2 | 3 | 4 | 5 | 6 | 7 |
|--------|------|------|------|-----|------|------|
| 90·9% | 1·1% | 1·2% | 2·9% | nil | 1·1% | 2·8% |

Although full-scale development of industrial plans in Bihar and elsewhere is certain in the long run to reduce foreign imports through Calcutta and therefore the existing proportion of about 90 per cent from Zone 1 stations, this effect is not likely to show itself to any material extent for a long time to come. As far as one can see the Calcutta area stations are likely to continue dispatching the overwhelming bulk of traffic to the north of the Ganges as hitherto. We may, therefore, calculate the lead differences on the assumption that Zone 1 stations will continue to contribute about 90 per cent of the total via Mokameh Ghat traffic.

As regards traffic moving via Sakrigali Ghat and Bhagalpur, the proportions of traffic emanating from the seven zones are

|  | Zone 1 | 2 | 3 | 4 | 5 | 6 | 7 |
|---|---|---|---|---|---|---|---|
| Via Sakrigali traffic | 89·4% | 3·7% | 3·4% | 3·3% | nil | nil | 0·2% |
| Via Bhagalpur traffic | 88·3% | 1·3% | 1·2% | 3·3% | nil | 0·4% | 5·5% |

If the traffic via the three junctions is pooled the zonal proportions are

| Zone 1 | 2 | 3 | 4 | 5 | 6 | 7 |
|---|---|---|---|---|---|---|
| 90·4% | 1·7% | 1·6% | 2·9% | nil | 0·9% | 2·5% |

For reasons already given we shall assume the proportion of traffic emanating from Zone 1 stations to be about 90 per cent. If so, it would not make much difference if the remaining 10 per cent is distributed among the remaining six zones in any particular manner. We may, therefore, assume the zonal proportions given above for the pooled traffic via the three junctions for calculating the lead difference on the EI Railway. Assuming the total traffic from the EI to the OT Railway to be $T$ tons per annum, the increase in ton-miles over the EI Railway will be

$$0.904T(57) + 0.017T(6) + 0.016T(-30) + 0.029T(-41)$$
$$+ 0(-34) + 0.009T(-42) + 0.025T(-58)$$
$$= 48.133T \text{ ton-miles.}$$

Hence every ton of freight on the EI Railway would have to be hauled, on the average, 48 miles extra via the Patna route compared to the Mokameh Ghat route.

To calculate the lead difference on the OT Railway we require the proportions of traffic moving into the four zones of the OT Railway. We shall adopt the same method as in the case of coal traffic to ascertain the zonal proportions likely to establish themselves with the construction of the bridge. As before, we may take the average traffic to Assam to be $t$ tons and traffic to OT Railway via Mokameh Ghat to be $T$ tons. The value of the lead difference per ton is

$$\frac{T}{T+t}\{-57p-26q+39r+59s\}+\frac{t}{T+t}(59) \text{ miles.}$$

The value of the expression in brackets $\{\quad\}$ may be calculated by substituting $p = 0{\cdot}603$, $q = 0{\cdot}186$, $r = 0{\cdot}13$, $s = 0{\cdot}081$, which are the proportions obtained by considering the statistics of traffic moved during the 'steady' period 1934–5 to 1943–4. Hence the decrease in average lead per ton of goods traffic on the OT Railway is

$$\frac{-29{\cdot}3T}{T+t}+\frac{59(t)}{T+t} \text{ miles} =\frac{-29{\cdot}3}{1+(t/T)}+\frac{59(t/T)}{1+(t/T)} \text{ miles.}$$

To estimate $t$ we observe that the value of freight traffic forwarded from East Indian to Oudh Tirhut and Assam Railways via Sakrigali Ghat and Bhagalpur during the two years 1949–50 and 1950–51 was as shown in Table 55.

*Table 55.* Freight traffic in tons from EI to OT and Assam Railways.

| Year | Via Sakrigali Ghat | Via Bhagalpur | Total |
|---|---|---|---|
| 1949–50 | 28,716 | 37,025 | 65,741 |
| 1950–51 | 110,015 | 28,118 | 138,133 |

As the traffic is still growing and has not stabilized itself at a steady level we shall not take the average of these two years. The demand for the movement of freight traffic for this route is heavy. On the average about 200,000 tons (excluding coal) are being carried over the river-*cum*-rail route, and the estimated quantum of additional traffic required to be moved is said to be over 300,000 tons, of which 200,000 tons is food-grains on account Assam Government. This last traffic may not materialize by the time the bridge is built, if we are able to implement the plans for securing self-sufficiency in food-grains. However, whatever the actual value of the anticipated traffic, we may as usual assume $t = 138,133n$ tons where 138,133 is the 1950–51 tonnage and $n$ is an undetermined factor. The pre-war average of $T$ was 233,105 tons as against the war-time average of 66,118 tons and post-war average of 108,173 tons during 1949–50 and 1950–51. We may thus take it that $T$ would attain the pre-war average 233,105 after the construction of the bridge. Our value for the lead difference on the O T Railway is then

$$\frac{-29\cdot3}{1+0\cdot6n}+\frac{59(0\cdot6)n}{1+0\cdot6n}=\frac{-29\cdot3+35\cdot4n}{1+0\cdot6n} \qquad\text{(i)}$$

For $n = 1$, value of (i) is $+ 3\cdot8$ miles
$n = 2$, value of (i) is $+18\cdot9$ miles
$n = 3$, value of (i) is $+27\cdot5$ miles.

Hence the average net increase in lead per ton on both railways would be

For $n = 1$, $48\cdot1+ 3\cdot8 = 51\cdot9$ miles $= 52$ miles
$n = 2$, $48\cdot1+18\cdot9 = 67\cdot0$ miles $= 67$ miles
$n = 3$, $48\cdot1+27\cdot5 = 75\cdot6$ miles $= 76$ miles.

Thus with the present level of Assam traffic every ton of goods would have to be hauled 52 miles extra via the Patna route and may possibly have to be hauled more (as much as 67 miles) should the traffic for the Assam side increase appreciably from its present level.

FREIGHT TRAFFIC FROM O T TO EI RAILWAY. Proceeding as before, the decrease in lead on the O T Railway would be

$$\frac{T}{T+t}\{-57p-26q+39r+59s\}+\frac{t(59)}{T+t}\text{ miles.}$$

In the present case the value of the expression in brackets $\{\quad\}$ is found to be $-23\cdot3$, for the statistics of traffic during the ten 'steady' years 1934–5 to 1943–4 give the followings values of zonal proportions: $p = 0\cdot52$, $q = 0\cdot20$, $r = 0\cdot25$, $s = 0\cdot03$. Hence the lead difference per ton on the O T Railway is

$$\frac{-23\cdot3}{1+(t/T)}+\frac{59(t/T)}{1+(t/T)}.$$

In the present case the volume of freight traffic moving from

Assam and OT Railways via Sakrigali Ghat and Bhagalpur is as shown in Table 56.

*Table 56.* Freight traffic in tons from Assam and OT Railways to EI Railways.

| Year | Via Sakrigali Ghat | Via Bhagalpur | Total |
|---|---|---|---|
| 1949–50 | 92,446 | 8,769 | 101,215 |
| 1950–51 | 190,020 | 39,217 | 229,237 |

Here too the actual movement is only a small fraction of the demand. For instance, over 200,000 tons of jute alone moves by the river-*cum*-rail route annually and the Central Tea Board consider that given rail facilities they could offer over 20,000 tons of tea alone per annum. In addition, 50,000 tons of forest produce and 15,000 tons of oil products per annum are expected to move, given transport. The existing traffic could therefore easily be doubled. However, we shall assume $t = 229{,}237n$ tons, $n$ being an undetermined factor. As for $T$, the pre-war average was 277,579 and the post-war average 261,150 tons. We may therefore take it to be 277,579 tons. Our value for the lead difference on the OT Railway is

$$\frac{-23{\cdot}3}{1+0{\cdot}8n}+\frac{59(0{\cdot}8n)}{1+0{\cdot}8n} = \frac{-23{\cdot}3+47{\cdot}2n}{1+0{\cdot}8n} \qquad \text{(ii)}$$

For $n = 1$, value of (ii) is $+13{\cdot}2$ miles
$n = 2$, value of (ii) is $+27{\cdot}3$ miles
$n = 3$, value of (ii) is $+34{\cdot}8$ miles.

We have now to calculate the lead difference on the EI Railway. For this purpose we require the proportions of traffic moving into the seven zones of constant lead difference.

As revenue statistics published by the EI Railway do not show station-to-station statistics, the zonal proportions were calculated from specially compiled station-to-station statistics for the six months January, April, June, August, October, and December, 1951. These statistics gave the following zonal proportions for via Mokameh Ghat traffic:

| Zone 1 | 2 | 3 | 4 | 5 | 6 | 7 |
|---|---|---|---|---|---|---|
| 92·5% | 0·5% | 0·4% | 0·3% | 0·3% | 2·2% | 3·8% |

For via Bhagalpur and Sakrigali Ghat traffic the zonal proportions for the same period of six months were

| | Zone 1 | 2 | 3 | 4 | 5 | 6 | 7 |
|---|---|---|---|---|---|---|---|
| Via Sakrigali | 86·7% | nil | nil | nil | 0·2% | nil | 13·1% |
| Via Bhagalpur | 98·1% | 0·2% | 0·1% | nil | nil | 0·2% | 1·4% |

For the pooled traffic via the three junctions the corresponding proportions were

| Zone 1 | 2 | 3 | 4 | 5 | 6 | 7 |
|---|---|---|---|---|---|---|
| 90·9% | 0·3% | 0·2% | 0·2% | 0·2% | 1·0% | 7·2% |

It will be observed that over 90 per cent of the pooled traffic via the three junctions flows into Zone 1 stations. As the overwhelming bulk of traffic moves into one zone, viz. Zone 1 (and will continue to do so on account of the location of Calcutta port in this zone), it would not make any material difference to the calculation of the average lead difference as to how the remaining traffic is distributed among the remaining six zones.

Assuming the proportions given above for the pooled traffic, the increase in ton-miles via the Patna route over that via the Mokameh route would on the EI Railway be equal to

$$(0·909T)\,(57) + (0·003T)\,(6) + (0·002T)\,(-30)$$
$$+ (0·002T)\,(-41) + (0·002T)\,(-34) + (0·010T)\,(-42)$$
$$+ (0·072T)\,(-58) = +47·025T \text{ ton-miles.}$$

Hence, on the average, every ton of freight would have to be hauled 47 miles extra via the Patna route.

Thus the net increase in average lead per ton over both the EI and OT Railways would be

$$\text{For } n = 1,\ 47 + 13·2 = 60·2 = 60 \text{ miles}$$
$$n = 2,\ 47 + 27·3 = 74·3 = 74 \text{ miles}$$
$$n = 3,\ 47 + 34·8 = 81·8 = 82 \text{ miles.}$$

At the very least, therefore, the average increase in lead per ton of goods is 60 miles and may possibly be as much as 74 should the traffic for Assam side increase to double the present volume.

## (b) Comparison of Mokameh Ghat and Sakrigali Ghat sites

For a comparison of these two sites we have to group stations of the EI and OT Railways into zones of constant lead difference with respect to them. These zones, of course, will not be the same as in the case of the Patna and Mokameh sites. As far as the OT Railway is concerned all stations can be divided into three zones of constant lead difference as shown in Table 57.

*Table 57*

|  | Lead difference + when via Sakrigali route is longer |
|---|---|
| **Zone 1** |  |
| (i) Samastipur to Darbhanga | +71 miles |
| (ii) Darbhanga to Nirmali including Jaynagar Branch |  |
| (iii) Darbhanga to Bagaha |  |
| (iv) Samastipur–Muzaffarpur–Narkatiaganj |  |
| (v) Mazaffarpur to Bhagwanpur (exclusive) |  |
| **Zone 2** |  |
| (i) Hajipur to Bhagwanpur | +84 miles |
| (ii) Hajipur to Barauni |  |
| (iii) Ujiarpur to Barauni |  |
| (iv) All stations north and west of Hajipur including stations between Sonepore to Bagaha via Captainganj |  |
| **Zone 3** |  |
| All stations on Assam Railway and Assam Link and stations east of Katihar | −139 miles |

NOTE: This includes all stations except a few which do not fall in any of the zones, but as one half of them are closer to one site and the other half to the second, their contributions to the total lead difference would mostly cancel one another.

Similarly, all stations on the EI Railway can be divided into five zones of constant lead difference as shown in Table 58.

Having divided the stations on the EI and OT Railway systems into appropriate zones of constant lead difference it now remains to estimate the volume of traffic moving in and out of each zone.

## Appendix: The Bridging Problem

Since the lead difference for Zone 1 and Zone 2 of OT Railway is +71 and +84 miles respectively, we shall get a lower limit for the lead difference if we treat both the zones as one with a common lead difference of 71 miles. Similarly, an upper limit can be obtained by treating both the zones as one with a common lead difference of 84 miles. This would obviate the necessity of ascertaining the proportions of traffic moving in and out of the two zones. If *T* tons is the traffic moving to OT Railway west of Katihar and *t* to

*Table 58*

|  | Lead difference + when via Sakrigali route is longer |
|---|---|
| **Zone 1** | |
| (i) Mokameh to Moghal Sarai on the main line | |
| (ii) All stations west of Moghal Sarai | +131 miles |
| (iii) Saiyadraja to Mohgal Sarai on the Grand Chord | |
| (iv) Irki to Patna Junction on Patna–Gaya Branch | |
| **Zone 2** | |
| (i) Howrah–Bandel–Khana on the main line | |
| (ii) All stations on the Howrah–Burdwan Chord | −62 miles |
| (iii) All stations on Sealdah Division | |
| **Zone 3** | |
| (i) Rampore Haut to Sakrigali Junction on Sahibganj Loop | |
| (ii) Dhatrigram to Barharwa on Bandel Barharwa Loop | −131 miles |
| (iv) All stations on Azimganj–Nalhati Branch | |
| **Zone 4** | |
| (i) Madhupur to Kiul on the main line | |
| (ii) Karmnasa to Nimiaghat on the Grand Chord | |
| (iii) All stations on South Bihar Branch | +94 miles |
| (iv) Chakand to Gaya on Patna–Gaya Branch | |
| (v) Untari Road to Sone East Bank | |
| **Zone 5** | |
| (i) Gomoh to Sitarampur on the Grand Chord | +32 miles |
| (ii) Tori to Gomoh | |

the Assam Railway east of Katihar, the additional haulage in ton-miles incurred on the OT Railway by diverting all traffic via Sakrigali Ghat would lie between

Upper limit $84T-139t$, and lower limit $71T-139t$.

The limits for the average lead difference per ton would thus be

$$\text{Upper limit } \frac{84T-139t}{T+t} = \frac{84-139(t/T)}{1+(t/T)} \text{ miles}$$

$$\text{Lower limit } \frac{71T-139t}{T+t} = \frac{71-139(t/T)}{1+(t/T)} \text{ miles.}$$

We may now calculate these limits for freight traffic from the EI to OT Railway and vice versa.

FREIGHT TRAFFIC FROM EI TO OT RAILWAY. In this case, as we have already seen, we have $t = 138,133n$ and $T = 233,105$ tons, where $n$ is an undetermined factor. Hence $t/T = 0\cdot6n$, and our limits are

$$\text{Upper limit } \frac{84-(139)(0\cdot6n)}{1+0\cdot6n} = \frac{84-83\cdot4n}{1+0\cdot6n}$$

$$\text{Lower limit } \frac{71-(139)(0\cdot6n)}{1+0\cdot6n} = \frac{71-83\cdot4n.}{1+0\cdot6n}$$

For $n = 1, 2, 3$ the values of the limit are

| $n$ | Upper limit | Lower limit |
|---|---|---|
| 1 | 0 | $-8$ |
| 2 | $-38$ | $-43$ |
| 3 | $-59$ | $-64$ |

To calculate the lead difference on the EI Railway we require the proportions of traffic moving out of the five zones of constant lead difference. From specially compiled station-to-station statistics for the six months January, April, June, August, October, and December, 1951, it is ascertained that traffic via Mokameh Ghat originates from the five zones in the following proportions:

| Zone 1 | Zone 2 | Zone 3 | Zone 4 | Zone 5 |
|---|---|---|---|---|
| 2·8% | 82·2% | 3·1% | 2·8% | 9·1% |

## Appendix: The Bridging Problem

As regards traffic via Bhagalpur and via Sakrigali Ghat the corresponding proportions are

|                    | Zone 1 | Zone 2 | Zone 3 | Zone 4 | Zone 5 |
|--------------------|--------|--------|--------|--------|--------|
| Via Bhagalpur      | 5·7%   | 71·8%  | 11·5%  | 1·8%   | 9·2%   |
| Via Sakrigali Ghat | 0·2%   | 89·1%  | 0·3%   | 3·2%   | 7·2%   |

The zonal proportions for the pooled traffic via the three junctions are

| Zone 1 | Zone 2 | Zone 3 | Zone 4 | Zone 5 |
|--------|--------|--------|--------|--------|
| 2·5%   | 82·8%  | 3·2%   | 2·8%   | 8·7%   |

It will be observed that the bulk of traffic – over 80 per cent – from the EI Railway stations via the three junctions originates from Zone 2 stations which include Calcutta area stations, and that the next in order is Zone 5 stations between Gomoh and Sitarampur and Gomoh and Tori, from which about 9 per cent of traffic originates. We may take it that these figures give a fair approximation to the pattern of distribution that is likely to establish itself immediately after the bridge is built. For although with the industrial developments in Bihar, e.g. the Sindri factory working to full capacity, the proportion of traffic from stations in Zone 5 may increase, yet these are not likely materially to affect the proportion of traffic emanating from Zone 2 (Calcutta area stations), which would continue to forward the overwhelming bulk of traffic north of the river Ganges. If so, the increase in lead per ton on the EI Railway by routing the traffic via Sakrigali Ghat instead of Mokameh Ghat would be

$$0·025(131)+(0·828)(-62)+(0·032)(-131)+(0·028)(94)$$
$$+(0·087)(32) = -46·837 = -47 \text{ miles.}$$

Hence, over the two railways as a whole the lead difference per ton between via Mokameh Ghat and via Sakrigali routes would lie between the following:

|              | Upper limit         | Lower limit        |
|--------------|---------------------|--------------------|
| For $n = 1$, | $0-47 = -47$,       | $-8-47 = -55$      |
| $n = 2$,     | $-38-47 = -85$,     | $-43-47 = -90$     |
| $n = 3$,     | $-59-47 = -106$,    | $-64-47 = -111$    |

Hence at the present level of Assam traffic the route via Sakrigali Ghat would, on the average, be shorter by 47 to 55 miles per ton. Should the Assam traffic be double its present volume, this route would, on the average, be shorter by about 85 to 90 miles per ton.

FREIGHT TRAFFIC FROM OUDH TIRHUT TO EAST INDIAN RAILWAY. Here we have $t = 229,237n$ and $T = 277,579$ tons. Hence $t/T = 0.8n$, and our limits of average lead difference on the OT Railway are

$$\text{Upper limit } \frac{84-(139)(0.8n)}{1+0.8n} = \frac{84-111.2n}{1+0.8n}$$

$$\text{Lower limit } \frac{71-(139)(0.8n)}{1+0.8n} = \frac{71-111.2n}{1+0.8n}.$$

For $n = 1, 2, 3$, the values of the limits are

| $n$ | Upper limit | Lower limit |
|---|---|---|
| 1 | $-15$ | $-22$ |
| 2 | $-53$ | $-58$ |
| 3 | $-73$ | $-77$ |

On the EI Railway the proportions of via Mokameh Ghat traffic moving into the five zones of constant lead difference, as given by specially compiled station-to-station statistics for the six alternate months of 1951, are

| Zone 1 | Zone 2 | Zone 3 | Zone 4 | Zone 5 |
|---|---|---|---|---|
| 5.9% | 80.8% | 0.7% | 4.7% | 7.9% |

The corresponding zonal proportions of via Bhagalpur and via Sakrigali Ghat traffic are

| | Zone 1 | Zone 2 | Zone 3 | Zone 4 | Zone 5 |
|---|---|---|---|---|---|
| Via Bhagalpur | 1.9% | 93.2% | 1.7% | 2.2% | 1.4% |
| Via Sakrigali Ghat | 12.8% | 85.7% | 0.5% | 0.4% | 0.6% |

The zonal distribution of the pooled traffic via the three junctions is

| Zone 1 | Zone 2 | Zone 3 | Zone 4 | Zone 5 |
|---|---|---|---|---|
| 8.2% | 84.3% | 0.8% | 2.6% | 4.1% |

## Appendix: The Bridging Problem

Here again we may assume that the zonal proportions for the pooled traffic would give us a near approximation to the pattern of traffic flow that would eventually establish itself. Even if in the distant future a considerable proportion of traffic from Assam and North Bengal begins to move via the pre-Partition route, it is practically certain that the overwhelming proportion of traffic, about 85 per cent of the total, would continue to move into Zone 2 stations (Calcutta area stations) as at present. If so, it would not make any material difference to the calculation of lead difference between the two routes how the remaining 15 per cent is distributed between the other four zones. Assuming then the zonal proportions as given above for the pooled traffic, the lead difference on the EI Railway would be

$$(0{\cdot}082)\,(131) + (0{\cdot}843)\,(-62) + (0{\cdot}008)\,(-131) + (0{\cdot}026)\,(94)$$
$$+ (0{\cdot}041)\,(32) = -38{\cdot}816 \text{ miles}$$
$$= -39 \text{ miles.}$$

Hence, over the two railways as a whole, the lead difference per ton via the Mokameh Ghat and Sakrigali Ghat routes would lie between:

|  | Upper limit | | Lower limit | |
|---|---|---|---|---|
| For $n = 1$ | $-15 - 39 =$ | $-54$ miles | $-22 - 39 =$ | $-61$ miles |
| $n = 2$ | $-53 - 39 =$ | $-92$ miles | $-58 - 39 =$ | $-97$ miles |
| $n = 3$ | $-73 - 39 =$ | $-112$ miles | $-77 - 39 =$ | $-116$ miles |

In the foregoing calculation we have assumed that Assam traffic would increase beyond its present level. This is a valid assumption for the present. However, when a bridge is built, it would last forever. It is, therefore, not enough to keep in view the requirements of the immediately foreseeable future but also to look far ahead – into the distant future 50 or even 100 years hence. It is not entirely unlikely that the present conditions, which militate against the free flow of Assam and North Bengal traffic along the natural and pre-Partition channels, may no longer operate in the future. In that case the traffic which gives the Sakrigali Ghat its superiority over the Mokameh Ghat route would vanish or dwindle considerably. We have therefore also to examine the lead difference not only for values of $n = 1, 2, 3$, and so on, but also for values of $n$ below 1, e.g.:

$n = 0.75, 0.5, 0.33, 0.25, 0.1,$ and $0.$

Table 59 gives the lead difference on the OT and EI Railways for these values of $n$.

*Table 59*

| Value of n | From EI to OT | | | | | From OT to EI | | | | |
|---|---|---|---|---|---|---|---|---|---|---|
| | Lead difference on OT | | Lead difference on EI | Total | | Lead difference on OT | | Lead difference on EI | Total | |
| | Upper limit | Lower limit | | Upper limit | Lower limit | Upper limit | Lower limit | | Upper limit | Lower limit |
| 0 | +84 | +71 | −47 | +37 | +24 | +84 | +71 | −39 | +45 | +32 |
| 0·1 | +71 | +59 | −47 | +24 | +12 | +68 | +55 | −39 | +29 | +16 |
| 0·25 | +55 | +44 | −47 | +8 | −3 | +47 | +36 | −39 | +8 | −3 |
| 0·33 | +47 | +36 | −47 | 0 | −11 | +37 | +27 | −39 | −2 | −12 |
| 0·5 | +33 | +23 | −47 | −14 | −24 | +20 | +11 | −39 | −19 | −28 |
| 0·75 | +15 | +6 | −47 | −32 | −41 | 0 | −8 | −39 | −39 | −47 |
| 1 | 0 | −8 | −47 | −47 | −55 | −15 | −22 | −39 | −54 | −61 |
| 2 | −38 | −43 | −47 | −85 | −90 | −53 | −58 | −39 | −92 | −97 |
| 3 | −59 | −64 | −47 | −106 | −111 | −73 | −77 | −39 | −112 | −116 |

Table 59 shows that the route via Mokameh Ghat is shorter for freight traffic both from the EI to OT Railway and vice versa so long as the Assam traffic is not more than 25 per cent of the existing level. If this traffic rises above the 25 per cent of the present traffic level the via Sakrigali Ghat route becomes, on the average, shorter to an increasing extent, the lead being shorter for every ton, on the average, by about 50 miles for traffic from EI to OT and 57 miles for traffic from OT to EI at the existing level of Assam traffic. This advantage in favour of the Sakrigali Ghat route would increase still more should Assam traffic increase beyond the existing level. It is, therefore, clear that the relative superiority of the Sakrigali Ghat site over the Mokameh Ghat site depends entirely on whether in course of time the Assam Railway traffic will follow its pre-Partition channel or present-day channels. On the other hand, the Mokameh Ghat site is superior to the Sakrigali Ghat site as far as the haulage of coal traffic is concerned irrespective of the quantum of coal traffic for Assam and the North Bengal side as has been shown earlier. In fact, this relative superiority of the Mokameh

## Appendix: The Bridging Problem

Ghat site would increase considerably should there be any reduction in the level of the Assam Railway traffic. Taking, therefore, into account the present and future likely flow of traffic, the best course would be to build the bridge at Mokameh Ghat and to route the entire freight traffic for the OT as well as coal traffic both for the OT Railway and Assam Railway via this route, and to provide a car ferry at Sakrigali Ghat for purely freight traffic (excluding coal) to and from Assam from and to the south of the river. This could be done by transferring the car ferry at Mokameh Ghat to Sakrigali Ghat after the bridge is built at the former site. By this means we would be routing both kinds of traffic by their natural and most economical routes. It would also obviate the necessity of large-scale remodelling both on the EI and OT Railways which would be necessary if the bridge were sited at Sakrigali Ghat and the traffic routed via that junction; for the entire layout of both the EI and OT Railways has been designed to effect the interchange of traffic between the two railway systems at Mokameh Ghat and any change therein would involve an extensive programme of increasing the line capacity over the various sections further afield from the bridge site. On the other hand, if the bridge is sited at Mokameh Ghat the line capacity would be adequate to take in the entire traffic that would be forthcoming after the bridge is built.

### (c) Comparison of Patna and Sakrigali Ghat sites

It was shown earlier that the average lead difference per ton between routes via Patna and via Sakrigali is simply the difference between the two average lead differences pertaining to Patna versus Mokameh and Sakrigali versus Mokameh sites. Using this result we have the following corollaries.

FREIGHT TRAFFIC FROM EI TO OT RAILWAY. The average lead differences per ton ($d$) between the Patna and Mokameh sites for various values of $n$ are

$$n = 1 \qquad d = 52 \text{ miles}$$
$$n = 2 \qquad d = 67 \text{ miles}$$
$$n = 3 \qquad d = 76 \text{ miles.}$$

243

Likewise, the average lead difference per ton ($d'$) between the Sakrigali and Mokameh sites for various values of $n$ lies between

| | |
|---|---|
| For $n = 1$ | $-47$ and $-55$ miles |
| $n = 2$ | $-85$ and $-90$ miles |
| $n = 3$ | $-106$ and $-111$ miles. |

Hence the average lead difference per ton between the Patna and Sakrigali routes would be given by $d-d'$ and for various values of $n$ would therefore lie between:

| | |
|---|---|
| For $n = 1$ | 99 and 107 miles |
| $n = 2$ | 152 and 157 miles |
| $n = 3$ | 182 and 187 miles. |

Consequently, compared to the Sakrigali route the Patna route involves an exceedingly long detour for traffic as a whole and becomes rapidly more and more uneconomical at higher levels of Assam and North Bengal traffic.

Freight traffic from OT to EI Railways. Here $d$ was found to be, for various values of $n$,

| | |
|---|---|
| $n = 1$ | $d = 60$ miles |
| $n = 2$ | $d = 74$ miles |
| $n = 3$ | $d = 82$ miles. |

Likewise, $d'$ was found for various values of $n$ to be between

| | |
|---|---|
| For $n = 1$ | $-54$ and $-61$ miles |
| $n = 2$ | $-92$ and $-97$ miles |
| $n = 3$ | $-112$ and $-116$ miles. |

Hence the average lead difference per ton between the Patna and Sakrigali routes would be given by $d-d'$ and therefore, for various values of $n$, lie between

| | |
|---|---|
| For $n = 1$ | 114 and 121 miles |
| $n = 2$ | 166 and 171 miles |
| $n = 3$ | 194 and 198 miles. |

Here again, compared to the Sakrigali route, the Patna route is exceedingly circuitous for traffic as a whole and becomes rapidly more and more uneconomical as the level of Assam and North Bengal traffic increases beyond its present level.

We may, therefore, state that if the volume of Assam and North Bengal traffic is likely to increase beyond its present level in the future and if this traffic is *never* likely to revert to its normal pre-Partition channels the three sites may be put in descending order of merit, as far as the haulage of freight traffic is concerned: *Sakrigali Ghat, Mokameh, Patna.*

But if, on the other hand, the possibility of Assam and North Bengal traffic dwindling appreciably in the future either by its reversion to pre-Partition channels or otherwise (e.g. carriage by river-*cum*-rail routes to a still greater extent, possibly as a result of a rate-cutting war between the steamer companies and railways) cannot be entirely ruled out, the three sites may be put in descending order of merit, as far as the haulage of freight traffic is concerned: *Mokameh, Sakrigali Ghat, Patna.*

It seems that ultimately we would probably need two bridges over the Ganges, as the entire length of the river from Banaras to Calcutta (a distance of about 800 miles) is without a bridge. This is too long a length for a single bridge to suffice as a connecting link between the great belts of territory north and south of the river. In fact, as mentioned earlier, the Ganges has been bridged more or less regularly at an average distance of about 150 miles all the way from its source to Banaras. There is no reason why we should not be a little more liberal in providing communications over the river below Banaras. If so, the best course, from the traffic point of view, would appear to be to have first a bridge at Mokameh (which is more centrally situated between Banaras and Calcutta), and consider the location of a second bridge downstream at Sakrigali (or elsewhere) later. Meanwhile, the needs of traffic to and from Assam and North Bengal may be met by the transfer of the car ferry at Mokameh to Sakrigali Ghat supplemented by the existing ferry at Bhagalpur.

*Table 60*

| Commodity | Tonnage | | Increase in lead per ton at various levels of Assam traffic | | |
| | Via Mokameh Ghat | For Assam and North Bengal | $n = 1$ | $n = 2$ | $n = 3$ |
|---|---|---|---|---|---|
| | | | miles | miles | miles |
| Public coal | 253,666 | 53,995 | 37 | 47 | 55 |
| Loco coal | 324,250 | 104,396 | 52 | Not | required |
| Freight from EI to OT | 233,105 | 138,133 | 52 | 67 | 76 |
| Freight from OT to EI | 261,150 | 229,237 | 60 | 74 | 82 |

## SUMMARY

We may now summarize the main conclusions of this discussion as follows:

(a) *Mokameh Ghat versus Patna.* If the bridge is sited at Patna instead of Mokameh Ghat the average lead per ton will increase for the various commodities as shown in Table 60.

(b) *Mokameh Ghat versus Sakrigali Ghat.* If the bridge is sited at Sakrigali Ghat instead of Mokameh Ghat the average lead per ton will increase for the various commodities as shown in Table 61.

*Table 61*

| Commodity | Tonnage | | Increase in lead per ton at various levels of Assam traffic | | | | | |
| | Via Mokameh Ghat | For Assam and North Bengal | Upper limit | Lower limit | Upper limit | Lower limit | Upper limit | Lower limit |
| | | | $n = 1$ | | $n = 2$ | | $n = 3$ | |
|---|---|---|---|---|---|---|---|---|
| | | | miles | miles | miles | miles | miles | miles |
| Public coal | 253,666 | 53,995 | 68 | 58 | 42 | 33 | 22 | 14 |
| Loco coal | 324,250 | 104,396 | 30 | 20 | NR* | NR | NR | NR |
| Freight from EI to OT | 233,105 | 138,133 | −47† | −55 | −85 | −90 | −106 | −111 |
| Freight from OT to EI | 261,150 | 299,237 | −54 | −61 | −92 | −97 | −112 | −116 |

*'NR' means not required.          †Minus sign indicates decrease.

## Appendix: The Bridging Problem

### Table 62

| Commodity | Tonnage | | Increase in lead per ton at various levels of Assam traffic | | | | | |
|---|---|---|---|---|---|---|---|---|
| | Via Mokameh Ghat | For Assam and North Bengal | Lower limit | Upper limit | Lower limit | Upper limit | Lower limit | Upper limit |
| | | | $n = 1$ | | $n = 2$ | | $n = 3$ | |
| | | | miles | miles | miles | miles | miles | miles |
| Public coal | 253,666 | 53,995 | −31† | −21 | 5 | 14 | 33 | 41 |
| Loco coal | 324,250 | 104,396 | 22 | 32 | NR* | NR | NR | NR |
| Freight from EI to OT | 233,105 | 138,133 | 99 | 107 | 152 | 157 | 182 | 187 |
| Freight from OT to EI | 261,150 | 229,237 | 114 | 121 | 166 | 171 | 194 | 198 |

\* 'NR' means not required.     † Minus sign indicates decrease.

For $n$ less than one the Mokameh site begins to gain advantage over the Sakrigali Ghat route for freight traffic also. The average difference between the two routes is zero for $n = 0.25$ approximately and the Mokameh site becomes superior for values of $n$ below 0·25.

(c) *Patna versus Sakrigali Ghat.* If the bridge is sited at Patna instead of Sakrigali Ghat the average lead per ton will increase for the various commodities as shown in Table 62.

# Selected Bibliography

## A NUMERACY

Moroney, M. J., *Facts from Figures*. Baltimore: Penguin Books, Inc., 1956

Morse, Philip M., and George E. Kimball, *Methods of Operations Research*. Cambridge, Mass.: M.I.T. Press, 1951

Singh, Jagjit, *Great Ideas of Modern Mathematics: Their Nature and Use*. New York: Dover Publications, Inc., 1959

## B NETWORK ANALYSIS

Battersby, A., *Network Analysis*. Macmillan & Co. Ltd., 1967

Federal Electric Corporation, *A Programmed Introduction to P.E.R.T.* New York: John Wiley & Sons, Inc.

## C LINEAR PROGRAMMING

Vajda, S., *Readings in Mathematical Programming*, 2nd edn. New York: John Wiley & Sons, Inc., 1962. (*Readings in Linear Programming*, London: Pitman, 1958)

Gass, Saul I., *Linear Programming: Methods and Applications*, 2nd edn. New York: McGraw-Hill Book Co., Inc., 1964

## D THEORY OF GAMES

Williams, John D., *The Compleat Strategyst*, rev. edn. New York: McGraw-Hill Book Co., Inc., 1965

## E QUEUEING THEORY

Morse, Philip M., *Queues, Inventories and Maintenance*. New York: John Wiley & Sons, Inc., 1958

## F MONTE CARLO SIMULATION

Meyer, Herbert A. (ed.), *Symposium on Monte Carlo Methods*. New York: John Wiley & Sons, Inc., 1956

## G GENERAL

Mehta, A. K., T. R. Thiagarajan, and N. K. Jaiswal, *A Collection of Some Operational Research Problems from World War II*. New

Delhi: Defence Research and Development Organization of the Ministry of Defence, Government of India

*Operations Research on the South Eastern Railway (A Corporate Research Activity directed by Jagjit Singh).* Published by South Eastern Railway, Calcutta

# Index of Names

# Index of Subjects

average: arithmetic, 23–32; harmonic, 23–4; median, 27–8; mode, 27–8; weighted, 25–6

bit, 199
Bottleneck problems *see* queues
brain, storage capacity of, 200
Buffon's needle problem, 170–71, 177

computer simulation, 173–5
computers, storage capacity of, 199–200
confrontation theorem, 187–91
critical region, 33, 150

Errors, theory of, 57
Exponential growth, 57–8

Frequency distributions, 32–5; biomodal, 65–6, binomial, 35, 49–56; continuous, 35–6; equation, 40; exponential, 35; geometric, 35; normal (Gaussian), 35, 40, 56, 59–64, 202; Pareto, 35; Poisson, 35; rectangular, 66; single modal skew, 64–5
Frequency, relative, 36, 51–3

games: non-zero-sum, 127; of strategy, 125; real, 147; theory of, and rational decisions, 124–51; zero-sum, 127–32, 150

Histogram, 37–8

imitation game, 201
information content, of letter, 203
information, measure, 199

liar paradox, 148
linear programming, 103–20, 150, 184
logarithms, 42

matrix, pay-off, 120–21, 129
maximax and maximin criteria, 121–2
mean *see* average
minimax and minimin criteria, 128–30
Moghalsarai, humping capacity of, 152–3, 166–7
Monte Carlo simulation, 20
moves: dominant, 145–6; mixed, 132–41; recessive, 145–6

Numeracy, art of, 19, 22–86

operations research, 13–21: on language question, 199–206; on Northeast Frontier Railway, 187–98

pay-off matrix, 120–21, 129
probability, 22, 42–51

queue discipline, 156–7, 169
queues: arrival pattern, 156–63, 169, 182–3; mean queue length, 156–7, 163–4; mean waiting